Also by the Author

*The Raven, the Dove, and the Owl of Minerva: The Creation of
Humankind in Athens and Jerusalem*
"I AM": Monotheism and the Philosophy of the Bible

PERSONS AND OTHER THINGS

Exploring the Philosophy of the Hebrew Bible

Persons and Other Things

Exploring the Philosophy
of the Hebrew Bible

MARK GLOUBERMAN

UNIVERSITY OF TORONTO PRESS
Toronto Buffalo London

© University of Toronto Press 2021
Toronto Buffalo London
utorontopress.com
Printed in the U.S.A.

ISBN 978-1-4875-0898-2 (cloth)
ISBN 978-1-4875-3945-0 (EPUB)
ISBN 978-1-4875-3944-3 (PDF)

Library and Archives Canada Cataloguing in Publication

Title: Persons and other things : exploring the philosophy of the
Hebrew Bible / Mark Glouberman.
Names: Glouberman, M., author.
Description: Includes bibliographical references and index.
Identifiers: Canadiana (print) 20210145757 | Canadiana (ebook) 20210145781 |
ISBN 9781487508982 (cloth) | ISBN 9781487539450 (EPUB) |
ISBN 9781487539443 (PDF)
Subjects: LCSH: Bible. Old Testament – Philosophy. |
LCSH: Jewish philosophy.
Classification: LCC BS1186 .G66 2021 | DDC 221.601 – dc23

This book has been published with the help of a grant from the Federation
for the Humanities and Social Sciences, through the Awards to Scholarly
Publications Program, using funds provided by the Social Sciences and
Humanities Research Council of Canada.

University of Toronto Press acknowledges the financial assistance to its
publishing program of the Canada Council for the Arts and the Ontario Arts
Council, an agency of the Government of Ontario.

If the concept of God has any validity or any use,
it can only be to make us larger, freer, and more loving.

James Baldwin, Letter from a Region in My Mind

Contents

Contents

Preface

The Bible is a work of philosophy. It's to advance a thitherto unrecognized category of being, the category of the particular, that the philosophers of the Bible ("the Bibleists") come forward. In the theological idiom of the age, they proclaim the category – "I am the Lord your God" – and assert its indispensability – "you shall have no other gods before me." Indispensability to what? To the referents of "you." As the Bibleists see it, each person – each man and each woman – is a particular. Trees and fish and planets? They, according to the Bibleists, are (to put it in the philosophical idiom of *our* age) non-particular, non-general individuals.

Like all philosophical positions, the Bibleists' position ("Bibleism") is a product of reflection. In context, it's also a call to action. "Lacking the category of the particular, the other thinkers of the age represent persons in the image of non-persons. Running counter as a result to what men and women are, the ways of life that their belief-system signposts are ways that men and women should leave behind."

In the pages following I deepen the defence of Bibleism that I've mounted in the wider project that this book rounds out. *The other gods or God?* The Bibleists' objective of ensuring to persons an accurate understanding of themselves doesn't, we'll see, require other things to be misunderstood, and hence, theologically speaking, doesn't require the other gods to be forsworn. "No other gods before God" is not convertible with "No other gods."

The Bible is a work of philosophy – a philosophical testament; one from which instruction can still be taken. That's the project's overarching theme. This book is also my testament about the profession of philosophy. In the chapters that tackle the theme, I try to practice what I preach in the Preamble about the profession and about the men and the women who profess it.

I've drawn on material produced and published in the course of working out the book's ideas. I'm grateful here to the officials of *The Heythrop Journal*, *Iyyun: The Jerusalem Philosophical Quarterly*, *Philo*, *Philosophy & Theology*, and *University of Toronto Quarterly*.

For support that facilitated the research I am indebted to Kwantlen Polytechnic University.

More personal thanks go to Len Husband, Jonathan Katz, Richard Keshen, Eva Shorr, Chaim Tannenbaum, and a University of Toronto Press reviewer.

The book is for the girls: Chava, Noa, Adi, Esme.

PERSONS AND OTHER THINGS

Exploring the Philosophy of the Hebrew Bible

Preamble
... with a loosened tie[1]

To set the scene, I'll list the principal theses of the two books that precede *Persons and Other Things*. I'll then loosen my tie and, for the remainder of the Preamble, have a bit of serious fun.

In contrasting the belief-system that the Bible endorses and the one that the thinkers behind it are aiming to supersede, *The Raven, the Dove, and the Owl of Minerva: The Creation of Humankind in Athens and Jerusalem* establishes the following. (1) Its origin in pagan Greece has a lasting effect on (Western) philosophy. It's therefore appropriate that in the myth of *her* origin, Athena, philosophy's patron god, emerges from the head of Zeus. (2) The inbuilt tendency of the early philosophers to calibrate worth to robustness affects their anthropology. Men and women get ranked in value beneath wholes larger and/or less fleeting, for example nature, the political entity, history, atoms, even the dominion of death. (3) The conception of men and women dominant in the West, the conception of them as creatures each of whose lives has intrinsic worth, traces back to the culture of which the Bible is the charter. The conception clashes with the philosophical one; indeed, the conceivers develop it as antithetical. "You have Marduk (or Amun-Ra or Zeus); we have God." (4) Because of how men and women are conceived therein, the Bible advocates for modes of comportment, individual and social, that respect the worth of each person.

Reviewing the body on the sheets after *The Raven* had been put to bed, I began to feel uneasy. In formulating the meta-moral as I had – "the philosophical style of thinking ... is hostile to what the Bible teaches about men and women" (ix) – had I not elevated a species into a genus? Philosophical enquiry I understand to be the rational study of *invariants*: necessary features of being and of thinking and of acting. Philosophy as a practice is the enterprise of articulating claims about being and about thinking and about acting, claims that are true no matter what; and philosophy as an object is the set of such claims. Relative to this (quite mainstream) conception of philosophy, Abraham and Moses are every bit as philosophical as are Plato and Aristotle. Which is what I proceeded to show in "*I AM*": *Monotheism and the Philosophy of the Bible*. (1) The category of the particular, the invariant on which biblical thought turns, is identified and examined. (2) The absence of the category from Greek philosophical thought is accounted for both in terms of how this style of thinking came to be and in terms of how it is structured. (3) The connection is explained between Bibleism and the position of theology called "monotheism." The Shema Yisrael, the creedal formula of the biblical belief-system, is shown to be a religiously encoded affirmation of particularity.[2] (4) The relevance of the category for the various active branches of philosophy, morals, action theory, metaphysics, epistemology, and so on is demonstrated.

While extending the arguments of both of its predecessors, *Persons and Other Things* roughs out how men and women who see themselves in the Bible's pages (as, once the "religious" glare is reduced, I think most of us will agree that we do) are committed to conduct themselves personally, to arrange their social ties, and to act in the natural world.

Why don't the scholars/intellectuals recognize the Bible for the philosophical document that it is? In some combination or other, the following four reasons inform the thinking of many who think about these matters, as at an earlier stage they informed mine.

In *Surpassing Wonder: The Invention of the Bible and the Talmuds*, Donald Akenson remarks on the hauteur of classicists towards Jerusalemite thought. There is Greek culture. There is Roman culture. The rest is the picturesque and the mystified and the barbaric. The right to this snootiness – shades of the *Odyssey*! – isn't earned through study of the kind required of postulants and novices in their field. So much is the attitude unjustified that the upturned of nose owe a penance or two.

The tone-setting intellectuals of our culture recoil from the spectacle of religious leaders in clerical vestments quoting scripture to a quiescent flock; of congregants wrapped in prayer shawls chanting the liturgy in unison; of students, backs turned to the modern world, poring over the columns of the Talmud. "Aren't the tone-setters right to be troubled?" Before taking the writers/thinkers to task for the much later company that their product keeps, isn't it necessary to determine what the Bible meant in context?

The third reason for excluding the Bible is its narrative texture. Since many works of the Western philosophical tradition aren't argumentative, the reason would be laughable if the feature of contrast didn't enfold a point of significance. Philosophers of this tradition make a virtue of their discipline's distance from the variable and from the fleeting and from the contingent. The Queen of the Sciences doesn't have to consort with the common types who toil below stairs in the Palace of Wisdom. Bernard Williams (Smart and Williams, 118) puts the thought, and criticizes it, stylishly. "Philosophers ... urge us to view the world sub specie aeternitatis, but for most human purposes that is not a good species to view it under."[3] The Bibleists, I'm saying, urge no such thing. The Bible's basic and distinctive principle is sub specie temporis. The story-like form is not incidental to this. Those behind the text, that is to say, proceeded as they did in aid of their philosophy, not because they were engaged in historical-type reportage.

The Jewish thinkers through the centuries who thought of themselves as philosophers drew their philosophical materials from, ultimately, Greek sources, Maimonides from Aristotle, Philo of Alexandria from Plato, Mordecai Kaplan from John Dewey, whose pragmatism has roots in Protagoras. Coming as it does from the heart of Jerusalemite thought, and based as it is on the self-characterization of the most influential Jerusalemite thinkers, this fourth reason is especially forceful. I can even top it with a dollop of personal experience. My professional apprenticeship was served in the land of the Bible, a land where the national radio bookended each broadcast day with scriptural passages. Physically, the department to which I belonged was situated a few steps from the department specializing in Jewish thought; professionally speaking, the two academic units might as well have been in different towns. We in Philosophy didn't look at the Bible; they in Jewish Thought regarded us with suspicion, perhaps on the grounds stated by Yehudah Halevy – that although the wisdom of the Greeks has attractive flowers, its tree is barren of fruit.

On the basis of the specifics of my case that a Jewish philosophy exists, I turn this reason back against the Jewish philosophers. Getting his philosophy as he does from the Greek context (a *pagan* context, presided over by the other gods), Maimonides is, it emerges, out of touch with the Bible's basic teachings. He, like the other philosophers whom I listed, talks British while walking Yiddish. I'll add that, *pace* Maimonides & Co., the other gods should not, according to the Bibleists, be black-Baaled. A bit of English is needed. But the point I'm making here is from the other side. *God* must be given his philosophical due.

I'll now do some preliminary reorienting towards the text of the kind of reader who is likely to be looking at these words, a reader whose passing acquaintance with the Bible is combined with resistance to what are understood to be its teachings.

God is invariably characterized as exploding in anger when he discovers the transgression in Eden. Those who bracket off the influence of long-standing interpretation will as easily see a deity regretful about the implications for the pair of what they have wrought, yet approving overall of the outcome. "Because you ... have eaten of the tree about which I commanded you 'You shall not eat of it,' cursed is the ground because of you." In saying this (Genesis 3:17) God is detailing what will befall the man, not meting out condign punishment. The episode, that is, presents an act of self assertion. "Isn't it bad, sinful even, to declare independence of God?" Half an answer is that God himself had cut loose from Baal & Co. Since God is not Baal, the half must be eked out, as must the man, by a better half. Observe the resemblance of the man and the woman in their initial condition to domesticated animals, and it's hard to miss that what they do is an *imitatio Dei*. That the major drama in the Torah reprises the departure from Eden even the casual reader will appreciate. If according to God the Israelites had to make a break from the Nilotic breadbasket, shouldn't the leave-taking of the man and the woman from the garden located at the headwaters of the Pishon and the Gihon be cause for tempered celebration?

The harsh moral lesson that, worm-infested as we are, we are lost but for the intercession of "one greater Man," loses its bite. The Bible is telling us what we are – namely, more than parts of nature – and hence telling us that we are by nature transgressive. No criticism is being levelled for our not being unquestioningly obedient to the (extra-natural) deity.

Ruling in advance against the capacity of the rational reading of the Bible to generate *bona fide* religious commitments would be dogmatic. But it's consequent upon study that I say of Abraham's theophanies and of Moses's close encounters with God that they are best read as dramatizations of the life-changing discovery, which came to someone somewhere, of the pagan view's inadequacy. This discovery is what caused the fission within paganism of which we read a slanted story in the pages of the Bible alongside a colourized history of the formation of the Israelite communion.

Both protégés have rocky patches in their relations with their sponsor. In neither case is rebelliousness part of it. The discovery is, after all, *theirs*. When Abraham and Moses resist, either the degree of bad of paganism or the degree of good of God's way is being questioned. We must add, in Moses's case, the extremes of frustration at the stiff-neckedness of those who, given a map and a guide to the Promised Land, seem little inclined to fall in step.

A widespread belief about what I identify as Jerusalem's *Metaphysics*, its *Ethics*, its *Critique of Pure Reason*, is that the book's philosophical status is incompatible with its focus on matters peculiar to a single group. Although some of the Bible *is* specific, its core is, at least in intention, true for all and true no matter what. Rejection opens the comprehending rejector to consequences more serious than being viewed as odd.

Some of the Bible is specific to a group. To reduce the quantifier's vagueness, let me enlarge.

I am persuaded by the scholarly view that the Bible was put together in the decades after the destruction of Solomon's Temple, put together of writings produced at different times in different parts of the Israelite world. On the basis that the producers of the several writings couldn't have had the end-product in mind, many who endorse this view conclude that the Bible is uninterpretable. "Since some individual or group fashioned the whole, isn't it reasonable to assume a guiding idea?" Reasonable, yes. But not closed to doubt. Your house is aflame. Won't you grab whatever is to hand? It comes down to whether an integrated reading of the whole can be supplied. The novelty of my version of the affirmative lies in the thesis that philosophy is the integrator.

One, popular, way of reading the Bible is as the religious history of the nation. But there's a downside here, especially for the devout. An extended Israelite presence in the land of Goshen is no better attested than the presence of Merry Men in Sherwood Forest.[4] The question, however, is how *I* handle the story, which certainly dominates the Torah.

If the dating of the Bible is as stated two paragraphs back, a clear situational reason existed for the "Out of Egypt" motif. At the time of the Hurban, the people of Judea, or at least its elite, found themselves in exile. A story of redemption from bondage would have buoyed them up as, weeping by Babylon's waters, they wondered whether they would ever again see Zion. "Doesn't citing this as the compilers' basis work against the proposition that philosophy is what makes a book of the Bible?" The apparent conflict vanishes once we see that God's liberating the Israelites also dramatizes the new category's centrality. *To be in Egypt is (=) to subscribe to a mistaken philosophical analysis.*

In composing the story as they did, the writers/thinkers behind the Bible were pursuing what I identify as their primary aim, to write up the philosophy, while at the same time they ministered to the situational need. Unfortunately, the latter strain has come to dominate scholarly minds. I shall at several points in the sequel discuss the story of Elijah, a double of the story of Moses, a *double without either exile or nationhood.* Had the writers/thinkers behind the Bible produced their opus in a time of peace, a story like Elijah's would have been drawn from the repository of legends to teach the philosophical lesson.

In the beginning of my professional life, a tiny Olivetti Lettera 22 was the instrument that I used to communicate with the academic world. This typewriter gave way to a slightly larger portable, a Lettera 35, which in turn handed over the keys to a yet larger – transportable, I would say – Smith Corona Galaxie Twelve, which allowed the interchange of a few characters of type, most usefully for me "[" and "]." Operating as I now do on a word processor, I am astonished at having produced so much finished material on the machines, doubly astonished as QWERTYUIOP is Greek to my digits. Triply astonished, in fact. I produced one slab of a book in the Paleolithic way. There

is also the point that constant revision is for me a fact of life. Since to many today the typewriter is lumped with the quill pen and lamp-black, it may not be superfluous to add that in my pecking and carbon paper period, making changes was labour intensive. A few typos, and a whole page had to be redone to achieve copy suitable for the eyes of others. How (I sometimes wonder) did Augustine manage to write *The City of God* when his process of writing would feel to us like using a bucket with a hole to draw water from a deep well? During my career I've observed two super-prolific pre-computer producers up close, and what I saw sheds light on such prodigies. One of the two had a dedicated secretary who was occupied full-time in transcribing the legal notepad scrawl. The other moved from typewriter to typewriter in his study, tapping out each paragraph of the latest opus in several of the languages in which he was fluent. As for me, a dreadful keyboardist unable to produce near finished product at the first go, I simply had to put in the time.

I am not among the fortunate few able to produce polished prose without extensive emendation. It's a good thing that I like the labour-intensive process. Indeed, as I'll explain, I find it to aid the cognitive side of the activity. So perhaps the fortune of the few is not unalloyed.

In the course of my experience among the lifelong learners, I learned early on that if, reading good prose, you say "*I* could do that," you are in all probability overestimating. Why we are lulled into the false estimation by the fact that we use our writing skills daily is a mystery. Who would think to try out for the Olympics on the basis of catching the bus each morning?

Writing well is hard; in different areas hard in different ways. The skeletal structure of many a philosophical paragraph is this. "A, but B, however C, so for all that A." Can't some of the techniques of standard descriptive prose be used to counteract the numbing effect of paragraph after paragraph of this sort of thing? "Jack went up the hill to buy a jug of milk at the mall; there he bumped into Jill; Jill suggested a latté; but Jack had only half a crown; also, he feared that Jill would propose a tumble; so he begged off and made for the dairy case." The milk run can be dramatized in myriad ways. Jack can hide behind a pillar when he spies Jill. Jill might go sour on him when Jack rebuffs her. The dairy case might be bare. Judging from the literature, few philosophers entertain such possibilities. True, a philosophy article is not a short story or, Plato's early dialogues notwithstanding, a one act play. Neither however is it a technical report. Philosophy is a humanities subject. The liberal arts offer many examples of writing that has not been leached of flavour. History is a cornucopia. Think of Gibbon, of Macaulay, of Donald Creighton, of Barbara Tuchman, of Thucydides and of Tacitus, the Olympians. Moreover, philosophers even address the topic as part of earning their keep. In instructing students, they advise simplicity and clarity. These, certainly, are virtues. But although the student of the piano must go up and down the scales long and hard to gain competence for performance, remind me of the last performance of Czerny's studies that you attended.

P.F. Strawson figures in several of the chapters. In 1969, I attended Strawson's Inaugural Lecture as Oxford's Waynflete Professor of Metaphysical Philosophy. In characteristic *bout de souffle* manner, Strawson paid a handsome tribute to his predecessor, Gilbert Ryle. Ryle, Strawson said, "contributed not only to English philosophy, but also to English letters, something," he added after a dramatic pause, "not less great."

A witty rhyme of the time was "Le style c'est Ryle." Certainly, *The Concept of Mind* is inimitably written. The rataplan of synonyms and near synonyms, the pungent formulations, the verbal inventiveness, speak of equal parts thought and labour. It's like watching a juggler at work. The book is still fun to read, as is Ryle's *Dilemmas*, an "ordinary language" treatment of a number of tough philosophical nuts – Gilbert's Filberts. Did the longtime editor of *Mind* red-pencil the submissions to the journal? I'd be guessing. But at the viva for the first graduate degree that I took, Ryle did in fact apply an oral version of the editorial tool. In the gruff voice that across the decades I can still hear in my mind's ear he urged me to "work on the pellucidity of my style."

Strawson was at the time the central figure in English philosophy. I attended his lectures and pored over his writings, especially the excellent book on Kant, *The Bounds of Sense*, published halfway through my first term at Oxford.[5] These exposures influenced my writing. The tribute to Ryle indicates that Strawson gave thought to style. Did he attend to it when *he* put pen to paper? The average length of his sentences suggests not. It's to the reader like a climb up a glassy incline. Another negative indicator is the overuse of "but." True, because of philosophy's argumentative texture, the conjunction is an occupational hazard. That's precisely why it needs monitoring. The writing improves if its frequency is limited, as it does if sentence length is varied. Why not the occasional rhetorical question? The writing, I say, improves. For outing "but" necessitates other changes, which one actuated by a sense of style is likely also to make with care. "But no one notices." Chiselling away atop a massive statue of Athena, the sculptor Phidias (the story goes) was invited to take a break. To the column fluters he explained that the task commanded his full attention. "But no one will see the hair." "The gods," Phidias responded.

The gods among the readers will notice that the glossmeter often gives high readings when applied to the earliest parts of the chapters. On word processors, a document is opened at its start. For this reason alone, more attention tends to get paid *In Principio*. If changes in *these* chapters were tracked, it would be found that the author not infrequently moved back and forth numerous times between one word and another in the early lines, only doing so twice or thrice later. Opening lines are, for me, tough. Also, they are, and not only for me, important. First impressions last. As for the train as it departs, my experience is that when a piece of writing has detached from the murk the closer often writes itself. Its emergence is the sign that completion is nigh. The last line in several of the chapters came as a gift, the oasis finally seen as the writer struggled, parched and begrimed, to the top of what from the bottom he feared was just the next dune in an endless series.

A chapter of a comic novel by Wallace Markfield describes en route *To an Early Grave* the travails of a reviewer who, having composed an opening line about a collection of essays, slowly alters it, shifting an adverb here, dropping an article there, inverting a phrase, only to revert in the end to the initial version. It reminds me of someone I know. "Certainly, Professor Gombitz's essays, gathered together for the first time, yield pleasure of a kind, but a pleasure increasingly tempered by the realization that Professor Gombitz is not altogether his own man." I do hope that Glouberman's essays, gathered together here, yield pleasure of at least a tempered kind. Is the reviewer right about Gombitz the man? As the case may be, and in full consciousness that the breathing of those who proclaim that they won't be led by the nose is often stertorous, Glouberman says that Glouberman is, for better or worse, pretty much his own man. I echo God, as the Bible enjoins all of us to: "I AM."

Being one's own man, or one's own woman, has a downside. The people of the book have, all together, drawn criticism for it. Charles de Gaulle characterized the Jews as *un peuple d'élite, sûr de lui-même et dominateur*. If this odious pronouncement is a gloss on God's promise of greatness to the Abrahamites, de Gaulle gets it wrong. The greatness is in the philosophical revolution that the first members of the line initiated; the national inflection – chosenness – is an add-on. Didn't de Gaulle himself, in order to inspire a Gaul dispirited by the ease with which *le people du Capet* had capitulated, harp on about *la gloire et la grandeur de la France*? And if de Gaulle's "dominateur" refers to the biblical ascription of dominion, *encore il à tort*. The ascription does not single out Israelites. Indeed, as I show in the discussion devoted to the Bible's notion of dominion, it doesn't even place the featherless biped on a higher perch.

Not a few have complained about my style. So far as the writing goes, for the little it's worth I'll say that I work hard at it. The writing that I do is also, overall, amusing. Some of the peeved reactions to *this* feature recall to me the tut-tutting of our rabbi when the hubbub in the pews challenged the cantorial chanting. "Let there be decorum in the sanctuary." Is there a place and a time in the philosophical frame for folderol? I'll plead my cause in the course of commenting more broadly on the craft of writing.

One of the first philosophy books that I read was Whitehead's *The Function of Reason*. At the time (this was in high school), I memorized several passages from the brilliantly written pamphlet, one of which came to mind while I was composing "A Plea for Ontology." Here's the passage, as I recall it at this moment. "The obscurantists of any age are in the main constituted by the practitioners of the dominant methodology." Why would I have committed the words to memory when I had no diachronic sense of any discipline? In my mid-teens, did I even know what "obscurantist" means?

This memory report is no bid to enter *Guinness*. Against the reciters of π to 50,000 places, the bid would anyway be irrational. I have a substantive point in mind. Narrowly technical matters apart, how can a lasting piece of philosophy be produced from a standing start in the space of several months? Philosophizing is, or should be, an integrative process, a seven-course meal, with quite a bit of repeating, perhaps even a visit or two to the vomitorium, not an oyster sluiced down the hatch by a shot of chilled vodka. Yet the structure of academic life makes long memory a recipe for perishing.

In *Remembrance of Things Past*, Proust (605) contrasts the intellectual approach of the Marquis de Norpois and that of the writer Bergotte, both of whom deem ill-informed young Marcel's disappointment at Sarah Bernhardt's performance in a production of Racine's *Phèdre*.

> … when Bergotte's opinion was thus contrary to mine, he in no way reduced me to silence, to the impossibility of framing any reply, as M. de Norpois would have done. This does not prove that Bergotte's opinions were less valid than the Ambassador's; far from it. A powerful idea communicates some of its power to the man who contradicts it. Partaking of the universal community of minds, it infiltrates, grafts itself on to, the mind of him whom it refutes, among other contiguous ideas, with the aid of which, counter attacking, he complements and corrects it; so that the final verdict is always to some extent the work of both parties to a discussion. It is to ideas which, based on nothing, can find no foothold, no fraternal echo in the mind of the adversary, that the latter, grappling as it were with thin air, can find no word to say in answer. The arguments of M. de Norpois … were unanswerable simply because they were devoid of reality.

To M. de Norpois, who's on the wrong side of my point. I'll return in a moment.

It's a rare bird that knows its thoughts without giving them a public form, even if only in a tweet. To be sure, vocalizing or jotting down the thoughts is no more than a necessary condition for the knowledge. In the new world of electronic writing, a related point merits emphasis. Until you examine hard copy, you don't know what you've written. Even then you might not know. Familiarity dulls the critical faculty. "None," as John Stuart Mill commented, "are more likely to have seen what he does not see, than he who does not see what he sees." You're unlikely, then, to do philosophy effectively without writing; and, assuming that you use a word processor, without reading a printout. *Le Penseur*, gripe though he may that his solitude is disturbed, needs to be Euphrosyne to *L'Écrivain*'s Agleia and *Le Lecteur*'s Thalia. Scrabble (the board game) gives a nice parallel. Without shuffling the tiles and taking a look, then shuffling them again, half of what you've got will go unnoticed. It's the same with people. Only exposure under varied circumstances gives a gauge of a person, including the person who is being exposed. "What will I be like in Paris?" The armchair is a poor place from which to answer, just as purely mental shuffling will miss more words than it finds.

In several cases, the end-form of the pieces that became the book's chapters materialized like the proverbial rabbit. To me this underscores the necessity of writing and rewriting and illustrates the likeness of the process to magic. In each of the pieces to which I allude, I began, as I usually do, with an amorphous idea. Take "On one leg." The title comes from an oft-repeated anecdote about a person considering conversion who consults two rabbis. What first suggested itself to me was a contrast between paganism, as having several legs to stand on (pagan pantheons are characteristically centipedal), and limpet-like monotheism. The prospective proselyte is challenging the rabbis: "I can't stand on one leg for long. How can a belief-system with God as its sole support be stable?" As I continued my tinkering, the idea took an unexpected turn. A clearer version emerged of the point that, *pace* most interpreters, Genesis 1 and Genesis 2 do not do the same thing in different ways. *The first chapter of the Bible is the pagan story; the second is the Bible's departure from naturalism.* So the two legs are a pagan leg and a biblical leg. The prospective proselyte is asking a philosophical question about the explanatory powers of paganism and of Bibleism. Invariably trotted out as a poster boy for chutzpah, he deserves an apology.

A similar meander led me to the key point of "Where were you?" In this instance a difference that I had not up to then thematized turns into a distinction essential to the Book of Job's case for absolving God of complicity in the suffering of innocents, namely the distinction between being present *at* but not being present *in*, as when you're watching a hockey game from the stands, and being present *at* and being present *in*, as when you're out there on the ice fighting for the puck. The first of these corresponds to God's position relative to the world whose creation is described in Genesis 1, the second, his position relative to the world whose coming into being Genesis 2 deals with.

The Quine aspect of the same piece traces also to some thoughts, entertained in a Bible-unrelated context, about Quine's program of replacing unstructured singular terms with predicates and bound variables. The program, I came to see in the frame of thinking about the Bible, would deprive us of the resources to formulate God's "I AM." Quine himself (needless to say) did not connect the logico-linguistic regimentation of names with issues about – as God is sometimes denominated – the Name.

"To be is to be the value of a variable." "I am who I am." Talk about permuting Scrabble tiles! T-B-S-T-B, I-M-O-I-M! The productive manipulation of ideas is more art than science. Isn't wordplay a relative of non-formulaic ideation? This furnishes an extra-stylistic justification for punning. In wordplay, the mentioned habit of mind percolates in the register of humour.

Word games in class? Not really. Nevertheless, the remarks do spawn an observation about the curriculum makers. Recall M. de Norpois. One often encounters the type in the guise of the exponent of the program du jour. Given how frequently the erstwhile visionary's vision proves to be of the tunnel variety, it's depressing to observe the alacrity with which not a few departments of philosophy seal their fate for a generation through hiring, in the space of a few years, a few.

The Norpoises of the piece are produced by graduate schools. Life produces the Bergottes.

The small point that I want to make here is, however, more sociological.

The Jerry of "Jerry and Jewry" is Gerald Cohen, Oxford's Chichele Professor of Social and Political Theory from the mid-eighties through most of the aughts. Like me, Cohen was born in Montreal. After completing an undergraduate degree at McGill University, as I did, Cohen, like me, went on to graduate studies in philosophy at Oxford and then entered the profession. Does it say something about Montreal that Charles Taylor, the predecessor of Cohen's predecessor in the Chichele Chair, is, as Cohen was, a solid gold link in this career chain?

Cohen (who died in 2009) had a reputation as a mixture, in subfusc, of Jackie Mason, Frank Gorshin, and Tom Lehrer. He wove the levity into his extensive lecturing; the audiences fairly rolled in the Isles. Would Cohen have smiled at "another Oxford priest"? The play on his surname falls well below Cohen's standards. On the other hand, the motto on Montreal's coat of arms being "CONCORDIA SALUS," perhaps he would have deigned to chuckle out of solidarity. As the case may be, I have a point to make, and "priest" gives a leg up.

"The world would not be in such a snarl had Marx been Groucho instead of Karl." Had *his* model been Groucho rather than Karl, Cohen could have worked the Borscht Belt. If instead of Sir Isaiah his mentor had been the Berlin who authored the quip, he could have made a Broadway living. Cohen was infectiously funny. For most in the academic game, fame that elevates them to the dais is a necessary condition for colleagues in the pews to be receptive to their humour. This has a couple of effects. Often, the response to even Wilde-like cleverness when it comes from a fellow pew-sitter is akin to what one imagines that a frogged-jacketed footman's belch in the Queen's presence would elicit from the ladies-in-waiting. At the other extreme, and as I have observed with my own eyes in the case of a few eminent programmers du jour, an inability to rise much above the level of the potty joke does not contract the circle of deferential chortlers.

A lot of the personal dynamic in the academy (as these facts about laughter light-heartedly confirm) invites the label "Toad Hall." Rank-and-file academics

too often combine in their persons a mixture of inflated self-evaluation reflective of how the non-academic world sees them – a rating rarely shared, as
they are acutely aware, by the higher-profile colleagues on whom they depend
for preferment; of a sense of entitlement based on the kite-tail of letters that
streams from their names; and of guilt, since, even though they rise to high-Cs
of indignation should the institution of tenure be questioned, the feeling gnaws
that freedom from serious oversight allows them to get away with murder.
Not infrequently, the effect of the toxic cocktail is a touchy Prufrock. Theodor
Adorno offers a quotable. "Intellectuals … encounter one another primarily in
the most embarrassing and degrading situation of all, that of competing sup-
plicants, and are thereby … compelled to show their worst side to one another."
To which this deeper assessment of José Ortega y Gasset's about the type makes
a good colleague. "He is a learned ignoramus, which is a very serious matter, as
it implies that he is a person who is ignorant, not in the fashion of the ignorant
man, but with all the petulance of one who is learned in his own special line."[6]

The chapter on Christopher Hitchens is more literary than the philosophical
discussions that I usually write. I was therefore surprised that a journal specializing in religious matters and targeting a fairly wide audience passed on a free-
standing version of it, the editor remarking that he did not publish writing so
fine. Was "fine writing" sarcastic? If so, witness a case of what I spoke of above.
Otherwise, I shake my head.

   Hitchens's bestseller *god Is Not Great* is of professional interest to me. As
it happens, I also have a personal connection (well, a personal connection of
sorts) with the author. In my graduate student days, Hitchens was an undergraduate at the Oxford college that I attended. Remembering our time there,
I portray myself in "God Loves You" as a version of Dostoyevsky's Underground Man, erecting a complex relationship on a brush-by in Balliol's Junior
Common Room. As a matter of fact, Hitchens read a precursor of "God Loves
You"; a mutual friend passed it to him. By then, he had received a terminal
cancer diagnosis. (As is evident from the first few paragraphs, what he saw
was written prior to this sad development. If I hadn't gone back and made
adjustments, my remark about throat-clearing, which quotes a phrase from
god Is Not Great, would open me to rebuke.) After Hitchens got the diagnosis – his, he says in *Mortality*, the brave, posthumously published book, was
Stage Four esophageal cancer, "and there is no such thing as Stage Five" – a
few fastened on the phrase. A place awaits them in Dante's eighth circle. As
for me, my thought was that Hitchens might benefit from understanding that
his criticism of religion, the institution, is misdirected at the scriptural core of
Judaism. I also confess to having thought that Hitchens's saying, in print, that

Glouberman had enlightened him on this (or even saying, if it came to that, that the kid is out to lunch) would do me no harm. A fantasy all round, alas! The Augustinian contrast that I draw in "God Loves You" is in all likelihood the last word.

Hitchens's reaction to what I wrote was relayed to me. For being unable to do more than skim, Hitchens expressed regret. The therapy, he explained, left him muzzy-headed. He went on to throw two darts at my screed, both on the factual side. One had to do with the telephone call of which I tell, the other, with the female names that I mention.

The telephone call: Hitchens (contrarian to the last thrupenny bit) denied the thing possible. To make a call he had had, he said, to leave the confines of the college and use a public box on St Aldate's, across from the stone monument commemorating Cranmer, Latimer, and Ridley. Could it be that frequent use of the payphone, eyes fixed on the Martyrs' Memorial, hardened Hitchens against religion?

Did it occur exactly as I describe? The description is at least a reasonable approximation. Of that I am sure. Let's say that the call to the common room was from the porters' lodge, announcing some ingénue who to penetrate the precincts of the college would need accompaniment. As for the names: Hitchens claimed that I got only one right. My motivation had not however been straightforwardly reportorial. Had I written "the Fionas and the Nigellas," I would probably have scored zero while still striking the desired tone.

When I happened upon a publisher's notice of Yoram Hazony's *The Philosophy of Hebrew Scripture*, my interest was piqued. I had been keeping abreast of Hazony's activity in a philosophy-driven program of study of the Torah, the Tanakh, the Talmud. My cup of T runneth over. Was I apprehensive that what I was labouring on would be yesterday's news? I found when I read the book that rather than point mainstream philosophers to a lode which through the centuries had been mis-assayed, Hazony only argues that it's not God's authority that is called upon to secure the views advanced in the Bible. A Godless rewrite, then, of biblical teachings. Some Godlessnesses are more biblical than others, however. The move from "The Bible's authority doesn't come from God" to "God's role is superfluous" bypasses the Bible's distinctive philosophical content. God in the Bible can be likened to the ghost in *Hamlet*. What the Bible's God, Abrahamlet's ghost, stands for is essential. Why do I write about a book towards which I am so cool? "Godless" is an occasion to test the essentials of *my* position. To be sure, I could be wrong. By much the same token, the exposition therefore stands a chance of eliciting helpful criticism, all the more given Hazony's star-maker machinery.[7]

"I could be wrong." This overstates my diffidence. But in comparison with Steven Pinker, Glouberman, thy name is restraint. The aggressive comment that

I quote in "A Plea for Ontology" disentitles Pinker to an answer from Thomas Nagel.

A blurb on the cover of Hazony's book quotes none other than the afore-mentioned aggressor: a fortuitous link, then, between two of the chapters. "A deep and lucid investigation of the connection between the ... chief strands of our intellectual history. A great achievement." I am put in mind of an amusing put-down, quoting which situates me offside Ruth Bader Ginsburg's sage advice about disagreeing agreeably. Here are Philip Larkin's words upon hearing that a reviewer had described his *A Girl in Winter* as a top novel of the postwar period. "I'd like to shake the woman's hand. Has she been discharged yet, or are there visiting hours?" Lucid enough, deep Hazony's book isn't. And what are we to make of Pinker's praising Hazony's defence of the Bible while suggesting that Nagel, whose position reflects the Bible's anti-naturalism, should place a band of black on his hat as a mark of respect to his brain? As to the meat of the debate: my point is that philosophers as philosophers might have more to offer than either of the parties allows. The chapter on Nagel is, as its title states, a plea for ontology, specifically for the Bible's categorization of being. Here, Nagel is nearer to God than thee, Hazony.

In the chapter on philosophy and the Holocaust, "'Jew' as a Category Label," I refer to Sophocles's *Antigone*. Antigone's defiance of Creon is, I argue, a philo-sophical act similar in its message to the transgression in the garden. My experi-ence trying to interest classical scholars in the idea confirms Donald Akenson's observation that a generalist in this field stands as much chance of getting into the specialized journals as does a Camel into an emphysema ward. This for-mulation will, I know, be viewed as so much smoke being blown lest the dis-gruntled rejectee be seen for what he is. The purpose is however to highlight the genre of criticism that I encountered: refutation by paraphrase. This is the scholarly correlate of holding up an item with two fingers, your arm extended, while pulling a face. So far as *Antigone* goes, my thesis is that the speech about brothers and sons and spouses that flummoxed Goethe, no less, unlocks the play's meaning. The muddle is the message. Here is the reaction of the classicist who refereed a version of the interpretation. "It is claimed that Antigone's argu-ment is shocking, and that it frustrates those who see in Antigone a champion of family in general over city. The basic argument hinges on the irreplaceability of a brother, and by extension, of each human being." The description is not inaccurate, which, since it quotes my abstract, is no surprise. Crickets, though, about why insouciance is an apt response to a speech any normal reader's reac-tion to which is incredulity. "It is claimed."

My favourite literary ending is that of the work of Dostoyevsky's to the imag-ined writer of which I jokingly likened myself earlier. The writer's last words are these. "But enough; I don't want to write more from 'Underground.'" An edito-rial comment is appended, which I can quote in capacity both as writer and as editor. "The notes of this paradoxalist do not end here, however. He could not refrain from going on with them, but it seems to us that we may stop here."

Even more than do deliberate choices, imponderables and uncontrollables shape both careers and lives. How else can I feel myself but fortunate in having been exposed through my early schooling to a body of material whose interaction with the products of the professional study that I later chose to do – chose with no such interaction in mind – have kept me intellectually busy and, I think, instructed me more than academically? The constellation is a gift for which I am, to whomever gives such gifts, or, if no one does, then in a non-transitive way, grateful. I would be guilty of ingratitude if I were to have taken the gift for granted.

PRINCIPLES

1

Bibleism and Judaism:
Four and a Half Dogmas of
Bible Interpretation

Marcion Redux

As Marcion (c. 85–c. 160) saw it, the creator deity of the Bible is implicated in the corruption that characterizes the lives of even the least blameworthy of the creatures vivified with his breath. The true deity he identified as a being who inhabits a sphere separated sharply from the fallen world, and Christ as an emanation sent on a mission – of redemption – that could not otherwise be accomplished. "Who," as Job asks rhetorically (14:4), "can bring a clean thing out of an unclean?" Marcion therefore lobbied to exclude the Hebrew Scriptures and those of the Gospels that reflected its theology from the Christian canon.

My thesis shifts the Marcionite position back an age. The higher being of Judaism, I maintain, is not the god who figures in Abraham's annals. *Given its theology, Judaism should be decoupled from the Hebrew Scriptures.*

It was for the sake of Christianity that Marcion advocated not including the Hebrew Scriptures. I argue that distancing Judaism from the Torah is required for the Torah's sake. Judaism fits the Bible's core out in religious garb that obscures its shape.

Teaching as it does that the lives of men and women intersect with and are affected by an extra-physical region of (non-abstract) reality, Judaism is a religion. Conversely, the distinctions upon which the truth of the biblical position rests are as internal to everyday experience as is the distinction between human beings and other physical things. Bibleism thus lines up with the various isms of philosophical anthropology whose advocates are neither rabbis nor priests: naturalism, materialism, neutral monism, dualism. To assess the Bible, one must gauge the effectiveness of its conceptualization not to matters numinous but to the condition of men and women in the world.

Judaism regards the following as Bible-based.

The natural world is the product of God's creative activity.

Men and women have a distinctive status among creatures, a status for which God is responsible and which the account of the emergence of men and women in Genesis 1 and Genesis 2 describes.

Monotheism – the theological view that there is one and only one deity.

Immortality (eternity) divides God from men and women.

None of the above are present in the Torah. Present are either their negations or teachings unconnected to them.

The natural world emerges without God's activity.

Genesis 1 does not describe the emergence of men and women as the Bible distinctively sees them among creatures.

The theological view is not that there is one and only one deity.

God is in the same case as are men and women with regard to immortality.

Marcion ran up against the formidable Tertullian. To prevent the reader from immediately turning Tertullian on Mark ("What part of IN PRINCIPIO CREAVIT DEUS CÆLUM ET TERRAM do you not understand?"), I'll add that what is written *resolves to* the members of the second quartet once the real tensions between them are dealt with.

Say "when"

"God created the heavens and the earth" appears both at the start of Genesis 1 (verse 1) and in the retrospective overview with which Genesis 2 begins (verses 2 and 3). It cannot automatically be concluded either that according to the Bible God is the creator or that the heavens and the earth are products of his activity. Verse 1 of Genesis 1 is a summary of the cosmogonic description in the offing. Also, the part after "in the beginning" is best translated as in the NRSV: "when God created the heavens and the earth."[1]

Verse 1 tells us that we're about to be told what occurred. Setting to work, the tellers might have told us how it was with God. "... and God, blueprints in hand, headed to the job site." In the event, they tell us (verse 2) how it was with things: "and the earth was waste and void."

> Here's how it was in the beginning, when, in the first of days, God created the world and all that it contains. At the outset, there wasn't a world. Chaos is what there was. Then God said ...

The (as it is usually regarded) creative activity is an ordering of the less ordered; of, at the very beginning, the orderless. Leave aside the *how*. Focus on the *what*. A featureless welter gives way to a whole of distinct regions.

Long have theologians debated the resolution that God, *in principio*, creates *ex nihilo*. The decision has implications for whether God is the sole basic principle of reality. Suppose we find fault with the world. A creator who didn't start with a blank canvas might get our sympathy. "How valiant the attempt!" Anger could under the same circumstances be felt towards a deity who had *carte blanche*. "What the devil! D for effort!"

Ex nihilo or not? That the text doesn't remove the question mark from the disjunction signals that the issue is immaterial to its teachings.

"Immaterial? Isn't God's nature at stake? The issue can be immaterial only if the theological treatment is *irrelevant* to the design."

Irrelevant I hold it to be. God performs no creative acts. Debate, the theologians may, the order of priority of creator and (the raw material of) creation. It's not a debate about the Bible.

"No creative acts? What are there, then?" Processes of increasing differentiation. Processes don't always involve actors. If mixing is going on in the bakery, we can infer a mixer. But when the dough rises, it is not because the baker raises it. "The dough rises of itself," we might say. We would not say that it raises itself. It's something that happens, not something that, in the verb's progressive sense, is done.

To establish that the creation is dough rising, it must be shown that of the things that come about in the biblical story, some, the more the better, are not the products of doings. Also, it must be argued that each of the comings-about that are represented in the narrative as doings needs undoing.

Among the cases of increasing differentiation some are depicted to occur on their own (versus: the gardener plants the garden) and/or to unfold without ongoing monitoring (versus: the gardener tills and keeps the plants). "Let the earth put forth vegetation" (11). God does not bring the grasses out of the land. More revealingly, since a higher level of organization is involved and the process is observationally fugitive, the waters bring forth the marine creatures. "Let the waters bring forth swarms of living creatures" (20).[2]

On the basis of internal churning of earth and waters, and subject to their governing principles, the areas, it would seem, populate themselves.

One swallow does not make a supper. The merged waters do not precipitate out a firmament.[3] God *inserts* the divider. The region above the upper waters does not congeal the sun and the stars. God *sets* the heavenly bodies there.

In the case of the fish, the process-emergence pattern is used. Yet the case of the birds is *prima facie* similar. Here, to the obvious question, is my reconstruction of the Bible's answer, which in its specifics also explains why the heavenly bodies are handled like the birds.

When we view a tornado, it's the objects whirling about that are seen. Air itself is not visible. In any case, flying things are too substantial to be churned out of air, which doesn't seem like stuff. The waters contrast on both counts. They are no less substantial than the marine creatures, and we do see them churning.[4]

The account defaults to process-emergence. The plants are dealt with this way; some of the animals too. The more elemental differentiation into upper and lower waters doesn't follow suit because, from the armchair, it's hard to imagine it belonging to the club.[5]

By way of showing that the textual barrier to process-emergence isn't impermeable, let me extend the pattern; extend it right into the citadel.

"Abracadabra," incants the magician over the top hat. Many commentators see the description of the emergence of light in verse 3 as ascribing to God the power with which the magician is invested only through suspension of disbelief.[6] Examined from the standpoint of the "normal" pattern, the incompleteness in this case arguably bears witness to (greater) puzzlement about the internal principle. Perhaps we can unwrinkle the formulators' foreheads.

Squeeze a sponge over an empty glass. The wringing done, the glass is half full. After the light appears, God "separated [it] from the dark" (4). This suggests a like pattern. In the case of the creation of dry from moist, separation makes perfect sense. But from what prior thing could light emerge? You're motoring along. Suddenly, a fog bank. "Light," you say, as you flick the switch. Enshrouded in a milky soup, you remain in the dark.[7] For the beams to assist navigation, the aerosol's particles have to coalesce. What if cohesive forces get the better of dispersive ones as the particles lose energy? The clumping would "separate … the light from the dark."[8]

Many hold up "'Let there be light'; and there was light" as the paradigm of divine creativity. On the described way of dealing with the verse, light and dark come to be as do dry and wet. Greater unity is thus gained for the whole – always an interpretive plus. *Eo ipso*, the unification reduces the number of doings in Genesis 1.

Question: If one arrogates to oneself leave to interpret aggressively, why not reverse the movement across the barrier? Answer: Who of the view that God is active would introduce something that gnawed away at the activity in a manner that causes the ship to spring a leak? Upshot: It's more reasonable to hold that the active deity remains because the writers/thinkers can't see how to treat the subject-matter in the other way.

This interpretation *is* aggressive. Weights are assigned to components of the text different than the weights that (it is agreed) the authors assign. There had better be a compelling reason for reconfiguring so that doings, as they are represented in the text, give way to processes.

There *is* a compelling reason. *Genesis 1's story is not distinctively biblical*. In fact, *it is distinctly non-biblical*. It's a version of the pagan story. "Why, if so, is it in the text?" The pagan account of the beginning is the best thing going, and the Bible is encyclopedic.

An oft-repeated anecdote that comes to mind here reports the title page of a Yiddish edition of Shakespeare: "Translated and Improved." Genesis 1 is more than a translated version of the Old Babylonian story; it's an *improved* version. Consider these lines from Hesiod's *Theogony*, a scriptural work of Greek paganism.[9]

> Chaos was born first and after it came Gaia
> the broad-breasted, the firm seat of all
> the immortals who hold the peaks of snowy Olympos,
> Gaia now first gave birth to starry Ouranos,
> her match in size, to encompass all of her,
> and be the first seat of all the blessed gods.

The Bible's story is myth-free. Orderly and rational, it invites the description "proto-scientific."

"If Genesis 1 is a version of the pagan story, why do the writers/thinkers put God in in the first place?" God fulfills three roles.

NARRATOLOGICAL: The writers, not seeing how the nature/natures pattern can work, fall back on the God-makes template. This overcomes a gappiness that would diminish the story's effectiveness.

POLITICAL: God presides over the whole of the Bible. Consider the form "JFK put a man on the moon." Even though Kennedy did not live to see the landing, we dignify him thus because the project was initiated when he was president.

CLARIFICATORY: God's extra-naturalness makes clear the manner in which one sector that differentiates out differs. I am referring to the assertion that men and women have dominion. The other things and creatures occupy specific habitats (a fish out of water won't flounder for long). Men and women alone are not domain-specific. The appeal to God helps clarify the point because God *has no place* in the natural world. Men and women are "in [God's] image and likeness" in this religiously neutral sense.

Readers will know that God throughout Genesis 1 reacts to what comes into being with "good," which means "does its job; functions as desired/required/intended." The sun is placed in the heavens to give light. It gives light. So it is "good."[10]

Recall the dyspeptic book reviewer. *What's original isn't good. What's good isn't original.* The slogan applies to the Bible's foundational part. The Genesis 1 story of the creation isn't original. It's only with what marks the Bible as original that we first hear "not good" (2:18).

The God Principle

Although consistent in spirit with paganism, the Bible's treatment of the natural world is more attentive to reason. From Chaos, Hesiod says, Gaia emerges; then, from Gaia emerges Ouranos.[11] The earth congeals from the welter; then, the heavens fission from the earth. Earth without heavens? Reason rises up. Covering the same ground, the Bible states that God created the heavens *and* the earth.

The Bible advertises itself as a replacement for paganism. In beckoning Abraham to leave his "country ... and ... father's house" (Genesis 12:1), God is inviting him to a new system of belief. If Genesis 1 is a version of paganism, in what does the Bible's originality consist?

In the Canaanite settlement of Beer-sheba where he had planted "a tamarisk tree," Abraham "called ... on the name of the Lord" (21:33). What did he say? Had he spoken "In the beginning when God created the heavens and the earth," the herders of the region would not have been moved. "Apart from the mention of this character named 'God,' the story," they would have said, "is our story."[12]

What *did* Abraham say? Abraham declaimed Genesis 2. "In the day the Lord God made the earth and the heavens ..." (Genesis 2:4). This is something that no ears had yet heard.[13]

Verses 1 to 3 of Genesis 2 look back. Why, then, does the effective start of the story describe a static world? Wasn't the outset of Genesis 1 – "a formless void" in the NRSV, "waste and void" in the KJ – a blooming, buzzing confusion? Here, again, is verse 4 of Genesis 2 along with the first part of verse 5. "In the day that the Lord God made ... earth and ... heavens, when no plant of the field was yet in the earth and no herb of the field had yet sprung up ..."[14] The reason is that change that is initiated change and whose product can come to an end is exclusive to the world of Genesis 2. What, then, does God's getting things going consist in? Verse 6: irrigating the barren ground. Verse 7: forming a man and breathing life into him. Verse 8: planting a garden[15] and putting the man in it. These developments resist the process-emergence pattern. No gardener, no garden. No man-maker, no man. No irrigator, desiccation.

To men and women, what God is represented as doing in Genesis 2 differs from what he is represented – misleadingly, I claim – as doing in Genesis 1. In Genesis 1, "male and female he created them." Here, it's a single person. Although the language is masculine (Hebrew is a gendered tongue), that person is not described as a male. If the story had been biological, the narrative would have contained an absurdity like the heavenless earth of Hesiod.

"Male and female" isn't said in Genesis 1 of the non-human animals. The phrase is used in the human case to forestall the thought that in representing only our kind as created in God's image and likeness the Bible is doing more than distinguishing one species among the many. For, usually, we *do* think of each person as separate, thinking along these (non-biological) lines of non-human animals only in special cases (pets, for example).[16]

A conceptual point is present here; an ontological one too. Non-human creatures have natures; cultures they do not have. Absent the distinction, the commonplace that men and women – individual men and women! – act against their biologies, for example by fasting, by celibacy, by staying up all night, would be inaccessible. The ontological point follows from the Bible's analysis of nature.

Two mutually excluding exclusivities convey the ontological point: the singular form in Genesis 2; the plural form in Genesis 1. In Genesis 1:26, God is said to propose making humankind in his image; "in [his] image," it is then written in verse 27, "he created *them*." In Genesis 2:7, God, it is written, formed the man. Then it is said that God breathed "into *his* nostrils."

Going against the original of Genesis 2:7, where the noun term has the definite article, the NRSV puts "formed man." The same noun term – "האדם" – appears later in the verse, and again in verse 8. But in both cases, the NRSV has the definite article. In his translation of *Genesis*, Robert Alter homogenizes in reverse. The Hebrew in 1:26 is the common noun. We could see its unaccompanied appearance along the lines of "Man is the most intelligent of creatures." The form is available for types and sorts. Alter's "a [hu]man" in 1:26 is a mistake. Three Hebrew words later, the plural form of the verb, which requires "them," appears. If we stick to Alter's "a human," a mishmash like the NRSV's results. "God created a human. 'Let them have dominion' God said."[17]

The plural is vital to Genesis 1; the singular, to Genesis 2. The biblical position is that the sector of being to which we belong is unique, each of us an entity in their own right. The heavens and the earth had better be happy together. For Dick and Jane, a change of partners is an option.

The Bible is answering *the* question of philosophical anthropology. "What is man?" The answer combines what is written in its two opening chapters. Genesis 1: Among the (natural) creatures whose coming into being is described, we alone belong to a species that is made in God's image.[18] Genesis 2: *Qua* inspired with God's breath, each of us is more than a member of the species.

To get the gist of the second part, look up at Michelangelo's panel of God enlivening Adam. God's index finger and Adam's are slightly apart. Asked, most, in my experience, answer that it's an "after" picture. "The man is alive, is he not?" But aren't animals and plants alive without benefit of God's breath? The biblical deity imparts not life itself but life of a specific sort. In highlighting the difference between the plural pronouns of Genesis 1 and the singular ones of Genesis 2, I indicated, obliquely, what sort of life it is.

It's no wonder that while Genesis 1 describes the emergence of luminaries and of geographical regions, of plants and of animals, Genesis 2 focuses on the emergence of the man, and through him the woman – the origin of each man and each woman down the ages.

Why is it *God* who makes the contribution? The question brings us to the third of the teachings, concerning monotheism. For the Bible teaches that paganism is inadequate because the contribution is beyond the pagan powers.

Monotheism: A Misnomer

"Monotheism" is transliterated Greek. Given the supposed centrality of monotheism to the biblical view,[19] it's odd that the Bible lacks a term of its own. Odder still is confusion surrounding the Shema, the creedal declaration usually identified as *the* assertion of monotheism. The NRSV has "Hear, O Israel: The Lord is our God, the Lord alone." The KJ has "Hear, O Israel: The Lord our God is one Lord." Both are problematic. In Hebrew, the NRSV's "alone" is the cardinal "one." Putting "Lord" at the end of the sentence, the KJ runs afoul of the fact that the word in the original is a proper name. "One person" makes sense; "one Fred" needs special circumstances.[20]

The considerable non-stylistic variation attests that the translators are at sea. If monotheism is central, and if the Shema asserts it, one would expect uniformity.

What the translators are missing is of the Bible's essence. Would Greek religion have been monotheistic had Zeus occupied Olympus alone? If Yes, monotheism's connection with the Bible is incidental. Zeus, a nature god, cannot be functionally identical with God, a personal deity whose mode of being is extranatural. If No, the Bible's monotheism is not the view that only one deity exists.

The (true) response that Zeus *could not be alone* on Olympus is useful to our purposes. A person who observes that the weather deity requires his brethren, the earth god and the sea god, is sensitive to nature's being a system, a fact crucial to the biblical position. "Heaven and earth" is the template. No Garbo here.

Some specialists opine that monotheism flowered briefly along the Nile, and in this some of these some see a harbinger of monotheism's long biblical bloom-time. Akhenaten, within whose dates falls the conjectural date of the exodus, attempted an upheaval to the extant form of worship.[21] Abandoning the regnant polytheism, he promoted the sun deity to exclusive sovereignty. James P. Allen, dissenting from the mentioned opinion, quotes Egyptologist Jan Assmann (Allen, 89): "We stand here at the origin less of the monotheistic world religions than of natural philosophy. If [Akhenaten's] religion had succeeded, we should have expected it to produce a Thales [sc. a material monist] rather than a Moses [sc. a monotheist]."

Akhenaten's is like an attempt to eliminate all the Olympian deities but one. The project isn't an idle fantasy. When beads of water coalesce, the previous multiplicity leaves no trace. *Mutatis mutandis*, the various natural principles (each associated with a god) might be unified. The pot of gold at the end of this rainbow is, as Assmann asserts, monism.

What does the Shema state? It states that the deity is, in a strong sense, a one. Behind the Shema is the position of philosophical anthropology that each man and each woman is a separate entity, not essentially part of the system that is nature.[22] When the text is approached as a rejection of paganism, this, obviously, is what is being said.

I'll sum up.

> In verse 2:7, it is said of our sector of creation what isn't said in verse 1:26: we are particulars. Verse 2:7 says this by saying that a part of the natural world (a lump of clay) is inspired with God's breath of life. God is introduced because the natural world, qua system, has in it no (real, basic, and separate) particulars. The advent of particulars cannot therefore be explained on the natural basis. Not only is God, the deity of the Bible, non-natural; also, God is a particular: God is one (= God has one-ness). Whatever we make of God's surgical procedure on the man, the result is another particular.

What does the man do next? The transgression dramatizes his separation from the system. The man has the capacity to separate, as parts of the system do not.

The departure from the garden is not the absurdity of a car tire's rolling off on its own. In the garden the man and the woman already have particularity or separateness. But prior to its exercise they differ little from bullocks. The reader who reads the text religiously might ask: "If God planted the garden, why doesn't *he* tend it? Wouldn't it be child's play?" The garden is the distinctive place of men and women. It's an emblem of the (extra-natural) world of Genesis 2. In describing the garden as the product of God's planting, the thinkers behind the Bible make the point in their default, genetic, way. The claim that no garden would emerge naturally is parallel to the claim that individual men and women, as particulars, wouldn't either. If they don't want to be reclaimed by the wilds, like a neglected garden, they had better tend to and keep themselves.

Mortality

Treating the difference between Genesis 1 and Genesis 2 as stylistic is the Original Sin of biblical scholarship. In this final section, I will subsume the final teaching, about mortality, under the substantial difference between the two.

The world of Genesis 1, inclusive of the human sector, is a system. The way the parts interconnect is written into their identity. To conceive a tree in a forest as an entity in its own right is to misplace concreteness. The possibility of death presupposes a scheme of being that includes entities capable of more than mutation. Real beginnings and genuine ends must be possible. God's creation of the first man (in Genesis 2) is a real beginning.[23] God is represented as responsible for this, because only particulars can really begin, and God is the principle of particularity.[24]

On the absence of real change in the world of Genesis 1 the Book of Ecclesiastes is explicit. "The sun rises and the sun goes down, and hurries to the place where it rises. / The wind blows to the south, and goes round to the north; round and round goes the wind, and on its circuits the wind returns" (1:5–6). "There is nothing new under the sun" (9).

God is, as the liturgy has it, "without beginning, without end." Despite no end of repeating this, the theologians don't tell us that "eternal" is *an implication* of God's not being part of the not so merry-go-round. It may be inferred that men and women, finite particulars astride the painted ponies, have beginnings and ends essentially. Do the Torah's teachings make our deaths more palatable? Still, they do explain why the alternative isn't the gift that we wish for. When we think of ourselves as immortal, it's as being what we are. Deathlessness in the Genesis 1 sense, were it given us, would require a category change. Would you want to be a π in the sky, with its non-terminating decimal expansion?

The idea that a particular might go on isn't logically incoherent. Still, as I'll end by showing, the Bible doesn't say or imply that the transgression "brought Death into the World."

The crucial passage is Genesis 3:22.

Then the Lord God said, "See, the man has become like one of us, knowing good and bad;[25] and now, he might reach out his hand and take also from the tree of life, and eat, and live forever" –

Having eaten of the tree of knowledge, the man and the woman are like the speaker in this respect. The verse's second part says that if they eat of the other tree, immortality will be theirs. Does the verse as a whole say that eating of the other tree will result in their becoming "like … us"? If anything, the position is that the tree of life must be withheld because they will lose the likeness by acquiring immortality.[26]

Roughly the same goes for God's curse: "By the sweat of your face you shall eat bread" (3:19). The verse continues: "until you return to the earth." God is only saying that the man's life will be hard. As little as we have to grumble about in this part of the world, our trials, such as they are, will nonetheless be over on the day that only our mourners return from the burial place.

Abraham we last saw in Beer-sheba. Starting his mission to the people of the world, he declaimed Genesis 2. The assembled still did not listen, so, rather than pack it in, he redirected the message to his own. If the doctrine of Israelite exceptionalism were not present in the text, I would add it as a fifth dogma. As it is, the doctrine's connection to the Bible's ontological driver, particularity, is situational. I add it, therefore, as half a dogma. As for the message: without the

God principle, either the human sector is distorted, or it is excluded. Abraham's claim on the well in Beer-sheba comes to this. *He* had done the digging. The water, the water mentioned in Genesis 2:6, *he* had divined. Only through him can the pagans draw on it.

Some Remarks on the Literature

A thinker's position on creation *ex nihilo* will have an opposite value to their position on biblical naturalism. Most therefore assume that Judaism's most important apologetical writer rejects out of hand the naturalistic reading of Genesis 1. As an Aristotelian in philosophy, Maimonides is however receptive to the world's eternity. Some say that it's only the logical possibility of beginninglessness that he allows. Others hold him to regard the story of the world's creation in the Bible – a narrative starring God – as tailored to the needs of non-philosophers. Maimonides's project being the enlistment of philosophy to illuminate the Bible, the second construction seems to be indicated. "Maimonides had every reason to present his true [Aristotelian] position on this issue in a ... veiled manner ... By proving creation, Maimonides has removed the philosophic obstacles to a literal reading of Scripture on these issues, though he nevertheless rejects such a reading on many points quite explicitly" (Kreisel, 49). In other words: an exoteric position (creation *ex nihilo*) is presented atop an esoteric one (eternity, in accordance with Aristotelian philosophy).

I hold a position about the Bible structured like Maimonides's: the issues of divine action and of divine presence arise in respect only of the sector comprising individual men and individual women. But for me, the duality is *explicit*. The talk of God's image and likeness in Genesis 1, part of the naturalistic account, clarifies the characteristic of men and women called "dominion." The mention of God's breath of life in Genesis 2 is the core of the non-naturalistic account. Here, men and woman are the only creatures.[27]

If Kreisel is right, then Maimonides's reading has to be faulted. The Bible does not speak – speak literally – of creation *ex nihilo*. God *is* represented as presiding over the whole. That however is mainly by way of curtailing the worship of the pagan deities. About "In the beginning ... God created" I'll say more below.

Ken Ham, founder and CEO of the Christian apologetical *Answers in Genesis*, doesn't beat around the bush. "The Bible – the 'history book of the universe' – provides a reliable, eye-witness account of the beginning of all things, and can be trusted to tell the truth in all areas it touches on."[28] Even if we accept the claim, that by itself does not however put us in the know about what it is that the Bible tells us. Ham himself has no doubt that creation *ex nihilo* is what it tells us. He had better (if asked) cite revelation in support. But why, if that were the case, would he fuss over the text?

Especially troubling about *Answers in Genesis* is the hostility towards science: "to expose the bankruptcy of evolutionary ideas, and its bedfellow, a 'millions of years old' earth (and even older universe)." I would not have mentioned the source otherwise than for the sake of the contrast with other commentators who also speak up for the Bible.

Maimonides arranges a marriage between Athens and Jerusalem. He might even be seen as beautifying the biblical story to improve the prospects. Other defenders of religion who come forward as friendly to science take similar positions. In "Responses to Darwin in the Religious Traditions," Christopher Southgate states (372): "A hermeneutic informed by Darwinism will suggest ... that God put in place the processes by which the Earth could bring forth living creatures, and it leaves fascinatingly open, as Genesis also does, the question of God's further involvement in guiding or sustaining those processes." What do the Darwin-inspired hermeneuticists do? They comb the text for hints and gestures. That's what I do too, though I have argued that hinted at and gestured towards is an internal tension.[29] The writers appeal to non-naturalistic explanations because plausible naturalistic ones elude them.

To Southgate, Genesis 1's Darwinian complementation is consistent with "In the beginning when God created." As the quotation about "bara" four paragraphs hence confirms, the thought is that God's activity is *sui generis*. "It is one of the curiosities of the contemporary debate on intelligent design that in an effort to demonstrate God's existence by reasoning about the natural world ID so seriously presumes upon the biblical text."

Southgate, like (in my understanding of him) Maimonides, mishandles the distinction between Genesis 1 and Genesis 2. It's in the Genesis 2 act of artificial respiration that God's activity is found. Darwin's book is *The Origin of Species*, not *The Origin of Particulars*. So rather than defend in God's name what is regarded from a scientific standpoint as indefensible, Southgate and Maimonides defend what from that standpoint needs no defence.[30]

Here, in a more analytic style, is the difference between Genesis 1 and Genesis 2.

A natural process results in a man (only) because it results in men. Just so, when a cheese omelette is made according to a recipe, it's not the intention for the specific omelette that is plated to come off the griddle. "Too runny, sir? Not enough cheddar?" "No. It's as I ordered. I just didn't want this one." The deism of Southgate's reading of Genesis 1, *qua* consistent in content with science's story, does not transpose easily to particulars. The view of those behind the Bible is that it doesn't transpose to them at all; which explains why God is part of the story of the coming into being of the first man.

What does Genesis 1's "In the beginning ... God created" come to? "The main verb of the first verse is *bara'*, in its Qal form only ever used for God's activity – hence, by inference, for what God alone can do, namely bring an entity into existence from absolutely nothing." This is merely stated, and Southgate passes to other matters. Cued by his remark, we can pass to the literature on the Bible that looks closely at language.

Some language-sensitive scholars who make use in their analyses of comparisons with the pagan creation accounts maintain, as I do, that Genesis 1 has a pagan character. Ellen van Wolde, in saying that "bara" has the sense of separating, aligns the cosmogenesis of the Bible with the *Theogony* and the *Enuma Elish*, thereby contradicting Southgate. The very start of Genesis, God creating the heavens and the earth, seems a platform firm enough for van Wolde's vault. A *distinction* is made, a *separation* of upper and lower. But, as many have argued, this could be a summary.

On linguistic matters, I am an outsider. But I have a criticism whose force is independent of the technicalities.

The Bible is awash in puns, proof of authorial interest in the look, the sound, the feel of the words. Take the very beginning, which contains "bara," the word whose usual rendering into English van Wolde is contesting. "Bereshith bara" is usefully compared with the phrase that begins Genesis 12: "Lekh Lekha." Since the first is a verb phrase, and the second, an imperative, usually rendered as "Go," semantic comparison draws a blank. The two however repeat consonantal pairs: B-R and L-KH. Now "bereshith," although there are issues about it, is semantically unproblematic. It refers to the start, the beginning. Since "lekh lekha" marks the start, the beginning, of Abraham's mission, couldn't the alliterative similarity be deliberate? Consider a parallel for "bereshith bara": the song title "Begin the Beguine." "Beguine" is not a coinage. Cole Porter chooses the word for its snap. Isn't it reasonable to see "bereshith bara" as chosen for *its* snap? If so, to attack van Wolde by pointing to other texts/contexts in which "bara" has the sense of "create" is like offering meteorological correction to Chaucer's "Whan that Aprill, with his shoures soote" by citing Eliot's "April is the cruellest month."

Terrance Randall Wardlaw, Jr., van Wolde's critic, cannot on linguistic grounds alone confute van Wolde's view of biblical creation as separation. Instead of saying that it *means* "separated," van Wolde should have said that in many cases "bara" is used to speak of separation. And why is it used? For, in part, the literary reason.

The king says: "Let the people be taxed." Pharaoh: "Let there be a pyramid." The minions set to work. "And it was so." In such instances, "Let there be" is tantamount to "It would be good if such and such were the case." If the tax is imposed; if the pyramid is built; neither materializes like a rabbit from a top hat. Abraham says (Genesis 13:8) to Lot: "Let there be no strife between you and me, and between your herders and my herders." The earth does not part. Rather, Lot's group moves eastward, and Abraham's towards the south.

We understand why light would be (deemed) good. Who of us knows what it's like to be a bat? The text suggests that light comes about not from scratch – "the quick sharp scratch. And blue spurt of a lighted match," as Robert Browning puts it – but by separation, as in the case of the herders of uncle and nephew. Then "God separated the light from the dark" (1:4). In effect, verse 3's "Let there be" is a statement of the (desirable) project. The process by which light comes to be is described in the subsequent verse. It comes to be as upper and lower waters do, as dry land comes about. Poof! The magician disappears through the trapdoor.

2
Godless the Bible's Philosophy Isn't

Athens in Jerusalem?

Within the Jewish tradition, activity of the reflective kind is not philosophical. That's the view that has dominion in the academy and that the intellectuals among the devout sanctify. In *The Philosophy of Hebrew Scripture*, Yoram Hazony takes issue with this orthodoxy. The Bible, the deepest product of the tradition's founding thinkers, belongs with "works by philosophers such as Plato or Hobbes[;] works of 'reason,' composed to assist individuals and nations looking to discover the true and the good … in accordance with man's natural abilities" (1).

With the quoted words I agree. But Hazony excises God from the story, when the Bible's distinctive philosophy is conveyed by the role that God plays. His Godless reconstruction may give us a work of reason. It's not however a work of philosophy; not, *a fortiori*, accurate to Bibleism.

The case for "No"

Is there a Jewish philosophy? A few decades ago, the first professor of philosophy in modern Israel, Leon Roth, answered with a categorical "No."[1] In Roth's view, Moses, even had he been less Periclean and more Socratic, could not have changed it to a "Yes."

Roth's answer has for its basis the practice of the Jewish thinkers who *are* more Socratic. In the works of the greatest of this company Roth finds philosophy aplenty. But (the following quotations are from 5 and 6)

> the genuinely philosophical side … is derived from without, that is, from the non-Jewish culture of the … time. Maimonides … select[ed] from that culture such [genuine philosophical] ideas as would offer an account of Judaism which should be consonant with the spirit, or, if you like, the vocabulary, of the age.[2]

Maimonides *adapted* material from the (extra-Jewish) philosophical canon to the principles and practices of Jewish faith.

The originality consisted not in his philosophy, which was that of Aristotle … but in what resulted when he applied his Aristotelianism to Judaism.

If philosophy constitutes the core of the Jewish charter document, why doesn't Maimonides see it? Two reasons can be extracted from Roth's discussion.

NPF. No philosophical form. The Bible's texture is narrative. It contains none of the reasoning and the argumentation that have been the discipline's *modi operandi* since its genesis in Greece.
NGC. No general content. That which is specific to one group lacks the generality of *philosophical* truth. Jewish thought is concerned, specifically, with Jewish matters: dietary habits, patterns of civility, modes of social organization, ritual practices, national self-determination.

Roth's case is made relative to his mainstream conception of philosophy. "[Philosophy] is not the immediate sensation or feeling, or the recalling of an immediate sensation or feeling. It is a pondering on it, a considering of it, a weighing of it" (2). Roth continues (2–3):

Philosophy is not just the [reflective] activity of weighing experiences, any experiences. The experiences it weighs are of a certain dimension and importance. They may be, for example, those ubiquitous elements which seem to appear in all, or almost all, the things with which we come into contact – space, time, form, matter, or more abstractly and more difficultly, causation. These are *fundamentals*, pervasive factors the removal or alteration of which would change the nature of things altogether.

What Hazony calls "*the* true and *the* good" (my emphasis) sorts with Roth's fundamentals.

In asserting that the Bible is philosophical, Hazony is classifying it as a work of reason. Although Roth agrees with this, in his view the Bible's thinkers do not deal in "factors the removal or alteration of which would change the nature of things altogether." They deal in mutables.

The Bible is certainly trying to bring men and women onside and to keep them from defecting. But if many trees flourish in the arboretum of world wisdom, how can this be done? Here, in my words, is Roth's answer.

The Bible sets out a comprehensive way of life, illustrates men and women coming to live it, living it under challenging circumstances, even often deviating. The detailed picture leaves little about the way to the imagination. The way's sensitivity to the major ups and downs of life is displayed, and confidence thereby instilled regarding its capacity to meet insistent needs and to resist the corrosion of despair. True, resource-richness and resilience aren't unique to the Bible's way. So what? Does exposure to cricket cause an exodus from the diamond to the oval?

His defence of the Jewish way is based in the fact that Roth himself has a satisfying experience of it and values its means for weathering life's trials. "[Wisdom] is a tree of life to those who lay hold of her; those who hold her fast are called happy" (Proverbs 3:18). Is it *the* way and *the* truth and *the* life? Warm though Roth's testimonial is, that he doesn't say. "The Proverbist," he could enlist in support, "also doesn't say that happiness belongs only to those who hold wisdom fast." And so, while Roth encourages those born under the tree to continue to hold her fast, a Pauline impulse is alien to his thinking.

Hazony and NGC

Hazony (100) is critical of both supports – NPF and NGC – of Roth's "No."

> The teaching offered by the Hebrew Scripture [in regard to the covenant] has recourse to concepts of a general nature ... Because of their generality, such concepts require no prior commitment to the historic Jewish alliance with the God of Israel to be understood. Thus while they were written for the instruction of the Jews, there is no reason why the standpoint and argument they make should not be heard and debated among all nations.

And again (114):

> In Abraham, God is looking for a man whose name can become great, and of whom a great nation can arise. God's concern here is not merely to find a just man, but to raise up an individual who can lay the foundations of a just society ...

The contrast between the biblical view and other views doesn't pit competing conceptions of justice. The story of Abraham dramatizes the genesis of justice.[3] The Bible does (intend to) deal with matters that in Roth's sense are philosophically significant.

"Don't different cultures view justice differently?" As indicated, I too deny NGC of the Bible. Abraham *is* advanced as a standard; *pace* Roth, Abraham's *is* the way. On what grounds? Plato (in *The Republic*) defends the view of justice as *doing one's own* by arguing that rejecters end up in conflict with themselves. But where in the Bible is Abraham demonstrated to be *the* just man? Where is Abraham's way shown to be sustained by logic? Superfluous to belabour, rejecters offend the character named "God." The attitude, however, is part of the *explanandum*.

NPF

It's a motif of Hazony's book that philosophers *can* use the narrative form for their probative purposes. Citing Martha Nussbaum, Hazony asserts (68): "narrative works are better equipped than [standard] philosophical treatises to conveying the truths that emerge under … concrete circumstances."[4] The truth of NPF is compatible with GC. But in reference to the Bible, Roth's claim – NPF is a sign of NGC – is the claim that seems correct. The "concrete circumstances" appear relevant to the content of the truths.

Nor, as I will now explain, is Hazony helped by cases where recognized philosophers violate PF.

Kierkegaard composes fictional diaries; Nietzsche writes aphoristically; a canny marketer might vend Wittgenstein's *Zettel* in a shoebox-type receptacle. Diving into the positions, analytic philosophers usually recast the material in the form that *they* favour. Routledge's *Arguments of the Philosophers* series devotes instalments to each of these three.

On the strength of examples of this sort, a classifier of the Bible as a rational work could maintain that its story-likeness isn't the last word. A background reason can even be adduced for not equating what you see with what you get. Kierkegaard, Nietzsche, and Wittgenstein, each as knowledgeable as any of Plato and colleagues, have a point to make about the philosophical tradition.[5]

An incompleteness of parallelism blunts the force of these points. We know of no argumentatively structured scriptural documents from which the Bible-ists could have made a show of deviating. In any case, are the men and women behind the Bible writing for submission to *Mind*? Special reasons have therefore to be given for likening their writing implements to Jackson Pollock's turkey baster.

We are left with questions. Why agree that the Bible is general in its teachings? If one accepts GC, why agree that the Bible's non-argumentative form is essential to it?

Hazony has, or so it increasingly seems, locked himself into his position in advance. He filters the primary data through his idiosyncratic analysis of truth as stability, an analysis that mingles pragmatism (the true is what works) with postmodernism (the correspondence view is objectionably logocentric).

After discussing the issue of narrative and philosophy, I will move on to what I regard as the Bible's philosophical core.

The Liabilities of Narrative

"[The Bible] has recourse to concepts of a general nature." Hazony rejects NGC. If the thinkers behind the Bible do not argue for the right, how right are they to treat the concepts as unrestrictedly general? Isn't Greek-type philosophy needed? How does the case of Abraham in the biblical narrative show justice emerging for the first time "in a sea of injustice"? The narrative contains no sign that Terah experienced a Mesopotamian *Kristallnacht*. So why accept the Bible's description of the environment?

To illustrate the problem, I call upon another scriptural document narrative in style.

In depicting Odysseus's exploits, the epic named after him advances the Greek ideal. What Hazony says about Abraham and justice could be said, *mutatis mutandis*, about Odysseus and Greek values. Plainly, though, the *Odyssey* is propagandistic. With what justice are non-Greek habitations depicted as dope dens and covens, Penelope's suitors as parasites rather than as nobles concerned for her welfare? Doesn't the Bible figure Abimelech and the Gerarites as double-dealers? Shechem and the Hivites as rapists? Goliath and the Philistines as thugs?

The narrative mode is by its nature vulnerable to the problem. Any triangle that you draw overdetermines the properties that Euclid's *Elements* explores. Similarly, narratives can't but introduce superfluities. Even if the narrator has no axe to grind, must one not resort to analysis, abstraction, definition, and so forth, to separate the thematic gold?

The notion of *establishing* this or that by narrative – the uncouthness of non-Greeks for instance – is in any case problematic. "After inscribing a 60° angle, Euclid, using only ruler and compass, partitioned the angle into three 20° angles." As I add details, at some point I will describe Euclid doing something that the reader will see cannot be done. This approximates the form of argument called *reductio ad absurdum*. Similarly, the epic's representation of Polyphemus as outwitted by Odysseus (with only one eye, the Cyclops is after all a halfwit) clashes with its portrayal of a host with a biting sense of humour who observes the rituals of exchanging names and of distributing gifts, and who has a connoisseur's appreciation for fine wine.

Consider another scriptural document. Why should a person do their duty? *The Bhagavad-Gita* addresses this cultural master-question.

Two related clans are waging a South Asian War of the Roses. Arjuna, a warrior of the Pandava clan, is paralysed by the thought that he ought to resist the action that it is his duty to perform. "How can we [warriors] know happiness / if we kill our own kinsmen?"[6] Here's a capsule of the guidance that Krishna, in the guise of Arjuna's charioteer, gives to the perplexed warrior.

Doing nothing (as you regard it) does not make of you, as an actor, a black hole. You remain in the arena of causes and effects. Moreover, no matter how much fore-sight you exercise, willy-nilly your (in)action will have unanticipated outcomes, some probably as negative as the spilling of blood that you fear, and will likely lack the positive outcomes, in this case the stable order that vanquishing the opponent generates. In this as in all cases, it's best to abide by tried-and-tested practices.

An argument is supplied to support the social imperative of dutiful action. The argument, by our lights down to earth, appeals to the common knowledge that the Socratic among us are trained to articulate.[7]

Here, then, is a tradition as old as the biblical one, a tradition in which argumentation is appreciated to have a role in stabilizing stories. If storytelling and reasoning are regarded as mutually supportive, the salience of the narrative side in the Bible might be a significant fact about how the arguers and narrators view the ordinary truth, not an invitation to cobble up a novel conception that makes of biblical thinkers proto-postmoderns.

Pesach, Matza, Maror

The Passover Haggadah quotes a remark of Rabban Gamaliel. "It's a dereliction not to have said 'pesach,' 'matza,' and 'maror' during the festival." I would have thought that the charge would apply to anyone who, purposing to establish the Bible's root character, fails to say "paganism," "monotheism," and (of course) "God."

Strikingly, the chapters describing the primordial creation are shunted to the margins in Hazony's book. *This* is where the basis of the Bible's philosophical position is found, and not just because we all live in the same world.

His situating the Bible's centre of gravity at its end goes some way to explaining Hazony's averted gaze. The sack of Solomon's Temple, Hazony points out, lit a fire under the Bible's composers. With the spiritual centre in ruins, a substitute was needed to keep the dispirited Judeans from adding two to the ten lost tribes. What better than a book around and through which the members of a dispersed people could maintain their unity? "But this formulation," Hazony hastens to add, "is too simple" (ibid.). God says to Abraham (Genesis 12:2) that *all nations* will be blessed through their collaboration. "God's concern … is … to … lay the foundations for a just society" (114).

The Bible doesn't begin with the call to Abraham. It begins *bereshith*. "Who declaims the cosmogonic part?" Hazony would have done well to ask. The declaimer is, I argued, the self-same Abraham to whom God speaks the words lately mentioned.[8] Obviously, it's as the gainer of a new understanding of the foundations that Abraham does the declaiming, not as the founder of a new nation. In this assertion we can see Hazony running the two together. *The Israelite cause is* [philosophical] *because it is, in fact, the cause of all mankind"* (59: italics in original). If the Bible's concern is human nature, that it comes to expression in the Israelite document is no more relevant to its substance than is Newton's English nationality to the *Principia*.

The Bible's philosophical concern is not social/political. It's more basic. What is it to be a human being? Hazony's silence about the Bible's opposition to paganism is revealing. That the first critics of pagans were of Abraham's line is an excuse, not a reason, for linking "opponent of paganism" or "monotheist" to "Israelite national."

The Burning Bush

Pagan thinking, representing men and women as (just) parts of nature, is committed to the view of nature as a system of reciprocally dependent parts.[9] The Bible contends that each man and each woman is independent. The physical world begins as a system, "the heavens and the earth." The origin of each of us, of you and of me, of him and of her, is not the species. "Don't verses 26 and 27 of Genesis 1 describe the creation of humankind, 'male and female [God] created them'?"[10] In fact, Genesis 1 is tracking the pagan account. It's Genesis 2 that makes the Bible more than a myth-free *Enuma Elish*. The mix-up is visible in Hazony's "the cause of all mankind." The man, not mankind, is what God is the cause of.

The dramatics and the use of his name apart, what's this got to do with God? *Pagan deities personify the principles behind natural forces. God is outside nature.* Although he *acts* on nature, God's nature is not *expressed* in nature. *Pagan deities form a system. God is alone.* God's status, extra-natural, and essentially one, is a match for the what-it-is-to-be of each of us, as the Bible understands it.

This confirms that the basic role of God is the creation of the man in Genesis 2.

Organic life is not what God is said to breathe into the man. The act has God imparting to one sector of the world a bit of himself – his one-ness. "Why God?" From the world that pagan resources can handle, one-ness is absent. Monotheism, then, is the view that the deity is a (genuine) one. "Hear O Israel! The Lord is our God, the Lord is one" (Deuteronomy 6:4).

The Bible presents monotheism as an article of theology. In actuality it's a piece of metaphysics-cum-ontology built on the distinction between (1) the system and its inalienable constituents, and (2) the system-independent items and the dissolvable collections that such items form if they come together.

Why should the Ten Commandments be integral to the Bible? Is morality not an add-on? In pagan thinking about the world, "good" applies primarily to the whole. The Bible's moral teachings depart from this. Each is *basically* what counts. Each *counts*. Each counts *equally*. Good therefore requires each having its own. If each decides to do its own, we might uncork the champagne. No one is under any moral obligation, however, to make that decision. Consequently, the frictional quality of communal life is no cause for complaint against the sovereign of the world.

More than the imparter to Abraham of the new idea, God is its principle. The Bible does not dogmatically assert the existence of the extra-natural deity. The existence of the pagan gods is, after all, far clearer: the wind in your sails, the sun on your face, the emotions by which you are buffeted, these press home the existence of Boreas, of Apollo, of Aphrodite, of Eris. The Bible reasons, reasons hard, for the acceptance of God. "Without the principle, the account of things is deficient; the human sector in particular is either distorted or excluded."

The transgression in Eden isn't central to the Bible's story for conveying this psychological point: we are unruly. Nor for imparting this moral message: we are bad. What counts is this message of ontology: each of us is a separate reality. The transgression is a break from the system.[11] Since God himself, in the back-story, breaks from the pagan view of deity, isn't what the man and the woman do the *imitatio Dei* that God's breath of life in them mandates?

Hazony sees the Akedah as asserting the value of human life. Doesn't Plato, a pagan, assign it value?[12] If Hazony were right, then Plato, for whom human life derives its value from the whole – the state – of which men and women are citizens, could dismiss the Bible as question-begging. The Bible's argument against paganism is a (philosophical) defence of *its* conception of human life.

"I am the Lord your God" heads the Commandments (Exodus 20:2, Deuteronomy 5:6). An imperative follows: "you shall have no other gods before me" (Exodus 20:3, Deuteronomy 5:7). "I AM" should recall God's self-identification to Moses. "God said to Moses, 'I AM WHO I AM.' He said further, 'Thus you shall say to the Israelites, I AM has sent me to you'" (Exodus 3:14). According to the Bibleists, to accept (only) the other gods is to subscribe to a view of things that, being natural through and through, plays human reality false.

Moses's encounter with God is, then, an encounter with the holy in an unmysterious sense. When *they* encounter the holy in scripture, secular folk should therefore park their qualms at the door. As for the devout, they should conquer the urge to reach for the shoehorn. God is the holy one because he is, archetypally, *one*. Wholly one, he is. The burning bush is an emblem of holy status. "The bush was blazing, yet it was not consumed" (Exodus 3:2). A perfect image, this, of disconnection from the cycle of nature. At "Horeb, the mountain of God" (1), the natural and the non-natural meet, not the immanent and the transcendent. That same meeting point is depicted at Genesis 2:7.

Doesn't Moses (Exodus 3:5) "remove [his] sandals"? In response to God's bolt from the blue, doesn't Abraham bolt from his previous way? Our condition is not theirs. Who among us expresses wonder each time unequal volumes of water are displaced by equal masses of copper and iron? Abraham and Moses were Neil Armstrongs of their time.[13]

It should be clear that, *pace* Maimonides, the Bible's deity is not the principle of pure being, or its epitome. God is the principle and epitome of particular being.

Intent on defending the Bible from the charge that its reportage cannot be known to be true, Hazony averts his gaze from the cosmogonic parts. The thinkers behind the Bible would agree about "cannot be known to be true," *but only to a point*. So far as Genesis 1 goes, they are doing their best. Not so Genesis 2. Here, for their enterprise, it's do or die. To be sure, the Bible's analysis of personhood could be faulty. But why should Bibleists not have been as competent as Plato and as Aristotle to offer it? Because Hazony runs the two chapters together, the baby of the second spirals down his drain with the bathwater of the first.

The Bible's Philosophical Logic, and the Bible's Form

The Bible offers the world of thought a new principle of being. God's absence from the pagan pantheons is the theological expression of the principle's absence from the repertoire of Greek philosophy. The Bible's form, narrative, is adjusted to the principle. Hazony is on a wild goose chase in looking to the specific stories for a distinctive view of truth. Roth is wrong to read biblical sectarianism out of NPF.

Adequate representation of reality requires resources for capturing particularity. Only through narrative is the "I" properly represented. NPF is not a sign of NGC. It's the Bible's way of introducing into the story its distinctive principle.[14]

To abandon the Jewish way is to abandon the first person, and hence to abandon all people, each and every one a first person. In that respect, the Jewish way *is* general. It isn't general because of an analysis of the concept of mankind. It's general because it applies to the (particular) first man, and through that man to all other men and women down the chain. *Adam is the first edition of a universal fact*. This is a non-Platonic sort of generality.

The Passover Haggadah contains this line: "in each generation, each one of us is obligated to see themself as though they personally came forth from Egypt." It would be apt for this wider claim to be part of the liturgy: "each one of us should identify with/as the first man that God made."

"What about these characteristics of the Jewish way: valorization of family; community-based institutions that offer relief to the less fortunate without absolving them of responsibility for their plight; respect for learning; discouragement of excess in the use of intoxicants; aren't they optional?" Each responds to the ontological insight. Take drugs. If the one-ness is basic to being, chemicals that smudge the particular's boundaries result in a reversion to Genesis 1 from Genesis 2.

On an interpretation (like Hazony's) that treats God's appearance in the Bible as a dramatic way of saying that each of the major characters had an insight unlikely to be had in the ordinary run of events, the resulting position is atheistic. If diplomacy doesn't prevent it, you'd have, if that's your view, to liken the "religious" appropriation of the text to the founding of a cult around a pop bottle tossed from an airplane. *I* have argued that God is the vehicle of a substantive point about reality's structure. The point concerns what from the perspective of a whole (pre-biblical) system of thinking is a new compartment of concrete being.

Sometimes, a Shepherd Is Just a Shepherd

That in its examination of the lives of men and women the biblical narrative is exploratory should impress all readers. If those behind the text are open-minded, should we not be so also? Hazony's response to the to-ing and fro-ing is rather more philosophical. He offers a convoluted view according to which "true" means something like "stable."

Since open-mindedness has nothing to do with the nature of truth, a diagnosis is needed here. It's easy to assemble Hazony's train of thought. God is said to be immutable: a rock. In fact, the deity of the Bible is often of two minds. "And the Lord was sorry that he had made humankind on the earth, and it grieved him to his heart" (Genesis 6:6).[15] What kind of deity is this? A non-dogmatic deity, perhaps. But isn't a deity who is fallible non-Godmatic? Thinking along these lines – recall that the variable cannot be extracted from the invariant – Hazony thinks that the only course is to plasticize truth.

God, according to the Bible, is the emblem of particularity. Where's the fickleness? Where the fallibility? Some biblically central things follow. Particularity is a presupposition of *mortality*;[16] of *morality* also. What doesn't follow is a unique way of life. It doesn't, for the pedestrian reason that there are many paths for the upright to walk. After "God ... caused it to rain upon the [frozen, static] earth" (Genesis 2:5), things do not remain as they were. Thus Jacob's chilling *aperçu* in the dream at Bethel. God lives with him, on the stony ground that he must traverse. "Surely the Lord is in *this* place – and I did not know it!" (28:16, emphasis added). The Godliness of men and women is salvific only in the sense that it saves them from un-Godliness.

Hazony quotes God's words to Cain after the sacrifice (Genesis 4:7). "If you do well, will you not be accepted?" This doesn't mean that if it doesn't stay the course the falsehood of what up to then was held to be true will be revealed. The meaning is commonsensical. *In evaluating ways of life that are shaped by changing circumstances, only time will tell.* This implies nothing about the truth and or the falsehood of before and after.

Having quoted verse 7, Hazony goes on (108): "God accepts the offering of a man [Abel] who seeks to improve things, to make them good of himself and of his own initiative." Hmmm. Isn't God only saying that Cain's sacrifice might be accepted too – at some future time? If anything, *Abel's* sacrifice marks *him* as lacking initiative. God also wants more. Cain's desire for more is pleasing to him.

Under the microscope are the socio-economic callings labelled "shepherding" and "farming." The Bible is highlighting that the shepherding way is clear of the potholes that immovable property introduces. Cain can hardly shift his field to accommodate the herders. Hazony says "farmers and shepherds" (105). Yet he does not treat the story as farmers versus shepherds in a world increasingly complex in its modes of production and its social relations. The crook in this instance is just a crook. As for that thing that's called a spade, why, it's a spade.[17]

Hazony is trying to get as far back in the story as he can to find a normative type. He gets as far back as Abel, whom, on the strength of a wisp of smoke, he proceeds to treat as a biblical paragon. But the Bible's philosophical basis is laid down even earlier, in Genesis 2, where we find a couple cast rather more in the Cain mould.

Cain's "am I my brother's keeper?" (Genesis 4:9) is rhetorical. The part of the narrative under examination treats, in moralized terms, the transition from gathering (Adam and Eve) through shepherding (Abel) to agriculture (Cain) and on to city dwelling (Enoch, Lot). The beat goes on. In my lifetime, dictaphones have made stenographers redundant; electronic switching circuits have put switchboard operators on the dole; supermarkets have sent milkmen to pasture. Will our grandchildren know of taxi drivers?

If God's question is self-answering, and if Cain is eventually accepted, why the criticism? It's because Cain washes his hands of responsibility for Abel once Abel's way of life has become the stuff of Christmas pageants.

Hazony gives God's words a reading that looks back to Cain's interaction with Abel (and reads the words judicially) when the speaker is looking ahead (and speaks scientifically). "And now you are cursed from the ground, which has opened its mouth to receive your brother's blood from your hand. When you till the ground, it will no longer yield to you its strength" (4:11–12). Believing that they can, at last, stay put, farmers soon find the soil's fist tightening. Moving, which this necessitates, is more difficult than it was for the shepherd. It's true that Cain's activity causes the earth to become less fecund. What's this got to do with Abel? Similarly, the point about the ground receiving the brother's blood isn't a 9-1-1 call. The nomadic way has been extinguished (lifeblood spilled) *and* superseded (lifeblood received). "And *your* way," the Braudel of the piece is explaining, "is no idyll. The earth will not respond to your need as you didn't to Abel's."

Hazony underscores "oved adamah" – "worker of the earth" – in speaking of Cain, again seeing an unfavourable contrast with Abel. Isn't God too an *oved adamah*? "From the dust of the ground" (Genesis 2:7) he made the first man. The question that God asks Cain the text puts to God. Is the product of your work acceptable? The parallel goes further. The name of Cain's son is "Enoch," whose correlate in the parallel line of Seth is "Enosh" (Genesis 6:7), a synonym

for "man."[18] Also, Cain (Genesis 4:17) names the city that he builds "Enochville."
In effect, God's distinctive work is man; man's is the city. According to the Bible,
the city is a problematic venue for men and women. This is not at all surprising. Men and women are themselves problematic. That the biblical story ends
before the city is reconciled to doesn't mean that city life is anathematized. Lot
was abandoned in the story after he set himself up in a cave, a lair for beasts.[19]
The biblical narrative is furnishing a template for handling the dynamic matter
rationally.

It should puzzle Hazony that sacrifice appears a mere generation and a half into
the annals of men and women. At his "Cain inclines to piety" (107) the thinkers
behind the text would have chuckled. The Bible is *using* the sacrament, known to
the target audience from pagan practices and from Temple ritual, as a litmus test.
It's by representing God in the biblical story as favouring this over that that the
Bible indicates *to its readers* its normative attitude. "Why should *Cain* be the first
to sacrifice?" Cain's experience is the first time an untried way comes into conflict
with a going concern. This happens neither to Adam nor to Abel.

Another reading of Hazony's concerns the Akedah. The preceding treatment
helps to pacify this fraught episode.

The killing of Abel is a way of saying that a way of life dies out. Similarly, the
"loss of Eden" lamented in Milton's epic waves goodbye to gathering. On this
level of reading, Adam and Eve, Abel and Cain, are types. It's along these lines
that the sacrifice of Isaac should be read. The issue between parents is stability
of union; between siblings, cooperation; between father and son, succession.
What type is Abraham? So far as the Akedah is concerned, he is the nation-
founding type. On the altar is national futurity. The death of Isaac would be *its*
funeral. The biological falsehood that God asserts, that Isaac is Abraham's only
son (Genesis 22:1), verifies the reading. Compare 25:12: "[Abraham's] sons Isaac
and Ishmael buried him in the cave of Machpelah." It's Abraham the patriarch
who has but one child.

In figuring out the episode, the reader should consider these questions. Who
is prepared to kill Isaac? Who prevents the blood's being shed? Who is willing
to abandon the national enterprise? Who resists? Does the attitude in each case
have to do with human flourishing? Remember: Hazony has told us that Abraham is a man of justice.

It's not some exotic idea of truth that we have here. Issues that arise for men
and women as their lives become more complex are being explored. The Bible,
Hazony says in commenting on the Akedah, is always defending human life.
How does this fit with his idea of truth as stability? The Bible would defend
the life of the particular even at the cost of increased instability. The defence is
anchored in God, in the principle of particularity.

The Bible's culture hero is Abraham. He discovered God. Indeed, God stands
to Abraham on the intellectual plane as on the elemental plane God stands to

the first man. The first man embodies what Abraham discovers. The discovery
is elaborated in the story of Moses. The discovery, moreover, is philosophical. A
new category of being, the category of the particular, is the centre of the Bible's
philosophy, as the Form is the centre of Plato's philosophy, the individual substance of Aristotle's, the unity of apperception of Kant's, the equation of meaning and use of Wittgenstein's. Not only is it a category that Greek thinkers don't
supply; it's also one that Greek thought cannot accommodate.

Pale Fire

"The god of Abraham," the slogan goes, "not the god of the philosophers." I've
argued that the god of Abraham, although he is not the god of *the* philosophers,
is the god of philosophers. So my reason for saying that Athens has nothing
to say to Jerusalem differs from Tertullian's. Jerusalem possesses a *philosophical* principle that Athens lacks. In theological language: "You, Athens, worship
only the other gods." Hazony's position is that Abraham is a philosopher among
philosophers. But since he writes God out of the picture, he flattens the philosophical differences between Athens and Jerusalem.

The relationship between the position that I hold on the Bible and Hazony's
can usefully be schematized. The possibilities are these.

	The Bible's God	The Bible's Theology
P1	x	x
P2	√	x
P3	x	√
P4	√	√

Pointing out that appeals in the Hellenic frame to deities are figurative,
Hazony defends a like reading of the Bible. Of the biblical appeal to God I've
said the same. But where Hazony assigns no philosophical significance to God,
on P2, my position, God is, non-theologically, relevant to the Bible's philosophy.

Since the overarching assumption here is that the Bible is philosophy, I'll
pass over P3.

And P4? If the Bible is philosophy, mustn't what looks like biblical theology
be formulable non-theologically? We've already looked at a combination of this
sort: philosophy for the insiders, theology for the unlettered. What I said then I
say again now. Even for the unlettered there is no theology. That being the case,
a diagnosis is needed of how P4 could come to be held in the first place.

David Novak *assumes* that the Bible is theology; the thesis of his *Athens and
Jerusalem: Gods, Humans, and Nature* is that the Bible's theology and its philosophy are complementary. From Novak's rabbinic standpoint the assumption
is natural. For, as he observes, the rabbis and the Church fathers both felt a need

to counter the wisdom of the gentiles. That the seminarians of Christianity are theologians doesn't however determine that the Bibleists are. Novak underplays Christianity's tendentious appropriation of the Bible.

These few lines from Novak's treatment (79) of the Bible's philosophical core illustrate the ease with which he theologicizes the text.

> In the first creation narrative in Genesis we read: "God created humans [ha'adam], male and female, in his image [be-tsalmo]" (Genesis 1:27).[20] That means, in my view, humans are created with the need for a mutual relationship with God, and the need for a mutual relationship with each other. This begins with the mutual need of a woman for a man and a man for a woman. "It is not good for humans [ha'adam] to be alone [levado]" (Genesis 2:18). Or, as one ancient sage put it: "Either companionship [haveruta] or death." The need for a mutual relationship with God is first activated by humans when they begin to worship God. "Cain brought an offering [minhah] to the Lord from the fruit of the ground; and Abel he too brought [an offering]" (Genesis 4:3–4).

[a] The ordinal in "the first creation narrative" is gratuitous. The second narrative, not referred to as such, is immediately quoted. [b] "Mutual relationship"? The subject-matter of 1:27 is biological. And, as we know, in many species there is no further relationship between the male and the female who couple. [c] "If God creates males and females in Genesis 1, what need to create the woman from the man's rib in Genesis 2?" This obvious question passes unasked because Novak's primary interlocutors are the rabbis. The issue of companionship first arises in Genesis 2, since the man is created alone. [d] As to the mention of God-likeness in 1:26, it's to single out the difference between humankind and other species. Novak is silent about what this difference might be. [e] "Either companionship or death." What could this mean other than "reproduction or extinction"? Non-human animals therefore have companions too. [f] Doesn't death enter only in Genesis 2, where there *is* companionship of the sort that Novak has in mind? [g] In the episode of Cain and Abel, God isn't a partner in an (interpersonal) relationship. He is a strip of litmus. Not that Zeus could play the role that God plays. For "way of life that turns the strip the right colour" means "way that respects the particularity associated with God's breath." The way of life of the builders at Babel fails this litmus test, despite what seems an admirable harmony. [h] Novak's elision of the very different Genesis 1 and Genesis 2 is evident from the word "levado," which he transliterates from Genesis 2. "Levado" means "by [singular] himself." The Bible is referring to the first particular, the man of Genesis 2, who is alone, not to humankind of Genesis 1. The species has no end of company, internal and external.[21] [i] Earlier, Novak says that "very good" applies "because God declared it" (49). But "very good" means that all the parts work

together; and God applies that term on the basis of seeing that they mesh. Thus 1:31: "God saw [that it was good]."

Here's Novak's capsule of the contrast between Athenian and Jerusalemite thought. "It is a one-way relation [in the Greek context] from the lower to the higher to the [self-contained] highest" (118). God, in the Bible, comes down from the heights. "We have a two-way relationship" (ibid.).

Isn't the idea of striving for perfection – *Citius, Altius, Fortius* – attractive? Why not go with Athens? The absence to him of the Bibleists' response strands Novak with the traffic-flow contrast.

To Novak – to each of us – the Bibleists would say:

Your substance is the substance of the particular. To bend your efforts to emulating what goes on on high is to see yourself as a second-rate god, rather than – what according to the Bible you are – a first-rate person, warts and all.

3
"Jew" as a Category Label: Philosophy on the Holocaust

A Philosophical Event?

In and of itself, the Holocaust isn't of interest to modern Jewish thinkers[1] who operate in philosophical mode. It isn't, because each and every happening, past or present, trivial or momentous, exemplifies the truths that philosophical reflection seeks out.[2] Nevertheless, for the mentioned thinkers the Holocaust is a learning occasion. This is because the events of the first part of the twentieth century track, more closely than do any equally available ones, the genesis, dramatized in its early chapters, of the Bible's philosophical position. *The attack on the Jews of Europe is a reversion, in space and time, to the pagan way of thinking the critique that is the Jewish conceptualization's foundry.*

Although the discussion in these pages proceeds largely in general terms, I do consider a few Jewish intellectuals of a philosophical cast of mind who grapple with the Holocaust. Judging from what they write, they do not see past the horrors to the foundations of Jewish philosophy. We get, instead, variations on this or that Western philosophical position.

What Jewish Philosophers Assume

Enquirers into what was visited upon European Jewry seek explanations in the non-Jewish sphere. "What was it about the non-Jews, about their situation, about their thinking, that triggered the murderous onslaught against the Jews who lived among them?" Since ideas from economics, sociology, psychology, history, and political science are the natural candidates to do the explanatory lifting, taking up the Holocaust in philosophical mode seems odd. What's philosophy got to do with it?

It's more surprising yet that the (Jewish) philosophers who seek for an explanation in non-Jewish philosophy take Jewish philosophy as its *reversal*: a philosophical position implicated in the horrors has got to be flawed. Another possibility suggests itself. Philosophy itself, sc. Western philosophy, is at fault. Doesn't Plato, its Columbus, endorse inhuman treatment of men and women? We cry out in dismay at what the analysis of justice in the *Republic* thrusts up. Plato, were he a member of his model city's producer class, would, it certainly seems, approve *his* being treated in the manipulative manner in which they are treated.

To assume that in its thinking about the treatment of people a philosophical position implicated in the atrocities must be flawed is to take for granted that Jewish philosophy's hands are clean.[3] This is a second assumption, a double one: there *is* a Jewish philosophy, and in it is found the general basis for invalidating conduct of *that* sort.

I'll argue two things. One: Western philosophy itself *is* the culprit. The advocates of such positions do not have the resources effectively to argue against the horrors. Effective argument depends on something alien to their philosophy. Two: The Jewish position *is* its reversal. It possesses that something.

Since my claim is that in how it thinks about people and the treatment of them Western philosophy is flawed, I maintain that the qualifier "Jewish" in "Jewish philosophy" can be dropped once the flaw is repaired. The Bible is a defence of human, not of Israelite, chosenness.

A Deduction

Although the fact that to them it's personal explains the Jewish philosophers' interest in the Holocaust, it doesn't justify their interest in it *qua* philosophers.

Readers will point out that a non-personal explanation can be found in the post-Enlightenment intellectual sphere. A preoccupation with Jews, a preoccupation rooted in the religio-theological stratum of pre-modernity, features in the thinking here. The Jews don't fit. Socially and psychologically anomalous as individuals, as a people they are a relic.[4]

Not any old differential treatment presupposes difference. *Systematically* differential treatment does. Only a fringe among the philosophers would say that the men and the women who live the distinctive life differ in some deep sense. The style of life is available to anyone. The philosophers, this is to say, regard the (non-Jewish) view of Jews as subject-matter for *diagnosis*.

Effective diagnostic treatment *cancels* an idea's truth-credentials. If the representation of Jews as misfits is the intellectual correlate of a disease, then the Second World War joke about the bicycle riders is a biopsy of the tragedy. As (horrific) nonsense, the Holocaust is inaccessible to philosophy. It's as if we hunted a species because the sound of its name grated. If the Holocaust is not nonsense, then the diagnostic spade is turned before bedrock is reached. This implies that the differential treatment of the Jews, howsoever objectionable, did have a basis.[5] A dilemma.

An instructive parallel is found in the annals of philosophy. Kant's position in *Critique of Pure Reason* runs up against David Hume's delegitimating account of the concept of causal necessity. Hume (as Kant reads him) exposes the generally accepted idea that the connection between striking a match and the match's lighting goes beyond spatio-temporal adjacency. Hume "diagnoses" the surplus in psychological terms: we are conditioned by constant exposure to expect a flame. Kant, to defend *his* view, supplies (A84/B116) *a deduction* of the concept. Our ability to distinguish objective from subjective temporal relations requires, he argues, that (some) sequences of events within our experience be linked extra-psychologically. Hume, whose own account presupposes the distinction, therefore needs the validity of that which his diagnostic account invalidates. His position is, if true, false. So it is false.

Kant must deduce the concept of cause. *Mutatis mutandis*, the philosophers of the Holocaust must deduce the concept of a Jew lest philosophical interest in it be like the interest of physics in goblins.[6] As to the fact that the deduction validates the distinction between Jew and non-Jew, the response is that the truth of other things to which the perpetrators themselves are committed requires that they apply the concept of the Jew in their own lives, so that they are in conflict with themselves.

Jewish Philosophy and Holocaust Philosophy

The Holocaust is of philosophical interest because the concept of a Jew, which the horrors highlight, is itself philosophically significant. In this regard the actions of the perpetrators have a basis in the victims. Conflagration *is* the round holes' final solution with regard to square pegs.

The truth of the "because"-clause ("the concept of a Jew ... is ... philosophically significant") passes beneath the radar of the Jewish philosophers who take up the Holocaust. They supply a Holocaust-philosophy loosely moored in basic Jewish thought – thought that does make Jews ontologically distinctive.

The position of Emmanuel Levinas illustrates the disconnect. Arising as it does out of his experience in the dark night of twentieth-century Europe, the position instances a feature of modern Jewish philosophical thought that does a lot to explain the intellectual passivity of its major figures vis-à-vis the assumptions adumbrated at the outset. The problem that the disconnect raises is plain. *Twentieth-century Europe is past time to be coming up with the Jewish philosophical position.* True, it can take time for distinctions to become clear. But Levinas doesn't trace his ideas back to anything that could be regarded even unclearly as a Jewish philosophy. His attunement to Jewish life explains the harmony with basic Jewish thought of what is really an original position.[7]

I have several times placed a question mark next to "Jewish philosophy." Are there Jewish philosophers? An affirmative answer requires a Jewish philosophy. *That* depends on what philosophy is understood to be.

The conception with which I work is the one articulated in the Preamble and alluded to in this chapter's first paragraph. Whether there is a *Jewish* philosophy comes down, then, to whether an invariant but non-formal feature of being is identified that either is missing from or is unrecognized in other cultural environments. I believe that one is identified. It's (what I am uninformatively labelling) the idea of a Jew.

Roth's "No" to the question that titles his essay rests on two supports. One: Jewish thinkers who are accounted philosophers borrow their philosophy from the mainstream. Julius Guttmann, in the seminal *Philosophies of Judaism: The History of Jewish Philosophy from Biblical Times to Franz Rosenzweig*, states (3) that even the impetus to philosophy is borrowed:

> The Jewish people do not begin to philosophize because of an irresistible urge to do so. They received philosophy from outside sources, and the history of Jewish philosophy is a history of the successive absorption of foreign ideas which were then transformed and adapted according to specific Jewish points of view.

Two: Jewish points of view are exclusive ("specific") to Jews. Indeed, even among Jews the stereotypical norms of conduct and patterns of civility are precisely that, stereotypical.

Levinas isn't persuaded. Jewish thinkers need, he says (1984, 201), "to express in Greek those principles about which Greece [knows] nothing."[8] The Jewish context, that is, contains valid principles absent from Greek-based philosophy, principles that Jewish thinkers who think philosophically fail to recognize.

This last sentence adumbrates *my* thesis. I do have questions, though. Did no philosophically inclined adherent to Jewish philosophy ever dress the product in its native garb? Is it believable that on the basis of sibylline utterances and sphyngine riddles people bought into the all-encompassing way of life that "those principles" underpin?

Levinas works in the phenomenological tradition. When he speaks philosophically, the tradition's language is heard: consciousness, intentionality, pre-cognitive and cognitive structures. Shouldn't Levinas feel that his M.O. gets in the way of the Jewish case?

In saying that Jewish thinkers need to express themselves in Greek, Levinas could be conflating a need that arises because of the desire to make the message accessible with a need generated by the discursive inaccessibility of the subject-matter. If it's "when in Rome," the appeal to Greek resources is void of theoretical interest. If ineffability is the issue, how would the Greek gift help? "Whereof we cannot speak."

Levinas's assertion that Greece knows *nothing* of the principles of Jewish thought sits poorly with the second way of looking at the need. To back up so strong a denial, the denier had better be able to do more than whistle what the other doesn't know.[9]

Something seems to get in the way of Levinas's saying directly what it is.

Typically, those who work with Athens and Jerusalem as polar opposites give ethics Jerusalemite citizenship. Levinas is of this company. The heart of his position is the idea of an unqualified ethical obligation to the other.

By any measure, an ethics based on this idea is an ethics of saintliness. Happily for most of us, who are not saints, that doesn't make us sinners.

How does Levinas come to merge saintliness and morality? Think of his experience in Europe. The plight of the victims of the Holocaust could, and should, elicit the response of one-way obligation. A less grisly parallel is given by the nursery. What parent syllogizes a response to the infant's cry? What parent expects *quid pro quo*? That is why I said that Levinas's is a Holocaust philosophy.

The underlying Jewish view sees things differently. Genesis 2 gets as close in its foundational part as the Bible gets to the portrayal of a helpless infant. Yet in this panel of the narrative God, the life-giver, expects a lot from the human inhabitants of the garden. Showing the man and the woman the door, doesn't God say that they must sleep in the bed that they made?

Two Distinctions

To expound more fully the case that Levinas's position levitates above the foundation of Jewish thought, two distinctions are needed. One: The distinction between traditional Jewish thought and modern Jewish thought. Two: The distinction between philosophical Jewish thought and non-philosophical Jewish thought. These differ in logical character. To picture the traditional/modern distinction, a linear series with a temporal direction suffices. A pair of concentric circles would better fit the thought/philosophy distinction.

When did Jewish thought become modern? The Enlightenment is the watershed here as it is in the case of European thought. This is no coincidence. Traditionalists in the Jewish world repudiate many elements of (Western) modernity. *Their* world, they would say, is one from which modern men and women, Jews most relevantly, are excluded; excluded in the way that deaf people are from Beethoven. Informed that *they* are throwbacks, traditionalists might throw back that past is preferable. Modern Jews, they will say, inhabit an etiolated reality – a house of credit cards.

In the case of the other distinction, dispute over which side of the line something lies on is unlikely to generate real-world conflict of the sort that erupts between traditional Jews and modern Jews. It's more like determining which part of Einstein's activity in coming up with relativity theory was conceptual, which factual.

The set-up has made no reference to the Holocaust. I'll now bring it in, specifically in regard to the second distinction.

Here's a simple matrix of the two distinctions.

	Non-philosophical Jewish thought	Philosophical Jewish thought
Traditional Jewish thought	1	3
Modern Jewish thought	2	4

Cells 1 and 2 have occupants. The problems arise from how cell 3 is completed. If traditional Jewish thought has philosophical content, how could Jewish philosophy (cell 4) do more than come to sharp expression in the context of the Holocaust? If cell 3 is empty, why call the later development "Jewish"? Wouldn't "Holocaust Philosophy" be more apt? The philosophy would be Jewish in the way that empiricism is British.

My position is that traditional (sc. pre-modern) Jewish thought has philosophical content. The close association of the Bible with the men and the woman whose brand of religiosity Enlightenment criticism targets is one reason why modern Jewish thinkers look elsewhere for such content. But what the modern Jewish thinkers offer in the way of philosophy is Jewish mainly by association. Focusing on the Holocaust enables us to highlight a gap in Western philosophy. The gap's reality has nothing to do with events of the twentieth century. In this respect, a claim like the traditionalists' about modernity applies. The Bible-less world of Western philosophers is a diminished world.[10]

I'll now distinguish two varieties of traditionalism. Traditionalism-1 is the pre-modern, Talmud-centred, Jewish ensemble. Traditionalism-2 is the pre-rabbinic one. Traditionalism-1, I claim, acts as a screen between modern Jewish philosophers and where the philosophical action is.

The twentieth-century Jewish thinker J.B. Soloveitchik is identified with the view that cell 3 is occupied. This accentuates the problem. Soloveitchik gets his philosophy from non-Jewish sources.[11] Moreover, his traditionalism is rooted in the system of laws and regulations set out in the Talmud. The position that Soloveitchik takes in *Halakhic Man*[12] is not consonant with Levinas's thesis of sub-cognitive anchorage for ethical obligation. The Talmud is committed to reasoning. Its special flavour resides in the reasoning's casuistic character.[13]

The Talmud screens the biblical position from view. Levinas, taking the screen for a stained-glass window,[14] does not go back beyond traditionalism-1. *Pace* Soloveitchik, the normative model in the Jewish context is Biblical Man, the archetypal person of traditionalism-2.[15]

There are, in fine, tensions between the Bible and halakhah. The tensions come out in stories (told from the Talmudic perspective) about God's bowing to the rabbis.[16] These stories ignore the fact that God's authority over the man and the woman in the garden lapses once they depart. From the halakhic standpoint it is much as if the garden is the whole of the human world when, as Genesis 3:24 makes plain, the part outside isn't an annex. Should it be said that halakhah fills in the part outside, well, that is presumptuous. According to the thinkers behind the Bible, halakhah could be filling in a much-needed gap.

Decastich and Decalogue

Quite a few Jewish intellectuals who address the Bible from the standpoint of Western culture allude to Sophocles. Why Sophocles?

Levinas asserts that Jewish philosophy must be taught to speak Greek. Sophocles is a Greek with a Hebrew accent. The fact holds interest for its own sake. Classicists, because of their attitude towards biblical thinking, deprive themselves of an interpretive resource. Pertinently to our concerns, Sophocles's Hebrew-accented Greek bears also on a difficulty that many modern Jewish thinkers have in going back to the Bible: the presence of God. A further point of value to these concerns is the fact that Sophocles's position homes in on an exaggeration in Levinas's view about a dissymmetrical ethical obligation and, at the same time, locates a lacuna in Kant's moral philosophy.[17]

At the start I floated the idea that (Western) philosophy, the discipline itself, is the culprit. Sophocles's *Antigone* reads like an indictment of Plato's *Republic*. That Sophocles flourished before Plato saw the light of day does not disqualify the reading. A reflective person sensitive to what is essentially the philosophical current in Greece didn't need the *Republic* as a windsock. They would have appreciated that such a position is an entailment. Sophocles's plays, in this context, are a gift to the Greeks that they did not accept.

I restrict my treatment to the ten lines of *Antigone* that perennially baffle.

Antigone has sprinkled earth on the body of her brother, defying Thebes's ruler, Creon, who had proscribed the burial, asserting that a traitor – Polyneices fell in a failed coup attempt – forfeits the rites. Backing up what she did, Antigone cites family obligation.

Suppose that the dissident had been a child of Antigone's, or her husband. "Surely," the reader will think, "that wouldn't have made a difference." Yet she voices these words:

> Never, I tell you.
> If I had been the mother of children
> or if my husband died, exposed and rotting –
> I'd never have taken this ordeal upon myself,
> never defied our people's will. What law,
> you ask, do I satisfy with what I say?
> A husband dead, there might have been another.
> A child by another too, if I had lost the first.
> But mother and father both lost in the halls of Death,
> no brother could ever spring to light again. [18]

Relative to the backing, these words make no sense. As I see it, they are not *supposed* to. Antigone is "express[ing] in Greek those principles about which Greece [knows] nothing."

Recur to the point about Levinas and the child. A parent responds to only one of two needy infants. Family continuity depends more, it is explained, on the beneficiary of the care. Creon, disowning Haemon, commits a version of this offence. He can, he says, get another son, and he should, since this one, for not satisfying the needs of Thebes, is a defective product of the reproductive assembly line. Haemon, he says, should seek another wife, since, from the civic vantage point, Antigone, to whom he is affianced, is a bad fit. Antigone's speech in its first half repeats these things. "A husband dead, there might have been another. A child by another too." Then, the second half. The brother is unique. Creon treats "father" and "mother," "spouse" and "child," as functional terms. Functions can be improperly fulfilled. When this is the case, the filler should be dealt with as we deal with a treadbare tire or a carious cuspid. Antigone's (anti-Platonic) position is, then, that people are, each man and each woman is, non-fungible.

Levinas offers this clever inversion. *Greek philosophy is the love of wisdom. The wisdom of love is Jewish philosophy.* Antigone too is counterposing love to the Greek way of understanding. She asserts (590–1) of herself that she was

> born to join in love, not hate –
> that is my nature.

Although no one would characterize Antigone as loving – to her sister, Ismene, Antigone is ice-cold; one shudders to imagine the interactions with

Haemon – the remark, a philosophical one, is on point. Of all the human out-ward-directed relationships, love is the one that goes directly to the (non-fungi-ble) person. That's what she is saying. "I will lie with the one I love and loved by him" [85]. Many things can be replaced. But not the beloved. One does not love for a reason. Bossuet: "The heart has reasons that reason does not understand." Because of that a person can't be reasoned out of love.

Levinas sees his wisdom of love as elevating *ethics over ontology*. A contrast is intended with Heidegger, who professes to promote *ontology over metaphysics*. But on any standard understanding of "ontology," the ontologist's remit *is* basic ways of being and basic kinds of thing. At the deepest level, men and women are non-fungibles. And so, the political affinities of *Antigone* are liberal.

Plato's metaphysical way of thinking informs Creon's view. The world's objects are (=) exemplifications of general things. In Plato's language: reflec-tions in the (inherently non-general) spatio-temporal Receptacle of the (inherently general) Forms. The Receptacle supplies numerical distinctness; the Forms supply the features and characteristics. Irreducible particularity is lacking.[19]

Doesn't all of this make clear that Levinas's position is *au fond* that men and women are (non-fungible) particulars? The idea of the dissymmetrical ethi-cal relation runs two things together. Levinas (1998, 150) denies the Kantian view that general imperatives mediate our moral relation to others. "From the outset, the I–you comprises an obligation in its immediacy, that is, as urgency without recourse to any universal law." Duty (in the Kantian view) is general. If I have a duty, it's because my situation falls under the likes of "Promises are to be kept." But to say that the duty is to the particular is only to deny *abstract* generality, the generality of concepts. One can *generalize* over (non-abstract) particulars. What's distortive about speaking of you and of me as "we"? Which, in the Decalogue, is what the Bible does, albeit in reverse. The Commandments, applicable to all of us, are formulated in the singular. "You [singular] shall not bear false witness."

In *Foundation of the Metaphysics of Morals*, Kant denies that love can be com-manded. Despite that, the emotion can serve to specify the field of morals: par-ticulars. Antigone was, she says, born to join in love. The point is that love itself joins particulars.[20]

The gods, Antigone explains, require the brother's burial. It's the Greek way. But Antigone doesn't have return to nature in mind. Entombed for her transgression, she takes her own life. This is an act of affirmation: her life is her own. That a person's life is their own the Bible states in *its* way in Genesis 2.[21]

The Decalogue begins with "I am the Lord your God." Antigone is claiming that each person is an "I." In the Decastich, the claim is made without appeal to anything transcendent; even to anything that seems in the least religious.

Biblical Man (and Woman)

The Holocaust is a philosophical event not *per se* but because through reflection on it the category of the particular can be brought out – specifically, the point about Jews falling into that category and, as a result, being branded as misfits.

In this closing section I shall return to the source, to the core of the Jewish philosophy.

The Bible isn't a historical work, not in the ordinary sense. It's a work of philosophy. Since the Bible is a narrative, there are in it – there must be! – philosophical *events*. The transgression in the garden is one.[22] Deviating from the order therein, the man and the woman reveal themselves to be *misfits among creatures*. God's planting in Genesis 2 is itself, prior to that, a philosophical event. The Bible is making the conceptual distinction between nature and culture. A garden is a place that wouldn't exist unless kept and tilled: *an organic misfit*. The creation of the first man in Genesis 2 is a philosophical event. The being-theoretic characteristic, particularity, the characteristic unavailable within the (extra-human) natural world, is described as entering through the (extra-natural) deity's breath. The man is *a misfit in the world*. Like the departure of Abraham from Mesopotamia, the Exodus from Egypt represents the divide with paganism. You can walk like an Assyrian or like an Egyptian, or you can "walk in the company of God" (Micah 6:8). The Israelite nation, until the conversion of the pagans, is *a misfit among the nations*.

At the core of the Bible as a revolutionary document is the campaign against paganism. The Bible is the *Critique of Pure Paganism*, and its centrepiece is the deduction of the particular.

Paganism is the view that today answers to "naturalism." The pagan deities are personifications of the principles behind the forces of nature. The Bible is explicitly anti-pagan. In the various episodes of backsliding and apostasy, a pagan view is raised up over and against the biblical one.

Abraham's departure from his country is a leave-taking from the pagan culture in which he was schooled. To represent it as a rejection of idolatry is to misrepresent naturalism as idiotic. If naturalism is correct, the *biblical* story is a fairy story. Abraham's view is better characterized as *anti-naturalism*, not as *supernaturalism*. His new view is that naturalism is inadequate to the world, to the human part especially.

What about God? If the pagan deities, for example Baal or Zeus, are the principles behind naturalism, God is the principle behind anti-naturalism. What is God? An irreducible "I." One who takes God to be the principle of pure being misunderstands the biblical position. God is the principle of *particular* being. The Bible does not teach that there is one deity rather than many; it teaches that the deity is a "one," a particular. Recall the point about fungibility. The point was made in terms of predicates. God is the ultimate non-predicate. "Isn't God supernatural?" The question puts things back to front. The Bible's theology is subordinate to philosophy. God as a deity differs from the pagan deities. Pagan deities are expressions of the principles behind the wind, the rain, the thrusting up of mountains. Question: How do the biblical thinkers know that God is extra-natural? Answer: Abraham is a philosopher – the first professor of biblical philosophy. God's extra-natural status is the conclusion of his *Critique*. The claim that God exists belongs to the quasi-historical narrative.

I listed key philosophical events in the Bible. What about the creation described in Genesis 1? It is only loosely, by external association, a member of the class.

Soloveitchik (to whom I now return) appreciates that the Genesis 2 representation of men and women outranks the Genesis 1 representation in normative significance. But since in his view God is creatively active in both chapters, to defend the differential ranking he has to resort to questionable distinctions, such as the distinction in *The Lonely Man of Faith* between the majestic man of Genesis 1 ("Adam I"), who controls nature, and the covenantal man of Genesis 2 ("Adam II"), whose attitude is reverential. Incorrectly, this assumes that the chapters deal with the same kind of entity. Genesis 1 is a view of the world from a pagan angle. This world is a system of which humankind is a part in good standing. Indeed, the writers/thinkers bend over backward to prevent the reader from taking the Genesis 1 treatment of men and women non-biologically.[23] Thus the statement of the sex difference only of humankind: "male and female he created them" (1:27). Observe, too, that *after* saying in verse 29 that plants are given to mankind for food, God in verse 30 repeats this of the beasts and the birds. The placement of the non-human after the human again alerts the reader that the human/non-human distinction isn't dichotomous. True, humankind in Genesis 1 is set apart from all the other species. Would Darwin contest that the species we comprise stands in a skewed relation to the natural world? The idea of dominion is used in Genesis 1 to mark the skew. The claim is that men and women are niche-free. This niche-freedom is neither more nor less a doing of God's than is the niche-boundness of the cactus and of the polar bear.

"*What* role does God – does the character called 'God' – play in Genesis 1?" Role 1: Because the Bible has God presiding, God presides over the natural creation too. "Khrushchev launched Sputnik." Role 2: Being extra-natural, and hence having no (natural) domain at all, God is an excellent model for the idea of niche-freedom.

To lose the distinction between Genesis 1 and Genesis 2 is to lose the Bible's driver. No principle of particularity is needed within (non-human) nature. Observe that the creation in Genesis 2 is not of the species. It is of one person, then of a second. And it is, by name, the deity self-identified to Moses as

"I AM" who does the creating. And what does he create? The first being who can say "I AM."

The Genesis 1/Genesis 2 distinction is between (1) a view of the world as a system in which everything is in its place and all change is (therefore) exchange of matter and energy, and (2) a view of the world as (also) containing entities (men and women) that have real beginnings and that really go out of existence.

An understanding of core scripture has consequences for the authority of the Talmud. *Pace* the Hasidim, there is no cosmic drama for the *mitzvoth* to re-enact. The Bible's core is the argument against naturalism. Observance of the sabbath, the one stereotypical *mitzvah* in the Decalogue, is a way of marking through practice the extra-naturalness of each person. The sabbath is a temporal version of a cultivated piece of nature.

Phenomenology isn't needed to get beneath the general level. The Bible penetrates analytically. If the listed events are read as a kind of special history, one might well think, with Roth and Guttmann, that philosophy needs to be found elsewhere. But the events *are* philosophy. Commandment One is the axiom of the Ten. It's not that God commands obedience. Nor that the moral values informing the ordinances come from above. Rather, particularity, of which the biblical deity is the source, is the basis of morality.

The deduction of the concept of the Jew is the validation of the concept of the person. The Holocaust does not do the deducing. The philosophical event of Genesis 2 does. That, I mean, is the Bible's representation of it. But in the Holocaust is played out, as clearly as it can be through a historical event, the struggle between biblical philosophy and paganism. Like the Sphinx that Oedipus encountered at Thebes, the Holocaust obliges us to confront the issue expressed in the riddle: "What is Man?" This, aptly, is the original title that Primo Levi gave to his book: "Se questo è un uomo."

Is there a Jewish philosophy? Only in that it's in the Jewish *context* that a principle not acknowledged in Greece is identified. In character, it's philosophy plain and simple. And the special status of the concept of the Jew? This is the concept of a separate entity that is the locus of intrinsic value. The applicability of the full Kantian pattern can be contested. Some might be prepared to forgo the self-image as human beings. That would amount to withholding transcendental status from the concept. Is it possible to live one's life on such a basis? *To do it*, instead of just *pay it lip-service*, one must become an image and likeness of Plato's carpenter, prepared for liquidation if they don't fit. This is to exhale God's breath of life, to revert to the condition of men and women as described in Genesis 1 – the condition, in philosophical terms, of the architects and perpetrators of the atrocities.

4
Hero, Israel:
Troy and the Torah

Proto-Abrahams

The Bible's conception of personhood is first advanced in the scene from Chapter 2 of the Book of Genesis in which God breathes life into, alone among creatures, the first man.

Decoding the theologically encoded biblical message doesn't require an Alan Turing. Alone among creatures, persons belong to the category of the particular. A person is a non-general individual whose being isn't inextricably connected to a wider whole. Trees, non-human animals, planets, and so on, bound up with the system that is nature, are *non*-particular, non-general individuals.[1]

Had the first person, "Adam" as he's generally known,[2] been reflective, would he have thought of himself as Abraham comes to think of himself when he accepts God's call?[3] If he would have, aren't the chapters between Genesis 2, in which God performs artificial respiration, and the chapter, Genesis 12, in which Abraham gains the insight about himself, an interlude in the treatment of the issue of human nature? In fact, they are not. But they pursue the issue in a problematic way.

It's possible to join without leaving. God does however urge Abraham to leave – to leave those other gods of which the Ten Commandments speaks, the only gods recognized at the time. He is to leave Terah for Torah. The change from "Abram" (the name given by his father) to (the God-given) "Abraham" is a marker of the two-sidedness: *from* and *to*. Isn't it therefore possible that Adam didn't have the same self-conception, or wouldn't have had it if he had had a reflective streak?

Question: Would a reflective Adam have believed what Abram believed, or would his beliefs have matched Abraham's? Answer: Who is placed better than Adam to appreciate that his thinghood in the world isn't fully natural? The woman, he is aware, was fashioned by God. He is aware, that is, that constitutive of creatures like them – "bone of my bones, and flesh of my flesh" (Genesis 2:23) – is an extra-natural element. Although "Adam *converts* from another view" is overstatement, the words of 2:23 come after God's *failed attempt* to find for Adam a non-human partner. Adam will therefore have grasped this much at minimum: "Like that I'm not."

On the basis, also, of the following evidence, I would defend the claim that this is the view of those behind the Bible.

The respect in which Abraham's name differs from Abram's features Adam's name too. In the primordial case as in the proto-historical one, the Hebrew letter "H" is added to a set of letters. "abrm" becomes "abrHm." The word of Genesis 1 that we render as "Adam," namely "adm," becomes "Hadm" in Genesis 2.[4,5]

The indications in the text are clear. Adam at some level thinks of himself as Abraham does.

In the frame of the wider text, all this, though not in itself inconsistent with the Bible's message, signals either a tactical omission or else (what comes to much the same) the insertion of something in so recessive a fashion as to ensure that most readers won't notice it. Similar remarks apply to the genealogy of the descendants of Noah, a mythic account of the origin of different nations. It's not just that, after the flood, every person traces back to Noah. When I say that Noah is the next iteration of Adam, I mean that his family tree also has Abraham as its *terminus ad quem*.

Noah experiences an unnatural (and as he knows) God-made flood, as Adam encounters an unnatural (and as *he* knows) God-made partner. Noah has his experience in what for a human being is an unnatural construction, the ark that he built to God's specifications. Adam for his part undergoes his sentimental education in a garden that he later tills and keeps at God's behest. Noah, then, is in as good a position as is Adam dimly to envisage what Abraham comes to know face to face.

Both Adam and Noah are proto-Abrahams. The writers are composing from the vantage point of what they regard as the truth, and this truth influences how they write from the outset. God, the source of H, presides over the whole. So the writers, proleptically, place the major figures on God's side. No titanic battle for paramountcy, like the struggle between Zeus and his father, is waged.

The composers can't pull off the obstetrick of having the three central figures emerge fully formed from God's head. Adam glimpses the other side. Although Noah had a pre-ark life, he seems too passive to have processed it intellectually. Only Abraham encounters serious opposition. My view is that Abraham did weigh the philosophical options before he decided. But the composers of his story waffle.

In the case of each of the three, the Bible starts on the side of its good guys. Like the others, Abraham has an encounter with God. It is only however with the birth of Isaac to a Sarah whose childbearing years are past that he witnesses an unnatural thing or event.[6] Buying into a position on the strength of a promissory note isn't the way of a philosopher. Yet there is no filling in of Abraham's thinking to clarify why he banks on God.

This inspires the question whether among the pagans a person could be found whose position has in it a basis for the shift away from the other gods. If such a person exists, insight might be gained from their case into what change made Genesis 2's Adam from one of the members of the species of Genesis 1, and/or of what turned Abram of Genesis 11 into Abraham of Genesis 12.

There is a proto-patriarch among those who are not on God's side. That person, I'll show, is a little more than Adam in their understanding of themself, a little less than Abraham.

First, though, another feature of the text. The genealogy of Noah's descendants, given in Genesis 10, is repeated in Genesis 11.[7] It's significant that only the second extends as far as Terah. The significance comes out if we attend to the nine verses interposed between the two, nine verses on which a million times their number have been erected.

Often, the story of the Tower of Babel is interpreted as a lesson in excessive pride. Another aspect is more important for us. I think you'll agree that it's of greater importance to the Bible too.

The pronominal forms used in describing the enterprise – "they," "us," "ourselves," "we," "them" – are, all twenty instances, plural. The implication? *The tightly collective nature of the project is what draws the Lord God's reaction.* The reason is implicit in the Bible's anthropology. At Babel, the particular, God's reflection in the world, gets sunk in the project, as the world gets swamped in the deluge. The men and women at Babel have "one language" (11:1). A rare meeting of minds? Nothing of the kind. It's a collective mind, with respect to which individual dissent is the ab-norm.

Observe now that the plural language echoes Genesis 1. We are being given here a cultural line that goes back to a time from which Adam might, in being particularized by God's breath, be regarded as de-parting. The tower story is in effect a cultural version of the biological story of Genesis 1.

mankind : the man (= Adam) :: Abram : Abraham

We get a glimpse in the story of what the Bible thinks of the pagan cultures that precede God's appearance. Why only nine verses? Here's a conjecture.

Reaching the genealogy of Noah, the thinkers/writers appreciate the difficulty in the narrative. What's become of the anti-Abrahamic view? To correct this they insert the tower story, to which they add another genealogy. This time it's a cultural genealogy, not a standard anthropological story of groups diverging.

Observe again that, on the preceding reading, the tower story is internally related to God's view of personhood. It's less prideful self-aggrandizement that the thinkers/writers have in the crosshairs than ignorance of the truth about the self. The ignorance *can* be described as the rejection of God. You'll appreciate however that the description is applied from the outside. The Babelites know nothing of God. Now obviously, since one will need a lot of luck if one acts on false beliefs, isn't God sparing the builders an unpleasant fate in shutting the enterprise down? This assumes that the other view has no merit. The Bible's thinkers are trying to eat their cake while having it. They don't want to leave themselves open to the charge of ignoring a relevant reality; at the same time, they are loath to dignify that reality by giving it credence.

Patriarch among the Hellenes?

The people have been scattered to the four winds. We shall hitch a ride on a thermal of Zephyrus. The writers of the Bible know a lot about the northeastern region of the Mediterranean. We get copious mention of its peoples and its places in the genealogy of the sons of Noah.[8] Will archaic Greece supply us with proto-versions of Adam and of Abraham?

Like Abraham, the third patriarch answers to both a parentally given name and a God-given one. Courtesy of the heavenly favoured antagonist whom he wrestles, Jacob also goes by "Israel": "one who has striven with God" (Genesis 32:28). As it happens, the name chosen for him at birth, like the birth itself, is multiple. Wrestling his fraternal twin for firstborn status, Jacob emerges from the womb "gripping Esau's heel" (25:26). "So," the text explains, "he was named Jacob" (ibid.). Although "Jacob" quibbles on "heel," "crooked" is even more apt in view of the "smooth" (27:11) bearer's passing himself off as someone he is not in finagling the paternal blessing. Happily, the two etymologies can share the prize. The heel is right-angled, and 90° is as far from straight as an angle can be.

Suppose, with these episodes in view, we extend our gaze to Greece. The unlettered will associate Achilles's name with the tendon between ankle and sole. The more scholarly will know, also, that Achilles is party to a fateful act of impersonation. He consents for Patroclus to enter the battle dressed in *his* suit of armour.

"Doesn't Adam hide his nakedness with a leaf? Do not the annals of the first man thus contain a nether body part and a disguise? Indeed, aren't the male genitalia sometimes referred to in the Bible as feet? Yet who would see in Achilles a Hellenic progenitor of the species?"

In the sense of Kipling's expression invoking East and West, East isn't East and West isn't West. The parallels comprise a small sub-subset of the similarities. But, I submit, archaic Greek culture does for all that have a Jacob.

Capacity to improvise is the Jacobite marker. When it comes to quick thinking, Odysseus, the protagonist of Homer's *second* epic, "the man of twists and turns" as the poet introduces him (1:1),[9] sorts excellently with the second son of Isaac. The echo goes right down to onomastic bedrock. "Odysseus" has the sense, perceptible in English, of "being at odds."

The list is easily lengthened. Odysseus's story, like Jacob's, begins with a struggle against brethren and ends in a reunion. Jacob's Joseph, like Odysseus's Telemachus, devotes himself to finding the father he fears has expired in the intervening years. Many of the overlaps have a qualitative feel. Jacob inherits the patriarchal mantle; it is to Odysseus, not to the more Esau-like Ajax, the presumptive claimant, that Achilles's panoply passes.

The episodes are so alike as to hint of actual influence – like, perhaps, the influence of the *Odyssey* on Joyce's *Ulysses*.[10] The biblical narrative explicitly references archaic Greece. To take one instance: Japheth, the ark-builder-and-civilization-saver's third son, shares his name with the father of the fire-bringer-and-civilization-maker Prometheus.

Jacob sorts with Odysseus. But the wrath of the great warrior whose story begins with a grievance against Agamemnon need not be rekindled at another indignity. Achilles has even more illustrious thematic *frères* than Jacques over in Jerusalem: Adam and Abraham. The effort needed to elicit the parallels in this case is handsomely repaid. We find resonances of the foundational thought of Athens and the culture-constitutive thought of Jerusalem.

When plotted against the Bible's internal timeline, Achilles's career commences prior to Adam's. Achilles has one foot in the cultural version of the world of Genesis 1 – prior, then, to God's act of respiration. Also, Achilles's career ends before the lights dim on Abraham. He has a view rather like Moses's of the destination.

The thesis, then, has a descriptive part and an evaluative part, with the latter comprising a critical side and a restorative side. Descriptive: through Achilles are portrayed an essential feature of the development of the human self-image (this is the Adamic parallel) *and* an essential feature of the national one (the Abrahamic parallel). The features combine in the chemical way. Evaluative: the blend of features in Achilles clarifies the biblical thematic, even, arguably, corrects a theoretical miscue in it.

Here's the thesis, graphically. Conceptual development goes from left to right.

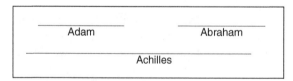

Adam and Achilles

Achilles's parentage includes one immortal, Thetis daughter of the sea god Nereus, and one mortal, Peleus king of the Myrmidons. Two elements of the runner's myth of origin are especially well-known. Element 1: The story of the apple of discord generates the *casus belli* of the Trojan War, Helen's leaving Menelaus for Paris. Element 2: Because his mother is divine, everlastingness is constituent to Achilles's nature, but, since his father is of flesh-and-blood, only in a recessive way. Thetis tries by topical means to repress the dominant gene. She dips the newborn Achilles in the waters of the Styx – an unsuccessful attempt, since, famously, the heel by which she grips the infant stays dry.[11]

Achilles, as this implies, is only potentially mortal. That, I mean, is how he is depicted. The *Iliad* is, *inter alia*, the story of this potentiality being actualized. What, exactly, does "potentially mortal" mean?

The first panel of Genesis, dealing with the emergence of men and women, tells of the same transition. In saying this, I am swimming against the current of Christian exegesis, which ascribes actual immortality to them. Theirs originally, the condition is later lost due to what they do.

This *actualist* reading is a misreading. After the pair violate God's ban on eating of the tree of knowledge, expulsion from the garden is necessary lest they "reach out … and take also from the tree of life, and eat, and live forever." Not having eaten yet of that tree, they do not at that point have life without end. Since the banishment puts the fruit out of reach, it's implied that they never have it.[12] The conclusion may be reached that the man and the woman are potentially mortal from the outset not just because it's logically possible for them to die. A person, to become bald, must lose their hair. To face a terminating future, *the man and the woman do not have to lose something*. It is true that, as the story is told, had Adam been left to his own devices, in some sense he would not have died. But this – the sense in which he is only potentially mortal – is what needs explaining.

The Jerusalemite resources aren't up to the task. That's the critical side of my thesis. On the constructive side, I'm arguing that Homer delivers the goods – or, to convert to biblical coin, the bads.

Achilles, in the myth of his origin, is potentially mortal. Homer, I said, adapts the mythic materials to his own ends. Here, from Book 9 of the *Iliad*, is a helpful passage.

Meeting with the ambassadors Agamemnon had dispatched to persuade him to retake the battlefield, Achilles gives voice (385–8) to a claim dissonant with the warrior ethos:

> One and the same lot for the man who hangs back
> and the man who battles hard. The same honor waits
> for the coward and the brave. They both go down to Death,
> the fighter who shirks, the one who works to exhaustion.

These lines constitute a hinge between the views of himself as only potentially mortal and as actually mortal.

The typical reader will question this construction. "Doesn't Achilles state that death awaits all?" In fact, he does not fully comprehend at this stage what he is saying, as is confirmed by the warriors' reaction of bewilderment rather than of – what they had to be prepared for – disappointment.

From the standpoint of the questioner, the exchange is a simple disagreement. This fact alone tells against the typical reading. It would be mad to say that the ambassadors are under any illusions about the prospects of those who wade into the battlefield. In composing the scene, isn't Homer saying something to the members of *his* audience about their position, something that they aren't aware of?

The tent to which a warrior returns at dusk is part of his field of action. Achilles's tent is outside this field, rather like the stove-heated room of Descartes's Meditator. Achilles is in transition, from one cultural ensemble to another. Achilles has an inkling of a way of thinking about life, about life's value, different from the one in which he was acculturated.

The Old Way

Here is a distillation of the warrior ethos, to which the ambassadors subscribe and by whose code they conduct themselves.

1. Men and women are fragile creatures. In the end the battle is always lost: death comes out victorious.

Comment: No tradition sees it otherwise.

2. Something so fragile could not be valuable for its own sake.

Comment: Why not? We sometimes attach great value to something precisely because of its intricacy and (hence, often) friability. The additional thought here is that the gods are immortal. It is because men and women measure themselves against the gods (or, at any rate, against the engulfing nature that threatens and eventually does away with them) that they ascribe to their lives diminished value.

3. What lasts is essentially more valuable than what is fleeting.

Comment: Aristotle was right to say that the white of a world without end is not one whit whiter than the white of a wink of an eye. Still, suitably qualified, the claim can be defended. A prolonged kiss might be awkward and/or tedious. But if the Stagirite thought a Lexus less valuable than a Lada, I have an automobile I might be persuaded to part with; and I will even be large enough to ask for no more than the Lexus.

4. While lacking intrinsic value, life is not valueless.

Comment: We grant that there is more than one kind of value. Money is not valuable for its own sake; it has instrumental worth. And many a thing, health for instance, is valuable both intrinsically and for what it enables.

5. Fragile though it is, life is valuable as an instrument that affords the opportunity for the person living it to achieve what is (regarded as) really valuable, something that lasts. And what is that? Survival in memory.

Comment: The activity of the Greek warriors is an attempt through their exploits to attract attention, to inspire a reaction of awe, so that they will be sung. They seek glory: kudos and kleos. The kind of attention they seek is the kind that nature, because of *its* power, attracts. They thus strive to be cyclones, floods, tsunamis, droughts, etc., in human form.

In gazing on this worldview, we do not feel ourselves to be gazing on a sphinx. If we envisage a life-environment much harsher than our own – for the warriors at Troy, the Trojan War is life itself – we can think ourselves into their skins. Nor is this an exclusively cogitative exercise. Leaping forward from Homer to an age historically accessible to us, it's easy to show the currency in Greek culture of the view that I find in the epic. *Plato*, some three centuries later, works with a version.

I refer the reader to Plato's sketch in the *Republic* of the life of a typical inhabitant of the ideal state. Regarding his identity as inextricably bound up with the function that he fulfils, the carpenter is content to leave when, due to chronic illness, he can no longer join. He thinks about himself as we think of a tire gashed beyond repair.

Plato's topic is not this painful happening or that unfortunate turn. Our lives, Plato is saying, are for doing what we do. Once the ability to cobble, to philosophize, or to play the flute effectively is lost, what's the point?

For Plato, as for the warriors at Troy, greatest value attaches to what endures. For Plato, the state itself is the thing that has primary worth. The citizens come and go. The state lasts. Functionally, though, the Platonic view inherits from the warrior ethos in welding worth to longevity.[13] From the perspective of the Bible, Plato's state is the political arm of the world of Genesis 1. *Qua* system, it contains no particulars.

Achilles never regards himself as deathless. The ambassadors are as aware as he is that all players born into this chess game are ultimately mated. It's a change in the attitude towards life (and hence towards death) that actualizes Achilles's potential mortality.

In Achilles's milieu, the life of a person is valued only instrumentally. To ascribe potential mortality does not mean that Achilles is beyond the sweep of the scythe. It means that he has not shifted, but might yet do so, to a view of life as intrinsically valuable. The *Iliad* is the story of the shift. Once he's made the

move, Achilles ceases to figure the loss of his life as the small price that a creature lacking in intrinsic worth has to pay to obtain god-like lastingness. Achilles
now figures the loss of his life as the greatest loss.

Such a change occurs in the biblical context too. Like Achilles, the man and
the woman originate un-naturally. That leads many to regard the pair as initially
sharing in the actual everlastingness that characterizes their maker. Whatever
else partaking of the fruit of the tree of knowledge comes to, it is an advance in
understanding of how things are with the partakers in respect to time. But, as
I'll now show, the Bible's "knowledge of good and bad" isn't culturally neutral.
Thinkers whose cognitive adolescence is long past might take a different view
of the same data.

Homer Goes Fission

How does the view of life as intrinsically valuable take shape in the *Iliad*? It
isn't enough for Achilles to have mused aloud that a life lived in anonymity is
a life with worth. Favouring the untrodden ways might merely mark a person
as eccentric. After all, a preference generates only likings. A value generates
prohibitions, obligations. There can be no private value system. Does publicity
require society? An attitude of respect for nature seems to make sense for an
isolate. Doesn't that attitude sustain a normative vocabulary? The isolate might
feel *guilt* if through their carelessness a forest goes up in smoke. But the attitude
presupposes the personification of (extra-human) nature and hence introduces
some other quasi-consciousness to which a duty of care is owed, a devastated-
looking quasi-consciousness in the case of the fire.

Confronting the embassy, Achilles voices ideas that, in his cultural
frame, make no sense. He must do more than deny the values to which the
go-betweens subscribe. "Demonstrably, a person who refuses to fight lives longer. But when such a one departs, it is to the world as if they've never lived at
all." Achilles must cultivate the alternative. Homer dramatizes its seeding and
fitful germination.

The event that precipitates the inaction of the *Iliad* (the epic is the story
of Achilles's *absence* from the battlefield) occurs *in principio*. Agamemnon
expropriates from him the girl Briseis – a trophy of war. At this stage, Achilles needs the good regard of his fellows, survival in the public memory
being that for which a warrior lives. His comrades, he fears, will mock him
because of the vacancy in his bed. Hadn't Menelaus, to expunge the shame
of Helen's removal, sprung into action? Feeling himself diminished, Achilles tries to run Agamemnon through – an action that makes as much sense
in the context of the culture as the Trojan War itself.[14] Poised to thrust, he
is restrained by Athena. This intervention from on high is the beginning of
his ethical change.

Achilles now has hesitations, reservations, misgivings, doubts, about the value system. The sentiments he expresses when the ambassadors come calling vocalize the turmoil.

Achilles has to say more than "I value my life; I see it as valuable for its own sake." The culture values life only instrumentally, and Achilles, when he speaks, speaks the language of the culture.[15] "What," we imagine the baffled ambassadors whispering to one another, "does he want? More in the way of recompense from Agamemnon? Yet the offer he spurns."

A value system isn't the possession of a single individual. How, then, can Achilles's sense that his life is intrinsically valuable fail to come over in that frame as a mere hankering to draw breath? What Homer does here is run Achilles through. But it's not Achilles's own life that Achilles comes to value. It's Patroclus's life. There is however a sense in which Patroclus = Achilles.

Patroclus, wearing Achilles's armour, is sent onto the battlefield as an Achilles-impersonator. Patroclus is not Achilles. Yet Patroclus is killed *as* Achilles. Observing (or imagining) Hector rounding on his friend, Achilles in a sense observes (or imagines) his own death. Dramatized for us is a fission of consciousness. Previously, Achilles saw himself as others saw him. The feeling of dishonour at Briseis's removal explains his withdrawal. Now Achilles himself sees himself (in Patroclus). This is (dramatized) self-consciousness. Achilles regrets Patroclus's death. He is attaching value to Patroclus's life. Once this becomes intersubjective and reflexive, we have a value system. And since Patroclus = Achilles, Achilles is attaching value to his own life, but not in a way that opens him to a charge of self-dealing.

Death, says Wittgenstein in the *Tractatus*, is not an experience. Even if it is, men and women never see their own deaths. Achilles, through Homer's artistry, sees the unseeable. He is and he is not Patroclus. *Is*: Patroclus, dressed in his armour, is identified as him. *Is not*: Patroclus is dead and he isn't. This two-in-one position supplies Achilles a new, non-self-regarding, appreciation of his life.[16]

A thesis of philosophical anthropology is suggested: no conceptual light will be shed on distinctively human reality by setting out with an isolated individual; social reality has emergent properties. A classic treatment is Rousseau's *Discourse on Inequality*.[17]

The elements of Homer's *tour de force* are visible in Moses's story. The fission of consciousness we get in the surgical intervention that extracts the man's rib. It is "not good," the text says, "that the man should be alone" (2:18). The man needs a "helper as his partner" (ibid.) "Ezer ke-negdo," the Hebrew, translates, part by part, as "helper as against him"; "helper vis-à-vis him." The apparent conflict of assistance ("ezer") and opposition ("neged") is eloquent. Without traction, your wheels spin to no effect. "Neged" also is cognate with a verb meaning "to say." So the second creature could be taken as one with which one might have (in both senses) converse. It's a kind of personal interpersonality: two poles in one.

Remember that in the course of the primordial creation God repeatedly saw that things were good. To say "not good" of the solitary condition is to say that the very idea of an ethical system, a value system, presupposes this interpersonality. Not that for not answering to "good" such a situation qualifies as bad. Rather, the conditions for good-and-bad are absent. The fission (or something like it) is necessary to supply them.

The stories differ clearly in this regard. Homer's Achilles is from the start a cultural being. The Bible, in its treatment of Adam, seems to be trying to deal with the emergence of self-consciousness – the portal to culture. It reads therefore as developmental psychology rather than as exploratory of the human condition. Also, certainly unjustifiably, the biblical story ties the advent of self-consciousness to Western culture.

I'll review. A sense of ourselves as mortal isn't the same as a sense of our lives as intrinsically valuable. Acutely conscious of their limited temporal horizon, the Greek warriors do not regard the leaving of this life as the loss of a thing valuable for its own sake. Death is to them no tragedy. Pain the warriors fear. In this they differ not at all from non-human animals. The questions are obvious. Why should God's threat "in the day that you shall eat of [the tree of knowledge] you shall die" (2:17) deter? Why should the woman have to be reassured – "tricked" (3:13) – by the serpent? The warriors require no reassurance. Their view is that they will die in a much graver sense if they do not put themselves at risk in the medical sense. *God's statement of the consequence of disobedience depends on the recipient's already regarding (personal) death as an evil.*

Achilles shifts from one value system to another. The sense that the man and the woman transition into value from a valueless condition obscures the underlying similarity of what befalls them.

"Adam is potentially mortal." Since Adam is figured in the story as a child, we might think to gloss the words thus: he *doesn't yet understand* his condition. It would however be unfortunate if this were the whole story. Walking develops from crawling. This doesn't mean that the study of crawling illuminates walking. Walking ≠ erect crawling. In fact, the Bible's claim that Adam and Eve, having eaten, are in an existentially problematic condition indicates that a *specific* view of life is acquired from the fruit of the tree of knowledge.

The Bible hides its commitment here. We aren't told about the view of life which doesn't torment those whose view it is even though life is characterized in it, and hence recognized by them, to be terminating. The view is, I am saying, (something like) the view of Achilles – of his culture – prior to the change that his trajectory dramatizes.

The serpent says to the woman that she will not die if she eats. This has a parallel in the story of Achilles. As he sends Patroclus into the fray, Achilles warns him to keep to the margins. But, more substantively, it is Achilles who will not die if Patroclus, wearing Achilles's gear, and hence indistinguishable to the eye from Achilles, departs the bivouac.

It is coincidental that Achilles's story begins with an apple too. In the spirit of the early part of the present discussion, one could bake a similar pie with it: because of an apple and a woman, Achilles, like Adam, becomes mortal.[18] There is another, less playful, respect of connection. Eve tastes death. Adam follows suit. Patroclus, in Achilles's suit, tastes death. Achilles, *his* mate, follows. But this parallel won't acquit the biblical account of incompleteness. If the parallel captures what the writers had in mind, their portrayal of the condition of the man and of the woman is misleading. The pair's not yet having eaten of the tree of knowledge has got to encompass their innocence of the *specific knowledge* that its fruit imparts.

Abraham and Achilles

The Achilles I've sketched is an Adam whose view is culturally committed from the start – an Adam+. The Achilles I shall now address myself to is an Abraham–. My claim is that the process that Achilles goes through in the *Iliad* tracks Abraham's conversion in the Torah to the new way. Abraham's shift is in one respect obviously a theoretical match for Achilles's. Abraham, like Achilles, begins as a member of a real culture.

In "Bibleism and Judaism" I amplified the echo between "bereshith bara" and "lekh lekha." We now appreciate the conceptual dissonance. In the latter alone is the movement transcultural. This is the feature that Achilles's case, while reduplicating what happens early in the Bible, exemplifies. But the view that life is intrinsically valuable cannot be taken up in isolation. From the case of Abraham, we see that the cultural move to monotheism is towards attaching intrinsic value to the lives of individual men and women. Once this is appreciated, our understanding is improved of what primordial creation is all about.

I mentioned the scene in which Athena stops Achilles from murdering Agamemnon. This event has at least three meanings. One: On the level of plot, Athena sides with the Greeks. Should Achilles carry through, the Greek cause will be lost. Two: On the level of theme, Athena's intervention gives sense to the quantum leap that is occurring. A cultural change is a function of all manner of imponderables. The idea is that the change in Achilles is, as it were, emergent. Three: Hera could not have done what Athena does. Nor could Ares. Athena has a special role in the Olympian pantheon.

In Book 4 of the *Iliad*, Athena is called "Tritogenia" (597). The appellation becomes thematically active when, in Book 5, Ares, injured with Athena's help by Diomedes, complains of Zeus's preference (1015–18):

> But that girl
> you never block her way with a word or action, never.
> you spur her on, since you, you gave her birth
> from your own head

Homer is referring to the mythic story of how the war of the generations of higher beings is ended, the war that sees Chronus disempower Ouranos, and Zeus in turn dethrone Chronus. It tells of how Athena bests Ares.

The cessation of strife on high is in Hesiod's *Theogony*. But Homer has a surprise in store.

How does it come about that Thetis and Peleus, a mortal, wed? True, the gods are masters of a variation on bestiality. But this union *sanctifies* a monstrosity. Here's the story.

Zeus fell in love with the sea goddess Thetis. To Zeus an oracle foretold that Thetis would bear a son greater than him. To disarm fate, Zeus bestowed her upon Peleus, a mortal king.

The account in *Theogony* has the internecine struggle terminating. Power is stabilized in the Olympian pantheon. But take another look at the words of the oracle to Zeus: "Thetis's son will get the better of you." Zeus wasn't told that Thetis's son *by him* would do that. *Homer, in the* Iliad, *tells the story of Achilles besting Zeus.*

This same story is told in the Bible. The focus of value shifts downwards from the eternal, the immortal, the all-powerful, to the finite, the fleeting, the fragile. The story is told in a way that has spawned religious attitudes on the Jerusalemite side. The difference is clear, but not distinct. Clear: In the biblical story, God sides with the mortals. He creates them and has regard for them. In the Greek story, the gods are over-and-against the mortals. Not Distinct: On the biblical side, God accompanies Abraham to a new place. In the Greek context, Athena comes down from high Olympus and causes a swerve in Achilles. Both God and Athena conclude covenants with the mortals. God promises greatness to Abraham:

> I will make of you a great nation, and I will bless you, and make your name great, so that you will be a blessing. (12:2)

Athena (1:248–251) promises Achilles threefold recompense for mastering his murderous impulse.

> And I tell you this – and I *know* it is the truth –
> one day glittering gifts will lie before you,

three times over to pay for all this outrage.
Hold back now. Obey us both.[19]

"Gifts ... three times over"? Achilles gets killed; Abraham's progeny end up in exile. Are divine promises idly made? What is promised does come to pass. Greatness, the promise in both cases, can consist in having made a great contribution.

Recall the oracle to Zeus regarding Thetis. Doesn't the story of the cessation of the strife among the gods have half the same twist? To stop a replay of sons deposing fathers, Zeus brings Athena into the world. This is his "dialectical" way of preventing the mother from making common cause with the offspring against the father.[20] Arguably, Zeus's foresight fails here as it did in the case of Achilles. Doesn't Athena best Zeus too?

It's overreach to situate Athena on the side of the Achilles who values a person's life for its own sake. True, she is associated with the strifeless equilibrium. True too, it's Athena who is plumed with founding the Areopagus, the first Athenian court of law. The idea of resolving disputes in a way that avoids bloodshed does not however require assigning primary value to individuals. Collectivist societies like the one Plato blueprints are not without legal institutions.

Absent here is something supplied through Abraham. Its theological face is monotheism; its onto-anthropological meaning is that each person is, like God, an autonomous being, and for that reason a (possible) locus of intrinsic value.

Abraham's deity calls him from out of the blue. "Go," he says. Achilles's deity, Athena, streaks down from the blue, grabs him by the hair. "Stop," she says. The difference between the green light and the red is appropriate. Of the two deities, only Abraham's can impart the momentum needed. Achilles has to power himself up after decoupling from the old engine.[21]

A Western Union of the Death of Adam

The change in Achilles, a change in the attitude towards life, turns his potential mortality actual. I used the claim to bring out the parallel between Achilles and Adam. Sticking to the denial that "in the day that you shall eat [of the tree of knowledge] you shall die" belongs to developmental psychology, here is one attempt, in biblical terms too, to make ontological sense of the matter.

Genesis 1 lays before us a system of parts: upper and lower, dry and wet, light and dark, and so on. The parts are inextricable from the whole. Humankind, the species, is bound up with the system. Thus the claim in verse 29 that the other parts are available to its members for sustenance.[22] In such a system, there is no death. Animals and plants, when – as we, anthropomorphizing unawares, say – they die, are reorganized into the wider whole.

In Genesis 2, God creates a single person. This entity, *qua* separate from the whole, *can* cease to exist. And so, the being of Genesis 2 has acquired mortality that is not a feature of the humankind of Genesis 1.

In a system, no element does its own thing. The representation of the advent of mortality through an act of transgression is, therefore, right. It has little to do with sinfulness.

The Bible takes a poke at Greek-type heroism. Lamech the descendent of Cain, its representative of the type, is by design a degraded specimen, bragging to his wives. The Bible is post-heroic. Or, if you prefer, God is its only hero. Homer, in the figure of Achilles, gives us a substitute for this hero in a God-less world.[23]

PASSAGES

5
"On one leg":
The Stability of Monotheism

A Plea for the Proselyte

The prospective proselyte goes right to the top. He goes to Shammai, a religious authority of the age. "May I ask the esteemed rabbi to explain to me the Torah's teachings? And, please, be so good as to do it while I stand on one leg." Brandishing "a builder's cubit,"[1] Shammai shows the man the door. Unfazed, the man applies to Hillel, no less authoritative on Scripture and on the spokes of practice that radiate from its chapters and its verses. Hillel rises to the challenge. "What is hateful to you, do not do to your neighbour: that is the whole Torah, while the rest is the commentary thereof; go and learn it."

Elaborators of the anecdote invariably rake the prospective proselyte over the coals for insolence; they criticize him roundly, too, for a devil-may-care attitude towards his soul's well-being. It's therefore no surprise that occupants of pulpits are so fond of the story. With cover from the columns of the Talmud, in telling it they convey to the pews that seriousness towards what is offered from the pulpit should be the default attitude, and respect the default mindset towards those who do the offering.

It is often added to the elaboration that Hillel, genial to a fault, is no pushover. "Go and learn it." Might it not be appended that Hillel's telegram also encodes a poke at the insolence? "What would you say of a businessman who bought a pig after only a peek? You are doing to yourself what you would not have done to you."

Why should a person not do to their neighbour? Many puzzle over this deep question of moral philosophy. How firm however is the basis for concluding that the person who applies to Hillel maintains that the short course suffices for receiving the scroll? If time for him is money, why would he have put himself in the way of a second bum's rush?

"On one leg" *sounds* chutzpahdik. "Spare me the rabbinic rigmarole." But, as the three questions posed just above suggest, perhaps Shammai, of whom the

Talmud may be speaking when it admonishes "the short of temper" by saying that they "cannot teach,"[2] was too quick to judge. Similarly, there is enough to sow a seed of a doubt as to whether the man's proviso indicates that he values his sales above his soul.

"On one leg." Plainly, the prospective proselyte has in mind the difficulty of standing thus for any length of time. But not only does a person *tire more quickly* in that attitude, they also *stand less steadily*. In glossing the story, why not focus on the stability?

Think of a table. How many legs make for stability? Assuming that it is otherwise sturdy, a three-legged table will always rest stably on the ground. Thus the use of tripods for long-exposure photography. A table with two legs is a dubious platform.

Who is the prospective proselyte? He doesn't (yet) belong to the Torah-based communion. In the context of the anecdote, it must be some stripe of paganism from which he is weighing departure.

Pagans worship other deities than do Jews. To become a Jew is to put the other gods aside.

The prospective proselyte's question should, I suggest, be understood along these lines. "How is it that the belief-system can rest stably on a single leg? Isn't it the case that even men and women can't remain for long in that position?"

The proof of *this* pudding lies in whether Hillel's reduction-of-Torah tastes like an answer to "on one leg," so understood. On the usual construal, the phrase's postural meaning is a cocktail umbrella.

The questioner is making a connection between the foundation of a religious belief-system and the supporting legs of, say, a table. Why should the instability of a two-legged table transpose to a one-principle belief-system? The analogy directs our attention to the vital point of opposition between the Torah's view and the pagan one.

Agreed: The person arrives at the rabbis' doors from the pagan part of town. Agreed: The Bible's view is theologically novel. Would it not seem reasonable for a comparison shopper to ask how the biblical view does all that the pagan view does, and if it doesn't do more too, does it better? Wouldn't the colourful way of asking be wittily consonant with the applicant's major doubt?

The issue is alive for all who situate themselves on God's side of the theological line or whose culture traces back to the crossing the Bible tracks. Most of us are numbered among this "all," the secular with the crossers. The issue has two parts. The purely theological point about deities aside, what are monotheists urging against paganism? Assuming that adherents to the Bible are correct about paganism's shortfall, might not monotheism's basis still need eking out?

The prospective proselyte isn't contesting monotheism's *reduction* of the number of deities. Their *rejection* is what concerns him. For it isn't as if pagans get no explanatory mileage out of their belief-system. Can monotheism, with its non-pagan principle, account for the condition of men and women in the world? That's what he'd like to know.

Why Not the Creation?

Critics of the pagan belief-system regard the truth (as they see it) of the proposition "One and only one deity exists" as significant to their lives. Obviously, those who accept this theological proposition will direct their devotions accordingly. But sacramental practices can't be the sum total of it. Behind the creedal difference with worshippers of many deities must be some disagreement expressible non-theologically.[3]

Saying this, I am putting distance between the issue of conversion and the question of the Bible's superiority. The contest couched in theological terms – "If the Lord is God, follow him; but if Baal, follow him" – is in the first instance about something extra-theological. One can speak, idiomatically, of Newtonians *converting* from an Aristotelian understanding. They came to see that it's not because of their ponderousness that unsupported bodies fall. Just such a change in how the everyday facts are understood lies at the base of *this* dispute. No one awakens one fine morning exclaiming "By Jove! There is one and only one god."

By the lights of adherents to the Torah, what do the pagans get wrong? In its first seven words, the Torah appears to answer.

A wayfarer arrives at the manor. Knocking, they expect the gatekeeper to appear. In the case of Bible Hall, the readers must wait twelve chapters before making acquaintance with Abraham. The very first verse does however find the reader in the presence of none other than the lord of the manor. Thus the answer: Abraham learns that God is the creator of the (physical) world.[4] The answer satisfies the desideratum. The existence of the world bears on everything that men and women do, not on their devotions alone.

It's worthy of remark, then, that Hillel doesn't say that without God there would be no world. Without God, he says, the world of men and women would not be governed by moral principles.

Hillel's focus puts us on a *proper* footing with respect to the "one leg" figure. He homes in on what he identifies as the point on which the pagans will appreciate the Torah's superiority. "Do not do to your neighbour ..." But is this "the whole Torah"?

Is Hillel's reduction-of-Torah anchored in God's cosmogonic activity? If it isn't, then the Bible, structurally, has an elliptical shape. One focus is the principle that underlies the world's creation, the other, the principle behind the conduct of one set of creatures. If this is so, then contrary to the Torah's advertising, monotheism isn't a comprehensive alternative to the pagan belief-system.

Four issues, Kant says, exhaust philosophy's mandate: the epistemological issue of what can be known; the moral issue of what ought to be done; the eschatological issue of what can be hoped. These three, he says, are summed up in a fourth issue; the anthropological issue of what people are. Is Hillel (also) saying that the Torah's teachings ultimately concern the human? If so, failing a deep-going idealism like Kant's, something's missing.

God and the Gods: Persons and Other Things

Pagans believe in many gods. That is generally true. But pagans don't have to be polytheists.

The reader will express puzzlement. "If a pagan believer needn't believe in many gods, can't a pagan be a monotheist?"

Each of the major deities of the Olympian belief-system, a typical pagan belief-system, may be viewed as the principle behind what occurs in some region of the physical world. Pagan gods thus express themselves in natural happenings. Zeus, the god of sky and thunder, expresses himself in thunderbolts; Poseidon, in tsunamis; Aphrodite, in the thunderbolts and tsunamis of sexual attraction.

Pagan religion, as the preceding illustration indicates, is nature religion. Question: Why *deities*? Answer: Nature is powerful in itself and powerful in its effects on the lives of men and women. Attitudes of awe and fear are therefore to be expected, the more so in a vacuum of understanding and in situations of helplessness.[5] Question: Why *many* deities? Answer: Nature is complex.

As they develop, pagan religions develop along the lines tracked in Hesiod's *Theogony*: from the chthonian muck (the coarsest features of the natural realm, the features in which men and women are immediately engulfed) all the way to the more ethereal regions of Olympus (the regions of the world that are more remote and hence whose influence is transmitted through intermediate causes).

The worship of sun and moon is, according to the Bible, idolatrous. Behind the ridicule heaped upon idolaters is a sound theoretical point: the multiplicity of deities in the pagan frame is a function of distinctions between aspects of the natural world. Early on in the cosmogonies, the aspects are figured as elements in competition: night with day, wet with dry, hot with cold, upper with lower. Eventually, they come to be seen as slices of physical spectra: dark-and-bright; wet-and-dry; hot-and-cold; low-and-high.[6]

The Bible's writers thus exhibit a keen grasp of pagan theology. The development of the natural basis in a religious direction they strongly oppose. But the facts they see much as do their pagan counterparts, which isn't surprising. The descriptions that a few thinkers behind the Tanakh offer evince a naturalist's appreciation of the extra-human world, and indeed an Aristotelian sense of wonderment. "Without having any chief or officer or ruler, / [the ant] prepares its food in summer, and gathers its sustenance in harvest" (Proverbs 6:8).

Monotheists stick these labels on the position that they oppose: "paganism," "polytheism," "idolatry." How do the notions interrelate? A pagan is one who holds that (concrete) reality is natural. "Polytheism" refers to paganism's (usual) theological elaboration. Although, *qua poly*theists, polytheists must believe in many gods, the natural belief-system needn't have any deities. Natural science is a form of paganism. "Idolatry" is applied to the religious elaboration of pagan-ism. It is applied *from the outside*. What internal point could there be to criticiz-ing pagans for directing their sacrifices to the principles that underlie natural happenings?

Nature being complex, pagan religions, stereotypically, have pantheons. But pagan thinkers who hold that a single principle underlies the variety of natural changes will, if they worship, worship (husbandless) Mother Nature. "Isn't such a religious position monotheistic?" If we feel unable to answer negatively, the terminology's the gag.

On the religious side, the biblical view is not, or not only, that there aren't many gods. It's the view that the deities, whatever their number, are not parts of nature or principles underlying natural happenings. God, in the Bible, is extra-natural. The ontological position is that reality is not exceptionlessly natural. We can put this more informatively by identifying what it is that according to the thinking of the Bible is extra-natural. It's not the deity as such; it's the deity as a person.

Why aren't persons natural? One: Pagan religions deify the principles that come to expression in nature. Natural happenings as they affect the lives of men and women attract the lion's share of attention. The story at the dead cen-tre of the Bible, of the emergence of men and women, lacks this centrality in pagan thinking. Human reality being from the pagan point of view generically of a piece with extra-human, this is as expected. Accordingly, the Bibleists will initially have identified a weak spot in paganism. If paganism deals poorly with human reality, isn't a revision of belief called for? Two: Like a blob of mer-cury, a pagan deity can fission. Like blobs of mercury, pagan deities can fuse. If the extension of *person* changes only through birth and death, *an argument* is therefore available for the inadequacy of paganism.[7] The argument informs the Bible's dramatics. In the Genesis 2 account of God creating the first man, God transfers a bit of himself to the (natural) lump of clay. *What bit? His one-ness.* In rendering the text into English, the KJ puts that the man becomes "a living soul." English supplies a happy homonym. The man becomes a living *sole* – a separate entity.

A widespread misconception is that in Genesis 2 *God brings a man to life*. Had God done that, Lear, weeping over the body of Cordelia, would commit a logical error: "Why should a dog, a horse, a rat, have life, / And thou no breath at all?" God *does not* breathe life into any horse, or dog, or rat. Men and women, as biological entities, like horses, rats, and dogs, also have life. God's intervention in Genesis 2 gives men and women, each of them, one-ness. The other living creatures are essentially parts of the system. Inspired with God's breath, the man is "alone" (18).[8]

Typology and Key Affinities

It will be helpful to tabulate these observations.

	Theory of being/ categorization	Theology/ religion	Sacraments/ practices
BIBLE	nature < concrete reality	monotheism: an extra-natural deity	Temple worship Sacrifices
PAGANISM	nature = concrete reality	polytheism: natural deity or natural deities	Maypole Stonehenge

Why should the being-theoretic position that the extra-natural category has occupants be linked to the theological position that one and only one deity exists? Why should the being-theoretic position that all concrete existence is natural be linked to the theological view that there are many gods?

Both links are affinities. The pagan categorization consorts with the many-gods view because *nature* is a system. Although, due to our interest in trees for food, for heating, and for building material, we tend to think of them as served by the rest of the forest, they serve no less than they are served.[9]

In the pagan context basic one-ness is absent.[10] The pagan pantheon may be likened in this regard to a cake. What sense is there to the claim that a cake removed from the oven consists of exactly eight slices?

The link between the Bible's non-pagan position on the constitution of reality and monotheism is also loose. The representation of a single extra-natural deity as breathing life into the human sector dramatizes the absence of one-ness from the natural realm. What counts is that the deity is a one, not that there is only one. If there were a biblical pantheon, the cake to which it is likened would be cut before the bake.

Ultimately, the Bible's position is that we must resist paganism because of its view of men and women. Pagans, when they get religion, deify the principles behind nature. The Bible, in its religious development, deifies the principle behind men and women. The apotheosis one can resist on both sides without losing the contrast.

Since Hillel's extract is true to its revolutionary character, the biblical posi-tion itself *is* a bit problematic. The equal treatment of each person that moral principles enjoin is incompatible with the thinking of paganism; a moral community is not at heart a system.[11] Pagan principles of conduct can *ape* moral ones. Under some circumstances of communal existence they can be justified on the grounds of conducing better to an independently desired result such as peace, or harmony.[12] This isn't however a moral justification. Those who desire different things aren't obliged.

Hillel's distillation does isolate the essence of the Bible. But only in the aspect that concerns men and women. The prospective proselyte's issue has to do with how the position in this aspect fits with the rest.

Back to the Creation

The results of the typological clean-up in hand, we return to the issue of the creation. Can the whole rest on one leg?

It's here that distancing the religious issue from the dispute between monotheism and paganism is most important. If the truth of paganism depends on (the existence of) pagan gods, then, assuming that monotheism is correct, what's left to talk about? But the natural world's (backwards) eternity is, logically speaking, an option. So the Bible's claim that the world was created is in opposition to more than a religious position that in all likelihood is false.

Here, then, paganism might best monotheism, best it by answering the inevitable question regarding the existence of the (extra-human) physical world. The problem for monotheism is yet more acute. Pagan gods express themselves through nature. Poseidon rules the waves and commands the currents. No wonder he is so turbulent. Nyx reigns all night. Her shadowiness is as it should be. But aside from giving us the smallest sliver of modal information possible, namely that God's being as he is is not incompatible with the physical world's being as it is, the findings of the naturalist deliver a blank, theologically.[13]

How did the physical world come to be? It's not because they are in possession of decisive grounds for answering that the Bible's thinkers tell the story of God creating. It's because they represent God as presiding over the whole. Like any question with several possible answers, "Does the world have a beginning?" can't be answered reflectively. True, the Bible's thinkers also do not know how men and women came to be. They do however have a view about *the nature* of men and women. The view they advance has to be evaluated on the basis of reflection as concerted as the reflection that generated it.

Continued misunderstanding of the theological formulation makes it an understatement to call "There is one deity" *potentially* misleading. Witness the ease with which the assertion gets paraphrased as the numerical "There is exactly one deity," rather than as – what it is – the ontological "The deity is a one."

Here's a striking passage from Proverbs (30:18–19).

> Three things are too wonderful for me;
> four I do not understand:
> the way of an eagle in the sky,
> the way of a snake on a rock,
> the way of a ship on the high seas,
> and the way of a man with a girl.

The way numbered "four" is a distillate of Hillel's distillation: the intersubjective sphere. This sphere the Proverbist sees as irreducibly different from the rest. Which gives a new perspective on Elijah's question to the Israelites (1 Kings 18:21): "How long will you go limping with two different opinions?"

The Actual Proselyte and the Potential One

The prospective proselyte has a leg to stand on. It doesn't follow that he should not take the plunge … into the *mikveh*. For it is true (or at least arguable) that his current belief-system misses what is essential to his own nature. He does not, to put it in the Bible's language, recognize God. On this missing essential Hillel's one-liner focuses. The "further study" that Hillel urges would however show that a second principle is needed.

I said that the Bible presents the lord of the manor before it presents the gatekeeper. This turns out to be, in a sense, incorrect. Abraham first meets God in Chapter 12. Abraham, the voice of the new tradition, then tells the story of the creation as the story of God's doings. In fact, the new thing that Abraham learned did not have to do with the creation of the physical world.

With a change of *dramatis personae*, the Talmudic anecdote can tellingly be retold. When it comes to his own nature, Abraham is of no doubt that paganism comes up short. On that conviction his mission is predicated. But he still has a question, about the natural creation. He goes to the top. "Let me take it upon myself to speak to the Lord, I who am but dust and ashes" (Genesis 19:27). "However it may be with how *I am*, don't the pagans have an effective answer to how *it is*?" Abraham must have hesitated about Genesis 1. What Genesis 1 contains is, after all, not much different from pagan accounts of the sort that Abraham would have been acculturated in before his life-changing afflatus. *Critique of Pure Paganism* isn't quite *The Twilight of the Idols*.

And the potential proselyte of the Talmud? Having received Hillel's answer, the man goes home and burns some midnight oil. Here's what he says when he returns to report on his progress. "What you told me, rabbi, is compelling. But it goes only so far. You told me of the principle of Genesis 2. What Genesis 1 tells of is as much needed if the overall position is to stand steadily. Otherwise, like a man on one leg, it will topple. He's got to put his other foot down. So, too, must you."

6

"Where were you?":
The Logic of the Book of Job

The same god who made you and me also made the rattlesnake.

Frank Griffin, *Godless* (Netflix)

Job Jobbed

The debriefing is under way. In answer to God's enquiry, Satan, singled out among the intelligence agents, reports that he has come "from going to and fro on the earth, and from walking up and down on it" (1:6). Has Satan, God asks (8), observed Job, "a blameless and upright man who fears God and turns away from evil"? Repeated reading of God's words suggests derision. "To and fro, you say. Up and down too, eh? I can assure you that in the case of Job, this assiduity won't add a feather to your cap." Satan doesn't quiver. "Have you not put a fence around [Job] and his house ...? You have blessed the work of his hands ... But stretch out your hand now, and touch all that he has, and he will curse you to your face" (10–11).

God accepts the challenge. Although Job, handed over to Satan, first exhibits the trait for which *his* name has become a byword, the mounting calamities eat away at his forbearance. Eventually, broken and bereft, he enters a grievance against God for having been, despite a glowing character and a record of devotion, jobbed.

It frequently happens that bad things befall the men and the women for whom *I* wish only good. My best efforts can't always keep them whole. I might even open them to harm in trying to obviate it. Yet none of this makes me unjust. Plainly, then, the issue of God's justice that the Book of Job tries isn't predicated on God's benevolence alone. Knowledge of the creation and supremacy count too. In a world over which such a deity presides, can bad things happen to good men and women without his being complicit?

The opening lines of the Book of Job provoke a composite question. "If God cuts deals with malign forces, isn't *the theodicy problem* a pseudo-problem? Doesn't the very existence of Satan call into question God's hegemony?" The argument of the Book of Job is that the world's being, as in the final verse of Chapter 1 of the Book of Genesis God himself pronounces it to be, "very good" (31), does not conflict with the blameless being afflicted. The writers of the Book of Job are not putting the Panglossian case: factor in all the factors and what seems bad turns out to be for the best. Like Leibnizeans, Job's comforters are dubious about accepting innocent suffering as a datum. God in their judgment would sooner have abided alone. Before pointing a finger, the afflicted should therefore look in the mirror. The comforters are, according to the Book of Job, mistaken. Job is as blameless as God says. Satan does not therefore function as the source of the bad. He is the Book's way of securing the datum, innocent suffering. The question for the reader is whether the place given to Satan in the story either is God's place (in which case the fault lies with him) or no place (in which case the defence is nugatory). With an eye on the answer, let me stress that rather than do what Satan suggests, God assigns *him* the dirty work. Satan is then said to "go out of the presence of the Lord" (12). The implication is that the harm is caused from a place where God isn't present.

Job suffers through no fault of his own. How does this square with the "very good"-ness of the world? If God did not foresee the problem and take steps, isn't he deficient in at least one of benevolence, power, and knowledge? What if a good and knowledgeable God could not have taken the steps? Commiserate we might. Revere less we would.

In the course of the discussion of the case for God as set out in Job, I will correct a mistake in the forums of commentary and interpretation. I hasten to add that the case is not available only to folk who acknowledge God. The heart of Job is an attempt to demonstrate that the suffering of the innocent protagonist doesn't clash with the goodness of the world as stated in Genesis 1. That goodness generates no religious commitments to God-ness.

The Perils of Epistemology

Even open-minded readers feel that Job withdraws his grievance prematurely. The answer that God delivers at the end seems to be based on an element central to the two God-defensive positions that are rejected because they deny the datum. Even Elihu, the least censorious of the comforters, claims that Job, in protesting his innocence, is – must be – missing something. Only God, with his knowledge of hearts and of the clockwork of the world, is competent to deliver the last judgement.[1] Leibnizeans say that the basis for judging definitively about good and bad goes beyond the reach of men and women.

Here is the beginning of God's response. The lines are from Chapter 38 of Job; the first line is verse 1; the next two are verse 4.

> Then the Lord answered Job out of the whirlwind.

> Where were you when I laid the foundations of the earth?
> Tell me, if you have understanding.

Isn't God pointing up the epistemological deficiency of finite men and women, the deficiency that lies at the intersection of the two rejected positions?

"Where were you?" Aren't we supposed to grant that God was, as verse 4 seems to imply, on the scene when the heavens and the earth came into being?

Why should God's primordial presence provide for an answer to Job? The reason is commonsensical. "I was there. You had better have in hand something that undermines the presumption that I know better." Through the Book of Job, God asserts, in a variety of ways, that he, God, has the goods and that Job is peering through the flyblown window. Here are verses 22 and 25 of the same chapter.[2]

> Have you entered the storehouses of the snow,
> or have you seen the storehouse of the hail[?]

> Who has cut a channel [through the firmament] for the torrents of rain,
> and a way for the thunderbolt[?]

Isn't the point that because of a deficit of knowledge men and women are in no position to judge? How else can verse 2 be construed? "Who is this that darkens counsel by words without knowledge?"

This certainly seems to be the point. But if it *is* the point, disaster for the Book of Job is in the offing. It's in the offing because, by the end, we do not have the knowledge that, on this construal of his words, God ascribes to himself. Under the circumstances, why moreover should we even accept the suffering of good men and good women as a datum? Perhaps "Look in the mirror" is right.

The words God is described as speaking do not come to the authors in visions. Their truth-content is known to men and women; known, then, to Job. God states that he fashioned the dome so that the upper waters could fall as rain and as snow and as hail. Although the scale is beyond us, the project – a sprinkler system – is workaday. But since we never doubted God's power, how does this advance the argument? Given that the defence is now complete, mustn't it be concluded that what God knows doesn't suffice for answering the question about justice and suffering?

If men and women have access to God's knowledge, then, since by the end of Job they have only the assurance that he, God, is in the know, Satan's challenge has not been met. If God's knowledge is inaccessible, how can a reasoned case, either way, be made?

So question-begging is the defence associated with the epistemological reading that something, we can't help feeling, has been missed.

In the course of his answer, God asks whether Job "can … draw out Leviathan with a fishhook" (41:5). It's time for *us* to fish or cut bait.

Being There: Two Ways

As I see it, the formulators of God's response were not clear in their own minds. The fact that God turns sarcastic solidifies our sense that the writers are groping. "Surely you [Job] know, for you were born [when I laid the foundations], and the number of your days is [as] great [as mine]!" (21).

In my view, Job is right to accept what God says. So before us is more than the task of making sense of a case that in its original form is elusive.

At the heart of the misunderstanding is an error regarding the core of the biblical position. Obviously, the deity the Book of Job speaks of is the deity of the Bible; the world in which Job lives is the world that Genesis 1:1 says this deity created. My reconstruction is restorative, then, of the proper connection with the Torah.

Consider these sentences from the preceding section:

"Where were you?" Aren't we supposed to grant that God was, as verse 4 seems to imply, on the scene when the heavens and the earth came into being?

We *are* supposed to grant it. The writers of the Book of Job, I mean, expect us to. This is what causes the difficulty in their case. For, arguably, God was *not* present when the foundations were laid. Recall here my claim that Satan, to cause Job's suffering, goes out of the presence of the Lord.

A standard view of verse 4 is that God is asserting that Job's position, representative of your position and of mine, is disadvantaged. "Job's position" is automatically taken to be an epistemological reference. "What do I know?" Might my disadvantage not however be due to what I am, not to where I happen to be? If a female is sought for a job, I am a non-starter.

A reader raises a hand. "God, you say, is not present when the foundations are laid. In Genesis 1:1, to which you referred, isn't God described in so many words as laying the foundations?"

Being present is possible in two ways. One: By being *on the scene*. A painter is present in this way when the canvas is filled in. Two: If, as in Van Gogh's *Self-Portrait with a Bandaged Ear*, the painter inserts their own likeness, they are (also) *in the scene*.

The distinction is a linchpin of Job's case for God. Equally vital is the fact that the opening part of the Torah contains two accounts of the world's creation, one in Genesis 1 and one in Genesis 2.

Taking the two ways of being present and the two creation stories, there are, then, four combinatorial possibilities.

God, I said, is not present when the foundations are laid. The reader who raised a hand takes me to be denying that God is *on the scene*. This I do *not* deny. God, I claim, is not *in the scene* that Genesis 1:1 depicts. God is not present in the world that is created.

I imagine that the reader, after pausing for a moment, will go back on the offensive. "The deity of the Bible is an extra-natural being. The distinction between being on the scene and being in the scene distinguishes nothing from nothing."

Not so. God is present in Genesis 2 in both senses. On the scene: "In the day that the Lord God made ... earth and ... heavens" (2:2). In the scene: "the Lord God formed [the] man from the dust of the ground, and breathed into his nostrils the breath of life" (7). God puts something of himself in the world of Genesis 2.

The key to Job is the contrast between Genesis 1 and Genesis 2 in the matter of the two modes of being present. God asks: "Were you there?" If God were stressing Job's puniness in knowledge, we *could* conclude the Book of Job's inconclusiveness. But God isn't pulling epistemological rank. He is saying that the world whose creation Genesis 1 describes is not a world that was created with Job in mind. In fact, it's a world in which Job does not exist. "You were not there then," God is saying, "and you are not there now."

Genesis 1: It's All Good

God is present in the scene in Genesis 2 but not in Genesis 1. In support, I quoted the assertion that God breathes life into the first man. Isn't humankind created in the Genesis 1 story? If God is present in the scene in Genesis 2, present specifically in the human sector (nothing else gets breathed into), isn't God also present in the scene, in the same place and in the same way, in Genesis 1 (nothing else is created in God's image and likeness)?

To begin answering, I'll quote another line from earlier.

> The argument of the Book of Job is that the world's being, as in the final verse of Chapter 1 of the Book of Genesis God himself pronounces it to be, "very good" (31), does not conflict with the blameless being afflicted.

At the end of Day 6, having applied "good" six times to what he brings into being, God says of the world "very good." Nowhere in the story is "bad" voiced.

Where, now, is this story? It's in Chapter 1 of Genesis. Let us label the world of this story WG1. "Bad," then, is not applied to anything in WG1.

Question 1: Why is "bad" absent from WG1? Question 2: Does "bad" later get applied to WG1?

"Bad" is inapplicable in WG1 because WG1 is an integrated whole. The luminaries are in the skies, the marine creatures are in their element, the land animals are on the land.

This doesn't mean that WG1 is changeless. Rather, the only kind of change that occurs is change that doesn't affect everything's being in its place. Picture a forest. Microorganisms metabolize organic material. Wind-wafted, seeds from the various plants alight on the forest floor. Nourished by the products of those processes, they develop, some into saplings that become mature trees whose shed foliage supplies more fuel for the microorganisms. Now and then a tree falls over and, decomposing, replenishes the humus. We have a system in equilibrium. Its parts – microorganisms, seeds, plants at various stages of development – aren't just changing individually. In the process they exchange matter and energy. God's judgment "very good" is to the effect that the whole is conserved through each thing's functioning.

"Bad" doesn't apply in WG1. The death of an antelope in the jaws of a lion benefits the whole. A weak animal is removed from the herd. "And if the antelope is robust?" The "success" of the lion enables an especially adept hunter to perpetuate its genes. So too would the robust antelope's escape be good. It challenges a lion whose breeding life is done and/or whose ability to collect food is on the slide. Again, if the "unsuccessful" predator is strong, the escape enables an agile antelope to breed further. One could as easily say that antelopes use lions to strengthen the herd as say that lions use antelopes for the good of the pride. In fact, the asymmetrical language is anthropomorphic. One location in the system is singled out from outside, by us, and judgments are relativized to that location when, in fact, proper judgments must be made in global terms.

The preceding description is incomplete. The balance can be disrupted. In such cases, disorder will rule until an equilibrium defined by different quantities is reached.[3] It's possible to read the early phases of Genesis 1 as a movement towards equilibrium. But by the end only changes non-disruptive of the overall structure occur. So far as WG1 is concerned, there is nothing new under the sun.[4]

Despite my mention of it, *death* is absent from WG1 too. Dying in WG1 is the termination of a phase of an ongoing process of transformation. Poetic talk of the dying day captures it. It's not the dying for which, when it occurs to someone near to us, we go into mourning.

Back to God's question, the one from 38:4, that was formulated sarcastically in verse 21. "Where were you?" The point is that Job and his like are not present in WG1. Humankind is a biological species, like lionkind and spiderkind and treekind. For humankind too, there is no bad in this world. The death of a human is no more bad than is the death of a tree. God could say to a tree what the god Krishna says to Arjuna. "No one dies. Your matter is recycled. You go on. The basic unit is the system." In WG1, everything gets out of life alive.

The objection is that God, in creating humankind, is also in the scene. Striking though its difference from other kinds is, the writers of Genesis 1 see humankind as part of the system. It's to clarify the difference that they say of humankind that it is made "in [God's] image, according to [God's] likeness" (26).[5] So if God is not in the scene in respect of fernkind and lionkind, neither is he in the scene in respect of humankind.

"Where were you?" The deity who asks is the deity of WG1. From the answer to Question 1 it will now be clearer that Job isn't in WG1. This is figuratively marked by the fact that it's from outside nature that God breathes life into Job's original. From the answer to Question 2 it will now be clearer that Job is never in WG1. God is not saying "*I* was there." No epistemological contrast is being drawn between Job and God. God is instructing Job in ontology. "You are not part of WG1 because I am not in it."[6]

WG2 and the Potential for Bad

In the clear sense in which the painter is not in the picture, God is not in WG1. The ontological significance of this will come out once we turn to the different creation story told in Genesis 2.

Genesis 1 is focused on the emergence of humankind, the biological species. What God creates in Genesis 2 is a particular person, a man, and then another particular person, a woman. From these two every particular man stems and every particular woman.

A (mammalian) species requires both sexes: "male and female he created them" is written when God is said to create humankind.[7] But in Genesis 2, the man, created first, is for a time present independently. The man's solitary condition through most of Genesis 2 is the Bible's way of making the conceptual point that although the species comprises both sexes, each particular person is a whole in his or her own right.

In creating the first man, God breathes life into him. Obviously, humankind (in the Genesis 1 story) exists without need for God's act of respiration. The life of which Genesis 2 speaks in the human case is different. It's the life that particulars have. It's God's kind of life. God, it may be inferred, is present in Genesis 2 in the way that Van Gogh is present in the self-portrait – though God's copies, carbon copies, are not generally circumcised of ear.[8]

Returning now to the absence of bad in WG1: bad puts in no appearance in WG1 because everything is in its place. Bad, it follows, is linked to being out of place – precisely what Genesis 2 relates. The story of disobedience in Eden is therefore more about what men and women *are* than about what men and women *do*.

In WG1, the good-and-bad coin always lands on good; or, better, no coin for tossing is two-faced. In a system such as a forest, nothing can do bad to anything. The possibility, in WG2, of the toss turning up bad is due to the presence of separate entities in interaction. Were dinosaurs more intelligent, they still wouldn't need legal systems. But the bad (and the good) that particular persons do one another isn't Job's issue. To cause Job to have a car accident, Satan would flash-flood the road, not ply another motorist with liquor.

The Case for God

The answer to the question of God's justice is in hand. *The source of bad that the Book of Job considers is WG1.* God is not present in WG1. God's nature – particularity – is absent from it. This explains why the Book of Job's Satan isn't a doer of evil. Satan is not, could not be, in the presence of the Lord when he inflicts the harm. Satan is cancer attacking an individual, or a tree, root structure compromised by heavy rain, injuring a walker when it falls. Cancer is as "good" in WG1 as is a sunny day. To be sure, if eating habits increase susceptibility to malignancies, or if arboriculture weakens trees, then Satan is only an accessary. *The source of bad is itself good.* So there is no faulting God for WG1. Men and women who suffer belong to WG2. They are particulars. *The suffering that Satan is said to inflict on Job comes from WG1.* The sufferers do not exist in WG1. So although there would be no undeserved bad if there were no men and women, where's the ground for grievance in that? *In fact, the existences of particular men and of particular women have value.*[9] *Job's treatment of the issue of undeserved bad therefore leaves no basis for asserting that God would have been more just had men and the women not been created.* The charge is that God would have been better had he created a world in which men and women do not suffer undeservedly. "But," the defence argues, "once WG1 and WG2 are up and running, undeserved bad is a standing possibility."

The effects of WG1 on WG2 are unavoidable.[10] Bad can affect us despite its causes' not being bad and even though we have no ground for complaint about how we are made. Job and his like come into being in WG2. The question of God's justice isn't asked from the standpoint of the (WG1) system that is nature. The creative act that makes the Bible the book that it is is God's breathing life into the first man. WG2, the world in which this occurs, is therefore a world in which there is more than God-likeness. God is present in the first man, and present, through him, in each one of us. So whatever justified complaints we, being in WG2, have, the complaint of injustice isn't one of them.

When his patience finally fails, Job snarls an imprecation. "Let the day perish on which I was born" (3:3). If the reference is to WG1's Day 6, Job is confused.

Neither was he conceived on any day in WG1, nor on any day in WG1 did he come to be. For the same reason, no innocent suffering (of a problematic kind) is found in WG1. If Job is referring to WG2, he is flying in the face of the basic conditions for his own (type of, namely particular) existence.

American Gods

Hinting of a connection between W.V. Quine, the American logician, and Job, the man of Uz, is Quine's thesis about enlisting the resources of first-order logic to take over the job done by unstructured singular terms.[11] It would be a gain in logical streamlining, he argues, if the proper name "Socrates" ceded to "the Socratizer," the artificial predicative element that incorporates in its meaning characteristics, baldness, snub-nosedness, loquacity, and so forth, appealed to in picking Socrates out. The bound variable would systematically replace the singular term. On the side of descriptive content, Quine's logic, as this illustrates, has only general terms. It's not "Socrates is snub-nosed." It's "The unique thing to which 'bald,' 'talkative,' etc. apply, also satisfies 'snub-nosed.'"

Pointing to the distinction between individuals and particulars, the ontologists behind the Bible would quarrel with Quine.

In and of itself, the defence of the proper name is being-theoretically insignificant. To what can a proper name not be affixed? The Bibleists' point is that the restriction to general terms and pronouns for purposes of world-representation affects (or reflects) the representors' basic understanding of the world's constitution. *The (non-general) constituents don't merely happen to exemplify general properties. Their being is that of general property exemplifiers.* Now general terms come as a system; the system of predicates is the linguistic face of the system of properties. Quine's proposal thus exemplifies this characteristic of Greek philosophical thinking: the particular is squeezed out. Quine, here, is a pure Platonist, Plato's metaphysical analysis consisting only of Forms, which are intrinsically general, and the (spatio-temporal) Receptacle, which is intrinsically singular. Of his mentor, Plato would have said that he is the (unique) Socratizer; the locale in the Receptacle of a unique suite of characteristics.

Quine's logic is suited to WG1. Since it's WG2 in which you and I, he and she, particulars all, exist, Quine's deck is stacked against us. Quine's commitment to science is the joker in this deck. Science too is pagan in character.[12]

A decision for (Platonic) metaphysics against (biblical) ontology should not be made by notation.

I distinguished particulars from other non-general individuals. Individuality is a matter of clear identification and reidentification conditions. Non-particular individuals can be parts of systems. The apparatus of first-order logic suits them to a T. It's always "something (in space and time) that satisfies general conditions C_1, C_2, C_3." This works for trees, for planets, for all the things found in WG1. The first particular in the creation inhabits WG2, not WG1. To say that God's breath of life inspires the first man is to attribute more than the God-likeness ascribed to humankind in WG1. The first man has a bit of God in him. "God" here functions as *the* name. In Beer-sheba, as the Bible tells us, Abraham "called ... on the name of the Lord." We need a P-logic, with *bona fide* names. A G-logic, with only general terms and quantificational apparatus, won't do.[13]

The Bible's principle is God. God is the basic particular. Logical formalizers must not eliminate the name in favour of predicates and bound variables. That, on the non-general side of the census of being, would leave nothing besides non-particular individuals.

Here's a Bible-inspired way of making the point. "There are in WG1 no separate places." Colloquially, one speaks of the place in which a specific tree is located. But the tree, to be understood, must be taken as part of the forest, the ecosystem. The whole of the system speaks through the tree. Places in WG1 are neither here nor there.

God, in answer to Moses's question about who he is, says "I AM." This also expresses the point: God is a basic "I." The pronoun is not dispensable. Since God is not in the scene in Genesis 1, there is no "I" in WG1.[14]

The imagery used for God in WG1 and WG2 captures the individual/particular distinction. In Genesis 1, verse 2, God is represented (in the Mechon Mamre translation) as "hover[ing] over the face of the waters." In Genesis 2, verse 8, God descends. He "planted a garden," no doubt dirtying his hands in the process. Only a particular can plant a garden. God's gardening prefigures the first man's transgression. A garden transgresses the natural system. Unkept, it will turn unkempt. A garden, then, has a bit of the (particular) gardener in it, as the lump of clay has in it a bit of God.

Quine's being-theoretic equation, "To be is to be the value of the variable," captures only the constituents of WG1. Bishop Berkeley, in formulating *his* view about existence, tacked "... or to perceive" onto "To be is to be perceived." Quine's equation too needs a disjunct. "To be is to be the value of a variable, sc. a (non-particular) individual, or it is to be a particular." Since, in the Bible, it's particulars that have intrinsic value, the value of all else being bound up with the wider whole in which it is situated, we can rephrase the equation in a more alliterative form: "To be is to be the value of a variable or it is to be a valuable."

A Text to Conjure With

Central to this reading of Job is verse 4 of chapter 38:

> Where were you when I laid the foundations of the earth?
> Tell me, if you have understanding.

Observe that apart from its usual epistemological sense, "understanding" also connects to Latin "substance" and to Greek "ὑποκείμενον," both terms central to the (Aristotelian, Scholastic) ontological lexicon. So perhaps God seems to us to ask an epistemological question because we've lost the connection.

The original of verse 4 runs thus:

איפה היית ביסדי ארץ הגד אם ידעת בינה

It's the last four words that interest me. The first word: "הגד," translated as "tell," although not cognate with the word for the copula, is close to it. To tell some-one something is to connect them in thought to it. The third word: one sense of the Hebrew verb "to know," as all are taught in studying Genesis 4:1, is sexual congress. The fourth word: a synonym of "understand," the word links also, in look and sound, to the verb "to construct." So we can render what God says thus. "Where were you, when the world was made? You can't connect with it intimately, can you?" More fully: "The world that was made is not of your kind, to know. What you are, what your being stands upon, your substance, is uncon-nected to that foundation." Or, to borrow the Genesis 2:23 words of the man upon meeting the woman, one of which, "עצם," translated as "bone," also means "essence" or "substance," it is not bone of your bones, flesh of your flesh.

7
"Let them have dominion":
The Bible and the Natural World

Don't know much about the science book
Don't know much about the Pentateuch
                              – Misheard lyrics of Sam Cooke's "Wonderful World"

The Evidence, the Charge, and the Plea

> Then [Genesis 1:26] God said, "Let us make humankind in our image, according
> to our likeness; and let them have dominion over the fish of the sea, and over the
> birds of the air, and over the cattle, and over all the wild animals of the earth, and
> over every creeping thing that creeps upon the earth."

Then Lynn White, Jr. said, "A main root of current environmental problems is
Judeo-Christian arrogance towards nature."[1]

The Bible, in which is crystallized the thinking of a small group who inhabited
the region of the Fertile Crescent three millennia ago, is a charter document of
our culture. In it are expressed some of the basic attitudes we have towards ourselves, towards our intimates, towards members of other groups, and towards the
extra-human world. To be sure, a lot of time has passed. Nevertheless, like the
bearded and bonneted figures in the family album of daguerreotypes, the characters through the description of whose lives the Bible's standard-setting ideas about
men and women are conveyed return a likeness. White appreciates this. But in
regard to attitudes towards nature, he does not like the likeness that he sees.

White charges the Judeo-Christian tradition with arrogance towards nature.
Genesis 1:26 is his Exhibit A. But the biblical attribution of dominion to
humankind isn't an attempt to rationalize an attitude independently held. The
attribution, I'll show, makes good analytic sense. Indeed, what the Bible understands by "dominion" hasn't even an affinity for the behaviours decried by the
environmentalists.

"If the environmentalists are wrong about the Bible, shouldn't the defence be able to secure an acquittal by summoning the experts?" Later, by looking at the view of an insider whose representative anti-environmentalist position[2] is that "[the natural world's] value lies in its serviceability to man,"[3] I will confirm that the defect in understanding is not confined to amateurs of Scripture.

In times nearer the inception, the text was I believe understood as I understand it. Since environmentalism has only of late taken over top spot on the food-for-thought chain, only of late have the polluting effects of the misunderstanding come to light.

How is it that the misunderstanding runs so deep? In the current environment of discussion, a pair of reasons, one interpretive, one philosophical, exercise an especially baneful influence.

The usual translations cloud the meaning of Genesis 1:26. Nor does knowledge of classical Hebrew work like Windex. Fortuitously, the most common English versions contain a clue to the real meaning, a clue that readers of the original are unlikely to pick up from the word translated as "dominion." Also, the difference between the world of Genesis 1 (in which dominion figures) and the world of Genesis 2 (which inaugurates the main storyline) is not factored into the overall treatment. God's creation of humankind in his image and likeness is taken for a stylistic variant of God's breathing the breath of life into the first man.

Here are two editorial comments from *The New Oxford Annotated Bible*, the first (2) a summary of Genesis's opening chapter as a whole, the second (3) a distillation of Genesis 1:26–7.

> Out of original chaos God created an orderly world, assigning a preeminent place to human beings.

> The solemn divine declaration ["Let us make humankind … and let them have"] emphasizes humanity's supreme place at the climax of God's creative work.

(1) God creates the world. (2) The creation consists in a shift from disorder to order. (3) Human beings are preeminent in the world. Of these, only (2) is correct. And (3), as I said at the start, is what especially draws environmentalist fire to the Bible.

God's Doings

The descriptions of God's doings "in the beginning" (Genesis 1:1) are neither eyewitness reports nor transcriptions of what a chosen few pick up on the transcendent bandwidth. Like Aristotle in the *Metaphysics*, the composers are delineating the structure of things and offering their best conjectures about the processes by which the world as we know it came to be as it is. The modality of the *analysans* is close enough to necessity for the reflectorium to be the appropriate venue of adjudication.

God bestows dominion on humankind. This isn't the issuance of a licence to men and women to act heedless of consequences except as they impinge on their own well-being. It's intended rather to explain how men and women differ from other (natural) creatures.

Appearances of God in the Genesis story are never self-interpreting. Often, a biblical claim that God does this or that God does that will be interpreted so that what God is said to do is done, but not by a transcendent being. On occasion, the interpretation will make clear that a deed is superfluous to what is being described.

When only mad dogs and Englishmen are abroad, messengers appear (this is described in Genesis 18) at Abraham's tent. Their mission? To gather intelligence about the person who had signed on as God's man. Is the human covenanter moving on the right track? The information furnished is intended *for the reader*. Emissaries from above are optional. Pleased at what they find, the messengers inform Abraham that Sarah will be delivered of a child. Given that Sarah's reproductive days are past, it's harder to see how this – a prophecy – could be built into the story without a special agent. Yet what is the tiding if not a way of indicating *to readers* the viability of the improbable child about whose prospects they, had they been present, would have joined in Sarah's belly laughter?

What of God's role in regard to dominion? As with the messengers to Abraham, God is appealed to by way of clarifying for the reader how the creatures singled out as possessing dominion differ. "What about the words 'let them have dominion'?" As I'll now explain, *the text doesn't in fact contain a Hebrew version of these words, taken as a verbal sign of an act of donation.*

Genesis 1:26: "let them have"

Johnny's parents hear a muffled ring. They find one of the devices in his schoolbag. "Honey, let him have the cellphone," says the mother to the father. Why not take what God is said to say in 1:26 as "Do not prevent them from having dominion," the implication being that dominion will be humankind's unless measures are taken?

This isn't in fact what I have in mind in denying that God is active in regard to humankind's possession of dominion. Still, observing that "let them have" can apply even when nothing is given points to what I believe to be, interpretively, the truth. Possessing the commodity called "dominion" links *internally* to being made in God's image and likeness.

It's a fine thing, this internality. Where else but in the product would the likeness that God is referring to be found? Omnipotent or not, God is highly

potent. The quality isn't however transmitted to humankind. Puny and fragile
we are, punier and more fragile than many God-unlike things with which we
share the world. Being God-like is therefore compatible with lacking characteristics that God has – compatible, therefore, with possessing characteristics that
God lacks. Were the link *external* we could therefore come up with no more
than this near-vacuous modal thing: it's possible for God-like men and women
to receive dominion. But isn't the distinction between humankind and the rest
made in terms of differential God-likeness? The implication is that in their
words regarding dominion the Biblists are clarifying what it is to be God-like.

Here's the Hebrew.

נעשה אדם בצלמנו כדמותנו; וירדו בדגת הים ובעוף השמים,
ובבהמה ובכל-הארץ, ובכל-הרמש, הרמש על-הארץ

The words

נעשה אדם בצלמנו כדמותנו

mean, nearly enough: "Let us make humankind &c." (The words could also be
rendered, less royally, as "Now [having completed these other things] we shall
make humankind &c.") As for "and let them have dominion," the corresponding
Hebrew is short and sweet:

וירדו

There is no "Let them." Here, with "Then God said" left out, is a closer translation. "Let us create humankind in our likeness, according to our image; and,
as so created, having dominion." That is: "Having created humankind in our
image, we have *ipso facto* created something that has dominion." It's not (to
adjust also the tenses), "Now that we have created humankind in our likeness,
we shall (proceed to) let them have dominion &c."

An instructive parallel obtains between this case and verse 3. "Then God
said, 'Let there be light'; and there was light."

ויאמר אלהים, יהי אור; ויהי-אור

"And [so] there was," "ויהי," is structurally identical to "וירדו." The implication is
the same. "Let them have" is misleading for suggesting a two-act play. In parallel
with the first's "and there was," the second might well be "and [so] they dominated."[4]

"Let them eat bread and milk." My meaning is captured by "Let them eat
bread and let them drink milk." The Bible being minimalistic, that there's no "let
them have" in regard to dominion doesn't decide against the NRSV. I am not

however relying only on the absence of a statement of permission ("they may be allowed") or of donation ("I give them"). Whatever the final judgment, it's a splash of cold water to the reader that "let them" isn't part of a word-by-word rendering.

I'll insert here the point that "Let them eat bread and milk" could sop up "Let them eat bread and then, suitably fortified, milk the cows." This, fortuitously, is closer to what I understand 1:26 to be saying! "Let them be like God and then, being that way, dominate."

Between being God-like and the having dominion a feeler gauge cannot be inserted. To be like God is (=) to have dominion. The creation of X in God's likeness is (=) the creation of something that dominates. It remains to defend this on the interpretive level.

"Dominion"

"Dominion" is the KJ's rendering of "וירדו." For three reasons, the English word is an inspired choice. (1) Latin "Dominus," cognate with "dominion," is an appellation for God. (2) "Dominion" is cognate with "dominate." (3) "Dominion" links semantically with "domain."

The link between "dominion" and "Dominus" supports the proposition that being God-like is (=) having dominion. For being God-like is being like Dominus. That implicates the idea of dominion on the level of words.

The Bible is focusing on a defining characteristic of God – of Dominus. God, being what God is, has dominion. What is it to have dominion? To be God-like, to be like Dominus, is to be like the Lord. The idiom "lord it over" is apt. While capturing the harsh feel of "וירדו," "lord it over" is at the same time emollient. How does Dominus, the Lord, lord it over? God is above and beyond the natural world. The prepositions-cum-adverbs here, "above," "beyond," "over," are positional. We could say that God is *outside* nature. It is in *this* core sense that God lords it over. He's the over-Lord. "Superior" carries both the evaluative sense and, in the Latin preposition, the positional one.

"Dominate," the cognate verb of "dominion," has a descriptive use. "The Empire State Building dominates Manhattan."[5] No tyrannizing here. Tyrannical or not, God dominates the world in this way. To say that they are God-like is to ascribe to men and women a like relationship to the (natural) world.

Neither of "lord it over" and "dominate" is of much help in illuminating the other. "Domain" supplies the independent wattage.

Men and women, bound up with space and time and matter, are not above and beyond. The Bible's focus is a difference internal to the physical world. Unlike polar bears, native to the Arctic, lions on the African veldt, barrel cactuses in the Mojave Desert, the human animal does not have *a specific domain*.

To have a specific domain, to be niche-bound, is be limited. To be limited is not to dominate.

To have dominion is to be especially versatile among the greenery. In the case of men and women, the Bible stresses omnivorousness: "every plant yielding seed … and every tree with seed in its fruit … for food."[6] Not the special bestowal of a catholic palate, this is the tail of the coin whose head is ubiquity. Wouldn't a niche-bound creature needful of niche-unavailable nourishment soon go extinct?

All this makes perfect sense without appeal to God. Starting with the strictly niche-bound, we move to (natural) things having a more versatile mode of presence, and then to an extra-natural being who has no (physical) domain at all. The niche-freedom that men and women perceive in themselves, felt even more strongly now that we have slipped our moorings from the earth, is expressible in terms of dominion. "X is niche-free" means "X doesn't have a specific, restricted, domain."

Doubt, if any remains that the theological infusion ("God's image and likeness") isn't intended to supply an aetiological explanation, vanishes once it is observed that the Bible draws a parallel with humankind inside the natural world. Humankind: "fill the earth" (28). The fish: "fill the waters" (22).[7]

The fish, in their watery habitat, move up, down, left, right, backward, forward, diagonally. In this their behaviour looks to have the plasticity of humankind's.[8] So the fish, as a group, can fill the place up. This reading is confirmed by the other recipients of a blessing in Genesis 1: humankind; the sabbath. Why the sabbath? Not being earmarked for any specific activity, it can be taken up by many, not only by work, as on weekdays. That the world does not receive a blessing supports the point that the whole, inclusive of the niche-free constituents, is a well-ordered system. As to the blessing itself, it's not that the mentioned things might stray in the moral sense. Rather, *qua* non-niche-bound, they will in the course of their careers necessarily interact with the rest – a challenge to their natural well-being.[9]

Genesis 1: *mundus Dei pro paganos*

In Genesis 1, the phases of the creation conclude with God's assessment: "good." The sense of "X is good" is "X does its job; X fills its intended function." The final judgment says that the parts, each designed for a local function, mesh into a whole. A general contractor will only at the end be able to say that the various subcontractors' products interconnect properly.

Genesis 1 tells of increasing differentiation. The various regions or domains come into being. Then, inhabitants for the various regions or domains emerge. Moreover, the inhabitants that emerge do so from within. They too are parts of the system, more differentiated.[10]

It's possible now to explain why, in Genesis 1, God does not create. Also, a general formula can be given for figuring out which of God's doings in the narrative are placeholders for genuine doings.

The cosmogenesis in Hesiod is similar to Genesis 1's. A primordial soup differentiates into broth and gobs. Further differentiations then occur, until the world as we recognize it eventuates. The difference is that, in Hesiod, no outside instrumentality is at work.

Genesis 1 is told by subscribers to the Bible, whose distinctive condition of belief is predicated on the biblical system's repairing a deficiency in the pagan account. The latter contains many deities: of the rain, of the tides, of the sun. No distinctive deity, however, of you and of me and of him and of her. The Bible's story of the natural creation is at base the same. Recall the editors of *The New Oxford Annotated Bible*: "[it's] only indirectly [bound] to God." But while it doesn't have to be, the Genesis 1 story is in fact told from the standpoint of God. "God separated heavens from earth" is thus akin to *Pravda's* "Khrushchev launched Gagarin into orbit."

This, then, is how to identify God's doings in the narrative of the natural creation that are placeholders for genuine doings. When what is done also comes about in the pagan story, God's doing of it is not representational.[11]

"If God doesn't create the physical world, why not a wholly demythologized version of Hesiod – Hesiod according to Hoyle, perhaps?" The making of the man – which is described in Genesis 2, not in Genesis 1 – is beyond the pagan deities. It, at last, is, in the Bible, a genuine doing of God's.[12]

A soft spot exists in the environmentalist's heart for pagan views. The men and the women who represent themselves as true to the biblical position also appreciate paganism's connection with nature. But they see it as a target of the Bible's animus. The link between paganism and environmentalism is obvious in any case. Worship of the pagan gods expresses reverence for nature. Since the gods, the natural principles, come as a system, to understand correctly is to understand from the standpoint of the pantheon.

Repudiation of idolatrous practices doesn't separate the Bibleists from non-mystical environmentalists. Also, the Bibleists see the natural world as more tightly unitary than do pagan thinkers. It's as if a unitary god-principle – a master Law of Nature – is postulated. The idea of understanding from the standpoint of the whole doesn't therefore fall to the objection that "whole" is misleading, the gods being so fractious. This is a second reason for telling the story in terms of God. It adds clarity to the idea of a unified system.

This, then, is the Bible's categorization of the natural world. Day and night, the seasons, dry regions and wet. A system of reciprocally dependent parts. You can't coherently separate Apollo from Nyx. Humankind too is part of the system, with the difference that its constituents are niche-free. The editors of the NRSV therefore err in according men and women pre-eminence.

Humankind's being in his image and likeness is not, then, a doing of the Bible's deity. The implication for conduct upends White. The certainty that the niche-free will cross paths with the niche-bound threatens the latters' balance. In view of the mentioned difference, the claim to Noah that "the fear and dread of you shall rest on every animal of the earth, and on every bird of the air, on everything that creeps on the ground, and on all the fish of the sea" (9:2) makes perfect sense.[13]

In Genesis 1 we have an advance on paganism, in whose stereotypical version the various gods – Zeus, Poseidon, Apollo – are niche-associated, and men and women, cultivating some coveted trait – Odysseus, ingenuity; Ajax, martial prowess; Helen, beauty – are thought of as protégés.

"Why do non-human creatures not share God's (Genesis 1) image and likeness?" The birds and the beasts, the fish and the insects, are niche-bound. If world-generation had ended at noon on Day 6, lionkind would not have been functionally equivalent to the kind on which the sun set several hours later. The lion would still lack what the fish are said to have.[14]

Why doesn't mortality, a standing concern in the Bible, figure in Genesis 1's treatment of humankind? "Die," in the sense of the word associated with the fruit of the tree of knowledge of good and – *what is absent in Genesis 1* – bad, does not apply to non-human things. Events of the sort that birth certificates and obituaries mark we do not have in the world of Genesis 1. We have recycling. Genesis 1's world couldn't sustain God's assertion that "my spirit shall not abide in [men] forever, for they are flesh; their days shall be [at most] one hundred twenty years" (6:3).[15]

I conclude by bringing it back to White and Green. White writes as if humankind is external to nature. The Bible's Genesis 1 story, conversely, represents the species as of the same whole as the rest. By differentiating the human sector of the creation in *natural* terms, the Bible supplies an analysis that makes the issue at once more realistic and less tractable. Given that men and women are as natural as the rest, the criticism of their conduct in nature is neutralized. There is no "bad" in Genesis 1. Yet our relations with the natural world are certainly problematic.

Black and White and Green

From White and Green I turn to Black and Green – "Black" here referring to Steven Schwarzschild, the biblical insider and champion. So exuberantly does Schwarzschild discuss the matter that one initially gapes in wonderment. *Initially.* A scene in Tom Wolfe's *Bonfire of the Vanities* (595) describes the progress of our admiration.

"Let there be decorum in the sanctuary." Myron Branoskowitz, the cantor of Congregation Schlomoch'om, Bayside, Queens, takes his place next the casket.

Aware that a Hollywood bigwig is present, Branoskowitz treats his part in the obsequies as an impromptu audition.

> [He] began in Hebrew in a strong clear tenor voice. His lamentations began to swell in volume. They were unending and irrepressible. His voice took on throbs and vibratos. If there was a choice between ending a phrase in a high octave or a low one, he invariably went high ... He put tears into his voice that would have embarrassed the worst hambone Pagliacci. At first the mourners were impressed. Then they were startled as the voice grew in volume. Then they became concerned as the young man began to swell like a frog. And now they were beginning to look at one another, each wondering if his neighbor was thinking the same thing: "This kid is out to lunch."

Schwarzschild reads Genesis 1 as an adjunct to Genesis 2. Citing Soloveitchik's view that there are two Adams, one aesthetic (Genesis 1), one practical (Genesis 2), Schwarzschild (361) swells in protest. He only moderates the criticism when he finds Soloveitchik subordinating the aesthetic to the practical. Schwarzschild quotes Leviticus Rabbah: "The first man was created for God's use and the disk of the sun for human use" (n81). This repeats the mistake. The sun is created in Genesis 1. The first man isn't. Moreover, no issue of use arises in Genesis 1; only one of interrelation and interchange.[16]

The first man is created in Genesis 2. Conflating the two chapters, Schwarzschild is blind to the textual basis for the rapprochement between White and Scripture. Insensible of the fact that the humankind of Genesis 1 is part of the greenery, he misses that the consideration of humankind's well-being requires considering things from the standpoint of the whole.

Schwarzschild sees in the early part of the Bible only the man of Genesis 2. The attitudes towards the world on display in the story of the garden are, for him, the normative ones. This omits the attitudes of Genesis 1.[17] Here, nature is not a garden and humanity has no privilege. A garden is a *cultivated* piece of the world. Without tilling and keeping, it will revert to the wilds. The grassing earth of the thinkers/writers responsible for the Bible can't conceivably be equated to their divine gardener.

Schwarzschild's essay is titled "The Unnatural Jew." Like "defective," "unnatural" is abuse. Schwarzschild, a professor of philosophy, will have known that G.E. Moore called good a *non-natural* property.

The opening anecdote is a foretaste of what we're being asked to swallow. Schwarzschild tells us that he doesn't get an invite to the annual departmental picnic. His colleagues learned early in his tenure that he is out of place among the frolickers. Here are three biblical grounds for objecting to Schwarzschild's gleeful curmudgeonliness. One: Genesis 2 has a garden. Two: A picnic isn't a natural event. Jewish festivals include Tu B'Shvat, the new year of the trees, and the holiday of Lag Ba'Omer, on which the celebrants go into nature and, often, picnic.[18] Three: Why should Schwarzschild liken his colleagues' activities to rites of spring around the Maypole? Doesn't God rest after his labours?

"Unnatural" is an irritant. The use of "anthropocentric" as a badge of honour is a provocation. "This," Schwarzschild writes (351), referring to the Bible, "is anthropocentrism … long before Kant." Schwarzschild's position on the environment – men and women should protect the environment if *they* benefit thereby – is anchored in the stronger claim that nature lacks intrinsic value. A defence of the claim can be mounted. Whatever the defence's quality, "anthropocentrism" is a misnomer. It's some stripe of (quasi-Kantian, non-Hegelian) idealism.[19] Parts of the Bible are receptive to the idealist construction. For instance: God's invitation to the man to name the animals implies that the output of cognitive processing of the world is peculiar to the human perspective.

The defence of a Kantian position isn't however a defence of the Bible.[20] The world of Genesis 1 is not understood from the perspective of human consciousness. To assert that *nothing* is intelligible once one abstracts from the relation to men and women is to depart from the Bible. At last Schwarzschild, who asserts this, qualifies as an unnatural Jew!

A final provocation is "pagan." Though hostile to paganism, the Bible is friendly to the underlying naturalism, *providing the naturalism isn't extended into Genesis 2*. Asked to name the animals, Adam doesn't go on safari. A zoo is constructed for the exercise. "Paganism" in Schwarzschild's hands is in this regard tendentious. True, the Bible repudiates the religious attitude towards nature that it implies. "I am the Lord your God …; you shall have no other gods before me." To bow to the imperative is to disenchant nature. But to admire nature; to appreciate nature; to respect nature's integrity: none of these presuppose a worshipful attitude.

These lines contain the core of Schwarzschild's position (351).

> The biblical and Jewish God is, indeed, absolutely transcendent. Nature is never in any way identical with him. It can serve him, as it can serve human beings made in the "image of God." What makes humans "images of God" is that they share with him the "will," the rational and the ethical.

The claim that men and women are made "in [God's] image" is found in Genesis 1. Explaining the Bible's point, I never used the word "will," nor did I speak of a faculty of choice. I also showed that God is superfluous to the truth of what is being stated in verses 26 and 27. Genesis 2 is the story that involves transgression and (therefore) choice. It is the story that features the worm. And it is the story in which God is, arguably, essential.

It's hard to decide which in Schwarzschild's case is chicken and which is egg: misreading of the text; minimizing the difference between Genesis 1 and

Genesis 2. There is another reason why readers and interpreters underestimate the difference. Apart from a few brief interpolations, for example the two verses in Noah's story regarding the raven and the nine verses that tell of the tower, the Bible pursues the Genesis 2 agenda.[21] The quantitative disproportion is not on reflection surprising, since the Bible's epochal novelty is the man of Genesis 2.

Schwarzschild's misunderstanding of how the Bible relates to naturalism has fallout. Pointing to the idea of incarnation, he charges Christians with crypto-paganism.[22] "Nature is never in any way identical with [God]." This verges on ruling out a common denominator between God and men and women. Providing that Schwarzschild averts his gaze from the obvious difficulty – it is as part of the physical world that men and women are fashioned in God's image and likeness – he might even think to help himself to my discussion of the Bible's opener. But were he to do that, he would, for accepting the difference between Genesis 1 and Genesis 2, owe an explanation of what God's breath of life means.

Here is the sense in which nature is never identical with God. *Qua* system, nature abhors the autonomous. Paganism/naturalism cannot be criticized from the standpoint of an independent understanding of the biblical view, which only revelation could vouchsafe. God's appearance to Abraham is (=) Abraham's appreciation that paganism's categorization distorts his own being. God does not say "come" to Abraham; his first words are "[g]o from" (12:1).

If you choose to link volition with particularity, be my guest. But it's not just that the idea of an automobile's steering wheel (a non-particular element of a functional whole) heading off from the chassis makes no sense. It's that the notion of volition presupposes a category of being not budgeted for in Genesis 1. So you can't explain the Bible's opposition to paganism by speaking, with Schwarzschild, of the ethical and the rational. As if towards rationality Aristotle has a take-it-or-leave-it attitude! As if when it comes to ethics Plato fills his mouth with water! To discharge your explanatory duty, you've got to prioritize the ontological difference. How are people like you and like me separate from nature? It's because it has an answer that the Bible exists. Schwarzschild exaggerates dangerously here. We men and women are not absolutely separate from nature. Rather, doing justice to what we are requires a principle not among the principles that suffice for dealing with the (purely) physical world. That world is of *individuals*, in Strawson's sense, not of particulars.[23]

Incarnation is another way the presence of God's breath in each of us can be understood. God is, in the Bible's view, immanent. Early Christian thinkers were much exercised by a theological issue that arises where incarnation meets Trinitarianism. Does God suffer on the cross? Schwarzschild's "God is absolutely apart from nature" prevents the issue from arising. But his biblical Unitarianism generates a corresponding issue. Since it is because each of us is inspired with God's breath that we are mortal, how could God not be implicated in the suffering associated with this new thing on which the sun rises in Genesis 2? If one is speaking biblically, saying what Schwarzschild says amounts to saying only that God is, or stands for, a principle that is non-natural. Appropriate for principles are the idioms of *A System of Logic* – "inconsistent with," "irreducible to" – not of *Star Trek*.

Grey Zone

At the Bible's core is a category absent from Greek-derived philosophical thinking. The theological form of the Bible's presentation notwithstanding, the portrayal of the coming into being of each one of us through God's pneumatic ministration carries the message that your being and mine, his being and hers, elude naturalist resources of analysis.

Equipped with his contrast between paganism and biblical thinking, Schwarzschild scans the literature produced by thinkers who reflect philosophically on the Bible. A whiff of paganism and onto the offensive he goes. When a reflective thinker who operates at a high level of abstraction distinguishes nature from human reality, he applauds.

The heart of the Bible, Genesis 2 and onwards, is anti-pagan. What draws fire is pagan thinking's incapacity to handle human reality. It can't be inferred that the Bible is anti-naturalist *simpliciter*. That the Bible doesn't seem to render unto naturalists is due to this: the departure from the then unchallenged worldview is the consuming concern.

God, Schwarzschild says, is absolutely transcendent of nature. Nature, symmetry entails, is absolutely separate from God. If nature has principles – if there are pagan gods – these are unavailable to the worshippers of God, to the theists. Black and Red, then: Marcion redux!

The biblical position in Genesis 1 is Platonic. Like the thinkers behind the Bible, Plato appreciates that men and women are unusual constituents of the system. But the Bible has two accounts of their square-peggedness. The first, in Genesis 1, uses the notion of dominion; the second, in Genesis 2, the idea of particularity. Plato collapses the distinction, though in reverse to Schwarzschild. Men and women go astray, in his view, not because they are wilful, but because they are ignorant. "To know the good is to do the good." The whole world according to Plato is the world of Genesis 1.

Schwarzschild attacks pagan thinkers among Jews: Philo; Spinoza; the neopagans of early Zionism. The criticisms are not nugatory. But to deny that pagan thinking has any hold in the Bible is to throw out Genesis 1 or to subordinate it to Genesis 2. Underlying the error here is failure to see that the Bible has a philosophy of its own on the Genesis 2 side.

Schwarzschild approvingly quotes (358) Avoth 3:9. It is, he says, his favourite mishnah.

Rabbi Jacob said: "One who walks by the road, studying, and interrupts his study and says "How lovely is that tree!" or "How lovely is that furrow!" – Scripture imputes it to him as if he had forfeited his soul!"

I've argued that the Bible's view is less shocking than the view that Schwarzschild sees here. Its view is that nature isn't the most important place for seekers after self-understanding to look.

The Bible neither subordinates specifically human interest to the integrity of the natural world nor figures nature as a combination of playground, supermarket, and garbage dump. Additional to the system story of Genesis 1 – the story featuring the notion of dominion – is the story of the man in Genesis 2. Since the man does not come into being along with the natural world, God's special relation to each one of us through that man isn't a ground for relativizing nature's value. The normative position recognizes both the integrity of the system, nature, of which humanity is a part, and the flourishing of the particulars, each man and each woman, who are not entirely natural. That accommodation has to be sought does not guarantee that it will be found once and for all. We are, then, in our activities in the world, required, if we follow the Bible, to perform a juggling act, to mix White and Black.

8

"Because ... God rested":
Philosophy on the Sabbath Day

"Remember the sabbath day, and keep it holy" (Exodus 20:8). In observing the seventh day as special among days, abiders by the biblical Commandment are acknowledging their own specialness (as they believe it to be) among creatures. The sabbath is a transposition into the medium of time of the Bible's view of the special sort of being that men and women have.

The holiness of the sabbath isn't primarily a theological matter, then. It's a corollary of the thesis of philosophical anthropology that is the core of the Bible's novelty.

To establish this, it first must be shown that the sabbath is rooted in God's handiwork as Genesis 2 describes it, not in the world-creative activity reported in Genesis 1. To that end, the distinction between the two chapters, a distinction usually elided, has to be brought out.

Chapter 1 of the Book of Genesis ends with verse 31:

> God saw everything that he had made, and indeed, it was very good. And there was evening and there was morning, the sixth day.

Here are the opening verses (1, 2, and 3) of Genesis 2:

> Thus the heavens and the earth were finished, and all their multitude. And on the seventh day God finished the work that he had done, and he rested on the seventh day from all the work that he had done. So God blessed the seventh day and hallowed it, because on it God rested from all the work that he had done in creation.

Why don't these verses appear as 34, 35, and 36 of Genesis 1? Shouldn't Genesis 2 have begun with what in our editions is verse 4?

These are the generations of the heavens and the earth when they were created. In the day that the Lord God made … earth and … heavens[.]

Although the chapter divisions and verse numbers used in formulating these questions are additions to Moses's secretarial product, the issue at issue is independent of them, as an experiment shows.

Presented with the opening fifty-five verses of Genesis, you're tasked with inserting a chapter division. You are likely to place 1, 2, and 3 of our Genesis 2 at the end of your first chapter. Verse 4 seems like a reveille. Since it resembles the opener of Genesis 1, shouldn't *it* be 2:1? The appellation for God is the same in the first three verses of Genesis 2 as it is throughout Genesis 1. Verse 4 sees the first appearance of "YHWH," which is used through the rest of the chapter.[1]

In the Bible, a summary of a phase sometimes commences the phase that comes next. To Robert Alter (7), it's self-evident that the opening three (or three and a half) verses of Genesis 2 exemplify this pattern. "The first Creation story concludes with [a] summarizing phrase …"

In my judgment, verses 2 and 3 introduce the theme of Genesis 2. The sabbath, mentioned in verse 2 and stamped "APPROVED" from on high in verse 3, begins a different creative phase.

I expect to be told that a passage like this one decides for Alter.

Six days you shall labour and do all your work. But the seventh day is a sabbath to the Lord your God; you shall not do any work … For in six days the Lord made [the] heaven[s] and [the] earth, the sea, and all that is in them, but rested the seventh day. (Exodus 20:9–11)

Yet it is as easy to understand the passage as saying that God blesses and consecrates the seventh day because *he doesn't do anything* on it as to understand it as saying that he blesses and consecrates the day because *he has left off what he had been doing*. Must the Wednesday idleness of an otherwise busy person celebrate the cessation of their Tuesday business?

Signs are present in the part of the text under examination that supports setting the sabbath loose from the preceding days.

Sign 1

"Thus the heavens and the earth were finished, and all their multitude." This, verse 1 of Genesis 2, could easily be repositioned at the end of Genesis 1. Here's the whole of verse 2: "And on the seventh day God finished the work that he had done, and he rested on the seventh day from all the work that he had done." Although the part of the compound sentence after the first prepositional phrase has the same content as verse 1, a change of subject is suggested by the phrase and by the phrase's repetition in the second sentence of the compound: "and [God] rested on the seventh day from all the work that he had done." The repetition draws the whole of verse 2 towards verse 3, which takes up the change. "This seventh day, of which Genesis 1 does not speak, God blessed it and hallowed it." Some may think that since a week has seven days, Genesis 1 does speak, implicitly, of a seventh day. This begs the question. Unlike the year, the week is a conventional cycle. The convention could as easily find its biblical basis in the sequence of days from the seventh to the thirteenth as from the first to the seventh.

Sign 2

The reaction attributed to God at the end of Day 6 is a closing bracket for the first six days, during which God half a dozen times perceives/judges what comes to be as good. What does Genesis 1's "X is good" mean? "X does its appointed job; X functions as it should." The intensified form, "very good," expresses satisfaction at finding that the parts mesh. This, which can be dramatized in a final stowing of tools after the general contractor is satisfied that the contributions of the various subcontractors dovetail, is a suitable internal ending. If the overseer now enplanes for the resort, that can't automatically be taken to punctuate the conclusion of the project. The holiday might have been planned well prior. It would be a different story if after the final whistle the general contractor headed with the others to the local watering hole. "How about a beer; the work is done."

Sign 3

Verse 3 describes God blessing and hallowing the sabbath. Blessing we already encountered, in Genesis 1. This is our first sighting of holiness. Again the suggestion is that verse 3 doesn't belong with the opening chapter. Also suggested is that the world of Genesis 1 has nothing sacred about it, even though it is God's handiwork. If we ratchet up the magnification, the suggestion resolves to the following: there is nothing holy about being good in the sense attaching to "good" in Genesis 1. This seems reasonable. A pail that is holey won't hold water. One that doesn't leak is hardly holy. As to the fact, which must disconcert the devout, that if sanctity is absent from the world of Genesis 1 the blessings given there cannot have anything to do with holiness, I'll deal with it two sections hence. Again, in fine, we have the pivotal feature: the blessing links to what has passed; the sanctification raises something new.

Sign 4

Prefacing the enunciation of the Ten Commandments is "the Lord God." But the treatment of the sabbath in Genesis 2 has "God." Isn't this evidence that the sabbath is as close (if not closer) to the topic of Genesis 2?

"Rest," the (translation of the) verb nominalized in "sabbath," is protean. One can rest *from* such-and-such. One can rest *for* such-and-such. One can simply rest. The sabbath is traditionally viewed in the first way. God rests from the creative labours. The translation of the Hebrew "כי" in verse 3 as "because" captures this perception. But "כי" can also mean "for." Which puts into play the other ways of understanding "rest."

Verse 3 appears thus in the NRSV:

> So God blessed the seventh day and hallowed it, because on it God rested from all the work that he had done in creation.

It is possible to render it, then, as:

> So God blessed and hallowed the seventh day, for that was when he rested from all the work that he had done.

Even more colloquially:

> So God blessed and hallowed the seventh day. The work all behind him, that, after all, was when he rested.

The sense is that the resting is sanctified. Modifying "work" with "tedious" or "tiresome" or "thankless" or, more coolly, "having first to be got out of the way," would seal the deal.

The latter rendering is consistent with the sabbath being a self-contained phase. Suppose the first day had been singled out for observance. Its specialness could not under the circumstances have been due to God's resting from X.[2] "Doesn't the location of the mention of the sabbath in the later part of verse 3 tell against 'for'?" The reading that I propose seems odd here only because of interpretive precedent.

Why are none of the signs ever said to associate more with Genesis 2? If A is closer to C than B is, A and B must differ in content. Although, certainly, the two opening chapters differ, the second chapter is usually discussed as if it gives a worm's eye view of one sector of the whole that the first looks at panoramically.

Those who run the chapters together find support in the blessing/sanctification of the sabbath. The blessing looks back to Chapter 1. The sanctification looks ahead.

In describing someone as blessed, we are saying that things are going well with them. So doesn't the giver of a blessing express the wish that the receiver prosper? Presupposed in either case is the live possibility of decline and fall. If "good" in Genesis 1 has the meaning that I ascribed, what sense could a blessing make in its world?

The wish that things *continue* to do their jobs is perfectly sensible. This wouldn't work here, though. One: The things in question are bespoke. "God set [the sun and the moon] to give light upon the earth" (1:17). They do nothing on their own initiative. So blessing the luminaries in this way isn't conceptually intelligible. Anyway, such a blessing is for the giver. Two: The characteristic expressed by "not good" isn't present in the world that Genesis 1 describes. The phrase only applies from the standpoint of some part or aspect of the whole system, or from an external position. Limited precipitation, rare in places where it has what we regard as negative effects, is not bad *per se*.

If "good" in Genesis 1 has the meaning that I ascribed, what sense could a blessing make? Observe that the fish also receive a blessing. "How," asks Robert Sacks (43), "is this kinship to be understood?

> The denizens of the seas indeed live a kind of watery existence. They neither follow the ecliptic as does the sun nor are they restricted in the direction of their motion as are the other animals … Man shares this openness of direction with the fish. The way was not marked for him in the beginning. It had to develop, and even then he was apt to wander from his path. Since man could err, he too required a blessing.

The fish move *everywhichway* in their watery world: up and down, left and right, forward and backward. Of men and women too it can be said that they have no set course. Their world is in this respect analogous. Men and women can therefore go wrong without outside interference.

Sacks's *the blessing is given because of this capacity to go astray* can't be right. The world in which men and women receive the blessing contains no bad. By sharp contrast, the world of Genesis 2 has no end of it. In talking of "wander[ing] from the path" and of "err[ing]," Sacks draws, irrelevantly, on the Genesis 2 episode of transgression.

Pace Sacks, the example of the fish is more than analogically relevant. To imagine them needing the blessing, one needn't imagine the fish as gilled persons. Although Sacks connects the omni-directionality of fish locomotion with both, neither the openness of human behaviour to moral evaluation nor the existence of different ways of life that can be compared for quality is on display until we reach the world whose beginning is described in Genesis 2. The violation of the prohibition against eating of the tree of knowledge is the biblical basis of the first; of the second, the move from the grazing lands of Abel to the acreage of Cain and on to Lotville. Obviously, unless the fish *are* thought of as persons with gills, they cannot intelligibly be imagined acting morally or immorally, or living good, bad, or indifferent ways of life.

In preparation for spelling out what the Bible is saying, I'll draw attention to a conceptual confusion in Sacks's discussion.

Sacks uses "they" in speaking of the fish. When it comes to the humans, "he." "Since man could err, he too required a blessing." To what is "he" in apposition? Sacks's translation disguises the logical impropriety of the question. The NRSV doesn't have "man." The term is "[hu]mankind."[3] Suppose Sacks had written: "Since mankind could err, he too required a blessing." If his formulation doesn't draw the red pencil, as this would, that is because his "man" can be taken as a reference to the first man. And, we saw, Sacks *is* thinking of Genesis 2.

In blessing the fish, God is blessing *the species*. "Be fruitful and multiply and fill the waters in the seas" (1:22). Sacks's "he" fosters the impression that in Genesis 1 individual men and individual women are the subject-matter.

The claim about the fish concerns the set or species. Also, it's a natural/biological claim. Its basis is the proposition that the fish lack a specific habitat. This, the angler knows, is biologically inaccurate. Because of their style of moving, the fish do however seem to be aquatic cosmopolitans. So the Bible is making use of a *falsehood* to get its point across.[4]

Shift now to humankind, and you'll see the position. The species's plasticity is not elsewhere exampled in the natural sphere. Members are ubiquitous: the tropics, the temperate regions, the desert, the jungle, tidal forests, highlands. Consistently with the biblical position, men and women are recruiting for Mars.

Why the blessing? The ways of members of the species open them to encounters of a sort, the unexpected sort, that the (other) animals, each in its specific niche, don't in the natural course of events experience. Since many of the encounters pose danger to life and limb, human beings can always use a bit of luck to pass on their genes. The blessing is therefore appropriate for a species that is not niche-specific. "Travel Safe!"

"Isn't the blessing appropriate for frogs too? For terns?" If "amphibian" implies that frogs occupy more than one niche, it's a misnomer. Going from shower to kitchen, does a person change dwellings? Similarly, terns, in their migration, aren't emigrating from the Arctic or immigrating to the Antarctic. Observe, too, that the idea of lacking a specific habitat is linked to the Bible's notion of dominion. To have dominion is (=) not to have a restricted domain. The biblical phrase "fill up the earth" means "inhabit the gamut of places," not "multiply to staggering numbers." In an extended sense, God, "Dominus" in Latin, is everywhere. Reality is full up of God.

The blessing of mankind in Genesis 1 is sensible for natural/biological reasons. The blessing of the fish, we see, serves two purposes. One: The look of the creatures gives an excellent model of biological plasticity. Two: The presence of the blessing works against the tendency to see the divine contribution to Genesis 1 as separating men and women from the natural world.

No reference to Genesis 2 is needed to make sense of the blessing. This opens the possibility that the sabbath, which occupies a place between Genesis 1 and Genesis 2, might go with the latter.

In what sense is the sabbath like the fish and/or like mankind? The answer, verbally, must be that the sabbath is an everywhichway day. Happily, this much is easy. Monday is washday; Tuesday is go-to-market day. Each of the weekdays has a direction. The sabbath? No busy-ness. Rest.

Saying that the sabbath is for nothing disconnects it from the (Genesis 1) story of creation, in which everything is for something. The one *prima facie* exception, humankind, actually proves the rule.

Why, then, is the seventh day sanctified, hallowed? The rest of Genesis 2 and *its* sequel contain the answer. In creating the world whose coming into being is described in Genesis 1, God doesn't put anything of himself into it. The sacredness, the holiness, has to do with God's presence. God it is who rests on the seventh day, and, in the narrative, the day's observance is anchored in that.

On the strength of verse 26 and its sequel, most readers conclude that God *is* present in the world of Genesis 1. "Let us make humankind in our image, according to our likeness." I've blocked the move. In being likened to them, men and women aren't getting anything from the fish the way a child inherits curly hair. Similarly, from God humankind gets nothing. The image-and-likeness claim is that men and women, like God, are not niche specific. They have dominion.

All this changes in Genesis 2. God isn't only *on* the world-generative scene. God is also *in* the scene that is generated. He breathes some of himself into the first person.

The feature that if not for his breath of life would be absent from the world is, we know, what the last part of the Shema ascribes to God. The assertion of God's one-ness is in contrast to what can be said of *each* of the pagan deities.

The idea of God breathing life into the first person encapsulates two points. One-ness is unavailable in natural terms, nature – "heavens [= Ouranos, in the Greek context] *and* earth [= Gaia]" – being a system. One-ness is uniquely a characteristic of men and women among creatures.

This is the core of the core of the Bible as a revolutionary document. God's self-identification, "I AM," is an assertion of that nucleus. The creation of the first person independently of any other person (a biological absurdity) captures, in dramatic form, the ontological crux.

Why is the sabbath hallowed? Nature never rests. The exchanges of matter and energy between the reciprocally dependent parts continue ceaselessly. Men and women are not natural things. They are not, because even though they live their lives within the natural system they are autonomous of it.

sabbath : time :: the first person : matter

The first person is a non-natural entity; the sabbath, a non-natural period. Both are made what they are by God. Both inherit God's one-ness.

The sabbath, then, is the emblem of the non-natural in the spatio-temporal realm. A non-natural construct for a non-natural world, the sabbath is therefore a suitable introduction to Genesis 2.

The natural world is up and running. Cue the real work. "Then the Lord God formed [the] man from the dust of the ground, and breathed into his nostrils the breath of life" (2:7).[5]

The idea of holiness requires extensive discussion. For here, I'll only offer a comment on God's response to Moses in the episode of the water and the rock.

God (Numbers 20:8) instructs Moses to command the rock. Moses (11) disobeys. For striking the rock with his staff, God (12) bars him from the Promised Land:

> you did not trust in me, to show my holiness ...

Moses treats the rock as one treats nature. But *this* rock's water is the water mentioned in verse 6 of Genesis 2, the water that "rise[s] from the earth." It's not the water that emerged out of the chaos. Moses is profaning the sacred. What he does isn't commanding – emphatic asking. It's superstitious causal manipulation. In addressing himself to God in this way, Moses is recrossing the Red Sea back into Egypt.

If it were a rebuke for how he executes the instruction, God's excluding Moses from the Promised Land would be cruel. The sanction has to do, rather, with the Bible's philosophical anthropology. Moses's act gives body to an ontological mistake. To men and women we (can) interrelate by speaking. "Speak to the Israelites and say to them." To get a person to perform, we needn't do what we do to nature: push, pull, poke, prod, pummel, pound. Moses's stick is a stick of dynamite. Contrast the performance of Elijah on the Carmel. "O Lord, God of Abraham, Isaac, and Israel, let it be known this day that you are God in Israel, that I am your servant, and that I have done all these things at your bidding" (1 Kings 18:36; see also 2 Kings 1:10). It's no wonder that while "no one knows [Moses's] burial place" (Deuteronomy 34:6), the Moses of the Northern Kingdom "ascended in a whirlwind into [the] heaven[s]" (2 Kings 2:11). One's separateness is sunk back into the whole; one is represented as impervious to physical passing.

The case of Moses sheds light on a feature of the Torah that repels many. In this case, the *harshness* comes out in stoning for sabbath violation. The pagan view lumbers men and women with an improper self-understanding. Not to understand oneself is, figuratively, to be dead to one's self. Which is what, in a chilling promise to turn figure into fact, King David says. "Those who make [the idols] / and all who trust them / shall become like them" (Psalm 135:18). Isn't exclusion from the Promised Land a national version of death?

The link to God's creation of the first person is the active ingredient in the sabbath. The sabbath's holiness is derivative upon that of particular men and particular women. The sabbath, as the proportionality indicates, is understood through the account of God's breathing life into the first man. And God's holiness is understood through the analysis of the position of men and women in the world, an analysis on which each man and each woman is separate from the system that is nature.

The base of the Bible is anthropological – philosophically so. Someone who appreciated this could have anticipated a connection between the sabbath and the person-creative activity of Genesis 2. *Pace* Orthodoxy, it's not God's wanting or commanding that mandates observance. It's that the practices reflect the special position of men and women among creatures.[6] The Enlightenment critique of naive religiosity doesn't lay a finger on the sabbath. Although the Bible wraps the special position in an act of God, the categorization of being is independent of the colourful paper.

Taking your cue from a task-terminator isn't the same as emulating a task-initiator. The sabbath is an entry into the creation of the specifically human world. More than stand in a preparatory relation to the creative activity, the sabbath is emblematic of it. The day itself is a disruption of the natural order, as particular men and particular women are surds in this order. It's therefore as it should be that procreative activity is (traditionally) encouraged on the sabbath.[7] Equally appropriate is the study of the Torah, which recounts the emergence of the specifically human, the "ones" who shares God's one-ness. As to the myriad sabbath day restrictions that Orthodox Judaism imposes on adherents, these, in the measure that they rest on taking the day as the termination of God's (Genesis 1) creative activity, must be reconsidered.

Jesus chides the Pharisees for rigid observance of the day of rest. "My father is still working [to sustain the world on the sabbath], and I also am working" (John 5:17). I believe that Jesus's strictures are defensible. But not for the reason given in John. True, on the seventh day the world-sustaining processes of Genesis 1 are not on sabbatical. The winds take no breather. Masses do not levitate. That does not however justify "my father is still working." The *natural* processes aren't expressions of God. The biblical representation of [God] resting gives expression to [God's] *non-natural* status.[8] In the (purely) natural order, no day is of rest. Sabbath is available only to beings who aren't completely natural, beings to whose creation Genesis 2 is devoted. The seventh day, "the day that the Lord has made" (Psalm 118:24), is the occasion for exhibiting mindfulness of non-natural status. By enacting God-likeness, sabbath observers acknowledge the presupposition of the moral modes of conduct that the second half of the Ten Commandments addresses.

Is lending a hand to the needy stranger destructive of that mindfulness? Need I say more in negative response than that non-human creatures do not lend a hand, and not out of stupidity or selfishness?

It's not because God is working on the sabbath that the pharisaical are wrong. It's because God *rested* on the sabbath.

9

"In the day that you shall eat":
Do *and* Die

"In the day that you shall eat of [the tree of the knowledge of good and bad] you shall die" (2:17). It's baffling, this assertion of God's, baffling in itself and baffling because the speaker appears to be a stranger to the truth. If upon their eating, death had come to the addressees of the words (for eat they do), *we* wouldn't be here.

Some readers will deny being baffled. "Genesis 2:17 asserts that in losing their innocence the man and the woman will come to be cognizant that the days dwindle down." True, as a person develops cognitively, they awaken to their short-livedness. But that isn't what the quotation means. Why, anyway, would God forbid the man and the woman the knowledge? "God is badly intentioned" isn't much better than "God is a stranger to the truth," is it? True, withholding knowledge doesn't always lay the withholder open to criticism. But it's equally true that ignorance isn't always bliss. A hard landing awaits those who believe they have wings. I'll add here that Christians will, on different grounds, resist the psychological construal. Since the construal implies that immortality was never a human possession, the possibility is gone of its loss through disobedience or otherwise. I'll be defending the proposition that the Bible teaches actual immortality and the loss of it. But in my defence of the proposition the loss has nothing to do with depravity.

To limit the potential of the Christian understanding to slant the treatment, I'll say one more thing. In context, Marcion's attempt to exclude the Hebrew Scriptures from the Christian canon was dead on arrival. Yet, theologically speaking, Marcion certainly had a point. Eusebius's view of the "Old Testament" as a *Praeparatio Evangelica* is as true as is Charles Kinbote's view of "Pale Fire" as a *poème à clef* about the dethroning of the King of Zembla. Perhaps Augustinian ideas about sin and mortality have merit. "What a piece of work is man!" But the Hebrew Scriptures offer no more than an excuse for echoing the Bishop of Hippo. Freud (no Christian) postulated a death instinct. And even he, well-versed in the Tanakh, did not look for corroboration to Moses. Bottom line: as

Marcion's proposal implies, it's best to develop these ideas independently of the Torah and those of the gospels that reflect its theology.

One might wonder why the composers see fit to give the words of 2:17 to the character named "God." Inclusion of the story of the creation is easy to understand. The good reason for its inclusion does not however seem to transpose.

Although it should go without saying, it doesn't. So I'll say it. *The Bible wasn't written for us.* Many of the men and women who constitute its target audience didn't view the origin of the physical world along the lines of the chapters and the verses. They didn't believe that God created it; didn't believe this, I hasten to add, not because they knew nothing of God. But they certainly didn't learn of their mortality, or come to fear it, through the pages of the Bible.

In his prior life as Abram, Abraham (also) knew nothing of God. When, out of the blue, God invites him to join (the signing of the covenant comes with a change of name, to "Hancock" from "Ancock" so to speak), God is revealing to him a deity of whom he hadn't heard in his father's house and his native land, and, in telling the story of the creation as the story of God's doing it, telling him a different story about that subject than any of the stories that he had up to then considered. It's not just that "Deity X is behind the world's being as it is" gives way to "God is." Such a shift is compatible with Abram's having believed substantially what the Bible teaches. There's also a change in how the world is regarded as being. The consensus back then was that the world had not been created; created, I mean, from nothing and/or according to a master plan. Deity X is not that kind of creator. Abram would have heard of a primordial chaos that differentiates into regions each of which comes to be occupied by inhabitants suited to it. Deity X is identified with a law of natural process (water seeks its level, temperature falls as volume increases, etc.) in accordance with which a welter takes on shape and form. Mavens of Greek culture know this story from Hesiod's *Theogony*. The corresponding creation story of Abram's Mesopotamia, the *Enuma Elish*, is alluded to in Chapter 1 of Genesis.

In further response to the psychological construal of 2:17, I'll observe that the contest between the one origin story and the other is an adult thing – a dispute about the objective facts. On the admittedly external ground that the composers are likely to have placed a premium on parallelism, this suggests that the shift with regard to mortality also has to do with what and how things are, not with what and how people think.

The Bible's treatment of ultimate origins differs otherwise than in its background materials – myths, legends, literary devices – from the treatments in the *Theogony* and in Hesiod's Mesopotamian counterparts. The Bible says that the world had a beginning. That's the excellent reason for its inclusion. Those behind the Bible are on a mission: to correct an error about how things came to be as we find them. But the story of mortality does not differ (it seems) in any exploitable way from whatever it is that men and women in the Bible's general catchment area held. To "The world does not have an absolute beginning" in the first case corresponds no "Men and women are immortal" in the second. "Abram might have believed the second" seems downright false. The difference looks sharper still if we bear in mind that philosophers among us who are not apologists for Judaism or Christianity continue to debate the cosmogonic issue. Besides, even if a view of men and women as immortal were found in the pre-biblical frame, we'd never expect a competing scripture to describe the condition's loss through mischief or malevolence. We'd expect to be told, rather, that spokespeople for false gods, taking a swatch from the tailors of the emperor, got them to believe that they weren't destined for oblivion. In the Second Teaching of the *Bhagavad-Gita*, the god Krishna tells Arjuna that the self is not born and does not die, using analogies like that of a business-suited person's surviving till morning in pyjamas. Shouldn't the story of eating of the tree of knowledge be a story of an awakening from such a falsehood? What on earth or in heaven could be sinful (or even bad) about *that*?

Parts that make sense when taken on their own lose their sense when brought together with the rest.

Not a few commentators on the Bible have no time for these subtleties. The Bible, the source critics maintain, is a compilation of elements produced at different times by different hands situated in different parts of the Israelite world. Like the button, the scrap of tinfoil, and the strand or two of pasta that make up a collage, the elements were produced with no thought of the end-product. "It's not surprising that the heads of those who assume that the Bible is a consistent narrative end up spinning."

"Who," those inclined on source-analytic grounds to deny that the Bible is interpretable should ask themselves, "would say that because the button, the silver paper and the noodles weren't produced with any thought of the final product, the collage is a mishmash?" To be sure, it *could* be a mishmash. That must however be determined on independent grounds.

The beginning of wisdom consists in recognizing that the first two chapters of Genesis tell different kinds of stories. The view that predominates among the interpreters is that only the emphasis or focus changes: Genesis 2 zooms in on one part, the human part, of Genesis 1's panorama.

Genesis 1 is a version of the pagan story. Also, it's a story of a deathless world. Genesis 2 contains the Bible's epochal departure from the pagan worldview. In theological terms: it introduces God. And death, thereby, becomes an unavoidable feature.

Hesiod's (pagan) cosmogonic story goes from chaos to order. First the largest things (upper and lower) emerge in the initial no-thing-ness. Then finer divisions (dry and watery). And so forth. The Bible's Genesis 1 tracks the development. A chaotic beginning gives way to heavens and earth. And so forth. The presence of God aside, the biblical story has two distinguishing features.

One: It's myth-free. Two: Not only do things happen; also, things are done. The grasses grass (verse 12); the churning waters solidify out marine creatures (verse 20). These are *happenings*. God (verses 6 and 7) inserts a dome to separate the waters that fall as drizzle and rain and snow and sleet from the puddles, the rivers, the lakes, the seas. God (verses 16 and 17) makes the sun and the moon and fixes them in the vault of heaven. These are *doings*. The doing-status of the occurrences that are assigned this status by the Bible's writers and thinkers is provisional. That they assign doing-status to *any* occurrences is a testament to their intellectual honesty. When they can't find a doer-less process within their (passive or active) experience that is a plausible fit for a natural coming-to-be, they don't pretend to have one. But the dynamic of the chapter (chaos resolving to order) indicates that if they could eliminate doings in favour of happenings they would. Given what we have since learned of nature – $F = G(m_1 m_2)/r^2$; $\delta q = Tds$; $E = mc^2$ – we can lend them a hand. A dome with valved spillways to control the fall of the upper waters (and hence a biblical smith to hammer it out) isn't needed. Evaporation and condensation account for precipitational cycling. The sun and the stars emerge from a soup of energy in the way that oceans and lakes do from moisty muck. Accepting what we offer, the Bible's writers and thinkers thus come to be able to replace the doings that remain in their story. The end result? *Theogony* and *Enuma Elish*.

God is present in Genesis 1 for three reasons, none theologically significant. One: Gaps would compromise the effectiveness of the story. Think missing link. So the writers, not seeing how to dispense with doings, fall back on the God-makes template. Two: The Bible is God's book. So it's written with God presiding over the whole. Consider the form "Queen Elizabeth sank the Armada." Three: God's extra-naturalness makes clear, through a structural parallel, the way in which one sector of the physical world that differentiates out differs. I am referring to the assertion that men and women have dominion. While the other things and creatures occupy specific habitats, men and women do not. Bound now for Mars and beyond, they are domain-unbound. The appeal to God helps clarify, for God *has no place* in the natural world. Men and women are (see verse 27) "in God's image and likeness" in this natural history sense. Although I don't list this as a fourth reason, it's worth adding that God's continued presence is helpful from a debating point of view. It rubs the noses of the pagan cosmogonists in the fact that many of the roles that they assign to the pagan gods are assigned with a hope and a prayer.

The end of Genesis 1 is a whole in equilibrium. Obviously, this doesn't mean that the world – our world – is frozen. But once the whole is up and running there are in it no beginnings and no ends. When a tree falls in the forest, it does not die. Its matter is recycled. A tree, an aspect of the wider ecosystem, stands to the forest as a season stands to the year. It's anthropomorphic to conceptualize the tree otherwise than as part of the forest. Philip Larkin is wrong when, in that wonderful poem whose final line ("Begin afresh, afresh, afresh") sounds the wind in their crowns, he writes of trees that "they die too." They no more die than summer does when fall arrives.

What goes for trees goes also for Genesis 1's humankind. The writers are referring to the biological species, which comes into being like everything else and which like everything else is part of the whole, albeit with the difference of not having a specific domain. This does not mean that there is death in the human sphere. Members of the species are in this regard just mobile trees.

What, now, of Genesis 2? Observe that its beginning is stasis. This seems so at odds with the Heraclitean character of Genesis 1 that one can hear the source critics licking their chops. The descriptions, though very different, are however compatible. Genesis 2 is not about happenings; it's about doings. The stasis-claim is that the world of Genesis 1, with which Genesis 2 starts, is doing-less. It's not "Nothing's happening" that's asserted by verse 5. Verse 5 asserts "There's nothing doing." Once we appreciate the significance of the distinction, the text is, we see, straightforward. Water, water everywhere, flowing and falling and rushing and coursing. Nor any gardener with rubber boots and a hose. "The Lord God had not caused it to rain" (2:5).

In the human sphere, the first doing is the eating of the tree of the knowledge of good and bad. This, I mean, is the first doing that the writers/thinkers present in describing the sphere. Prior to it, the man and the woman are for all intents and purposes domesticated animals. They go about their days with a regularity that features the rounds of the seasons, the orbits of the luminaries. This first down-to-earth doing brings about good-and-bad. It does so because it activates the category that is absent from Genesis 1.

Observe that the situation in the human sphere is a downwards reflection of God's situation. God's forming the man (verse 7) and God's planting a garden (verse 8) are, both of them, doings. Given that in the view of the writers/thinkers Genesis 1 (really) contains only happenings, they are the first biblical doings. *The doings are transgressions against the natural order.* Certainly, the principles that govern happenings would never produce a cultivated piece of terrain.

In the celebrated Schrödinger experiment, a person, by looking into an opaque box, collapses the objective indeterminacy therein with regard to life and death of a cat into its objectively determinate death. Similarly, the eating of the tree, an act of a conscious being, collapses the end-less world of Genesis 1 into a world in which (real) endings occur. There are now different discrete things capable of acting against one another in ways that aspects of nature's processes cannot (night does not kill off day, spring doesn't take back from it what winter stole from fall).

Death is original to the world of Genesis 2. It's there for a structural reason – the same reason that birth is there. Although at the cost of the story's effectiveness, the content of Genesis 2 would have been the same if the writers had portrayed the man and the woman as doing exactly what God instructed them to do. What's crucial is that they do it, that it not just happen.

It's not, then, because of what is gained by doing it that eating of the tree of knowledge is important. *Pace* Milton, "the taste" of the fruit of "that forbidden tree" isn't what "brought death into the world." The tasting did. The world, not just the cognitive condition of the doers, was changed thereby. The result is a world of a different kind, of the kind that we, unless we are very much mistaken, live in; a world comprised of things with real beginnings and that really end.

I'll say again why the disobedience of the man and the woman is an *imitatio Dei*, not an act of defiance. God's planting of the garden, a doing, transgresses against nature. God is putting a bit of his un-natural self into the world. Just so, far from marking us as incorrigible sinners in need of redemption, the transgression of those first editions of ourselves is how the God-inspirited come to be in the world.

An amusing story is told about Bertrand Russell (Spadoni, 37). "One day he was walking along Trinity Lane having just bought a tin of tobacco. Suddenly, he threw the tin up in the air, and at the same time uttered the words 'Great God in boots! – the ontological argument is sound!'" Abram has a similar epiphany, as a result of which he becomes Abraham. The pagans of his time regard themselves as mortal. That is: each shares the self-image of the man and the woman of Genesis 2. Abram's "Great God in boots!" is stimulated by the insight that they cannot make sense of this. The resources available to the philosophers of his father's land derive from and suffice to rationalize only the contents of the world of Genesis 1, a world not of doings but of happenings, hence a world whose newspapers publish no birth announcements and include no obituaries.

This tells us how to read the Commandment of Commandments: "I am the Lord your God …; you shall have no other gods before me" (Exodus 20:3, Deuteronomy 5:7) means "Each of you (like God) is a doer: a separate entity, not just an aspect of a process." It's not that the "other gods" are not gods. It's that they are not gods of "you" to whom the Commandment is given.

The incompatibility of my reading of 2:17 with the loss of immortality is only half the problem from the Christian point of view. *God* brings death into the world.

"In the day that you shall eat … you shall die." It turns out that the day on which the man and the woman eat is not just a day on which the eating happens to take place – as if they could have stayed away from the tree for a week or two more. Recall Job's curse: "Let the day perish on which I was born" (3:3). Were Job expressing the wish never to have been born, here's what we'd expect. "Woe is me that mine eyes ever saw the light." Job's words contain something deeper, and the deeper something shines a light on God's words. The world in which Job experiences what he experiences is of a different kind than the world of Genesis 1, which contains no birthdays. In eating, the man and the woman made the day. In making the man and the woman, God made the makings of that making. "This is the day that the Lord has made; let us rejoice and be glad in it" (Psalm 118:24).

PEOPLE

10

Eat, Pray, Smoke:
Halakhah for Everyone

The Carpatho-Rusyn Formula

Remembering the days of his youth in the 1920s and 1930s in Uzhhorod, a town in Carpathian Ruthenia, Arye Amikam describes how a local gentile saw the religious practices of the Jews she worked for as a domestic (Rosen, 214):

> The gentile maid goes home and they ask her: tell us, what are these Jews like? So she answers, well, they are very strange. They have a holiday in which they eat by the table and smoke in the bathroom, that is *shabbat*. They have a holiday in which they eat and smoke by the table, that is *simchat Torah*, and they have a holiday in which they eat and smoke in the bathroom, that is *yom kippur*.[1]

Since the maid is *chez elle*, we can infer that Amikam's description isn't a first-hand report. Aren't eating and smoking at various places in the home routine enough? Won't the maid anyway have seen her employers exiting the dwelling for a week each fall to eat and smoke in a flimsy shelter with no roof to speak of ("that is *succoth*")?

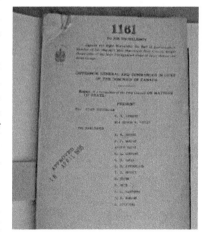

What we have here is, at least in part, an act of ventriloquism. In addition to being told from the Jewish point of view, the vignette conveys a thought unlikely to be thought elsewhere: the Jews are hypocrites. Certainly, the maid herself has no idea that smoking isn't permitted on *shabbat*, nor that both eating and smoking are banned on *yom kippur*.

I am, it happens, only two degrees of separation from the scene. Uzhhorod is my mother's birthplace and where she lived until immigrating to North America. Between 1927 and 1939, all the family members except for the father, Moishe Goldstein, who died of tuberculosis in 1931, made the move, the last of them disembarking at the Port of Quebec on 2 July 1939! In my possession is a copy of Privy Council document 1161, an Order in Council stamped "Approved, 18 April 1935," permitting my grandmother and four of her children to land in Canada. Presiding at the Privy Council meeting was none other than R.B. Bennett, prime minister of the day. Not that the innkeepers from Uzhhorod had the top politician's ear. Rather, the 1 March 1931 ban (Order in Council P.C. 695) on Asians, Jews, and others deemed undesirable required a waiver at the highest level for each and every exception.[2]

I can attest Amikam's description. These were the ways in which my mother and her siblings conducted themselves in their Jewish lives. Though never questioning that adherence was a factor in their identity, they carried to their Canaan the relaxed attitude towards the practices. They observed some; some not. Like the Jews of the vignette, they honoured Judaism in the eating and the smoking as well as in the praying. Strictly semi-Orthodox!

One additional factor I can single out as significant in the family's cultural formation: Zionism. My mother, in her teens, joined a left-wing Zionist youth organization: Hashomer Hatzair. Throughout her life, she retained an emotional link with Kibbutz Gan Shmuel, where several friends of her childhood put down roots. The family's Zionism didn't end at sentiment. It was transmitted in an active form to the next generation. Although even more relaxed about religious observance than their parents, quite a few immigrated to Israel.

If the product proves the formula, here, then, is a formula for Jewish survival without strict halakhism: exposure to Jewish practices in youth in an environment not friendly to Jews; immigration to a place also lukewarm to them, but in which their paths to advancement are open; commitment to a national form of Jewish existence in a geopolitical frame where it's not just a fantasy. As to the hypocrisy, let us, for the sake of Jewish self-identification and Jewish survival, all look both ways. Anyway, "hypocrisy" is tendentious unless identity as a Jew requires full halakhic observance.

Full halakhic observance is sufficient for Jewish survival of the sort under discussion. Shouldn't anxiety about assimilation lead the anxious to Orthodoxy? To characterize the demands of observance as too onerous is to invite the charge of placing expediency before principle. The Conservative answer, one of principle, is an intellectual/theoretical answer. My answer, also on our side of the Haskalah, falls into that category too.

Conserving Conservatism

The concern in these pages is with Jewish survival in America outside Orthodoxy: survival anchored in the Torah's system of belief. Why not take instruction from the Goldsteins? Although my mother's siblings all belonged in adulthood to Orthodox synagogues, the texture of their lives as Jews was more akin to that of members of the Conservative group.

There are however problems with holding up the Goldsteins as a model. Both their level of comfort with the traditional patterns that shape everyday life, and their strong internal bonds due to outside pressures, are considerably diminished among the bulk of Conservative Jews. Also, the Goldsteins' personal interest in Jewish existence on the national plane has given way among these Jews to formulaic expressions of solidarity, fundraising, and flights on El Al. The wider culture is seen by them as a culture in which they can freely pursue their life-goals. Accordingly, the discontents of Conservative Jews in America are much the same as those of their neighbours. Given these facts, the role of Zionism in the lives of the Goldsteins draws my attention, not for what it is but for what it does. In an environment in which sporadic adherence to the rabbinic letter neither provokes feelings of guilt nor attracts denunciations from those whose opinion one values, can the slack of casual observance be tightened in some other way? Trends in non-Orthodox American Jewry aren't encouraging. At any rate, the proposals made by leading figures are, as I'll show, deficient.

The Conservative movement in America has been the subject of heated discussion in recent years. The spark was the Pew Research Center's 2013 "A Portrait of Jewish Americans."[3] The numbers compiled in the report are concerning. In 1971, 41 per cent belonged to this stream of Judaism. The 1990 National Jewish Population Survey showed a fall of 3 points. As of 2000, the percentage had dropped to 26, and in 2013 only 18 per cent named Conservative Judaism as their denominational home.

Statistics, statistics. Mightn't the cultural odds have been stacked so heavily against the leaders that credit is due to them for stanching the flow? Despite the decline, couldn't it also be that Conservatism finds quite a few whom most would have despaired of? "I tell you, there shall be more joy in heaven over one sinner who repents than over ninety-nine righteous persons who need no repentance" (Luke 15:7). These constructions on the numbers do not however stand up to scrutiny. Certainly, Daniel Gordis and Roberta Kwall, the commentators whom I will engage with, see what the casual observer does: the writing on the wall. *The only proven model of survival that Gordis and Kwall have is the Orthodox model*, which they reject. Indeed, it's halakhah's *insignificance* to latter-day (non-Orthodox) Judaism that drives Gordis's thinking. As to Kwall, she reaches for halakhah mainly as a way of reducing the *threat* that intermarriage poses to Jewish survival.

Solomon Schechter, the founder of American Conservatism, worked to clear a space for men and women who found Orthodoxy too constricting and Reform too lax. The firmament that he inserted was a critique of Orthodoxy's theological/revelatory understanding of practice. Here, Schechter took the baton from

Zechariah Frankel, the originator of Conservatism.[4] The position, in a sentence, is this. Although the Torah is axiomatic to Judaism, halakhah, largely a rabbinic product determined by circumstance, is amenable to updating.

The coherence of Conservatism's middle way was soon tested. The *Responsum on the Sabbath* permitted the use of motor vehicles on the day whose observance shapes the life of the religious Jew. The reason for overriding the Torah's proscription of sabbath work was demographic. In postwar America, many who made the move to the suburbs found themselves in a dilemma: forgo an activity vital for an active connection to Judaism, or transgress the ban.

Here is Gordis's description of the effect of (as it's less Popishly known) "the Driving Teshuvah": "When Conservative Judaism declared, in its (in)famous 1950 'Responsum on the Sabbath' that it was permissible to drive to synagogue on [the Sabbath], Conservative Jews smelled a rat." The movement's leaders represent Conservatism as non-robotically halakhic; as responsive to the shifting consensus among adherents. But erstwhile adherents, once they twig to, as it seems, the opportunism, are left wondering whether their practice isn't a charade.

The pure facts of the matter raise doubt about "smell a rat." The Driving Teshuvah is dated 1950; the decline that Pew charts, four decades later. Stinkweed, I'm informed, has at most a latency period of half that! Gordis's description of the Responsum indicates that he's really talking about the ultimate significance to Judaism of halakhah.[5] As he sees it, there is none. For clarity's sake he might better have characterized the Driving Teshuvah as a window *for us* onto the real Conservative attitude. The drop in numbers is, it may be inferred, *irrelevant* to his stand on Conservatism. Survival is no proof of quality. This, after all, is Gordis's opinion of the survival of the something called "Orthodoxy."

Kwall (35) advances a similar point. "[The Responsum] made no practical difference to the majority of Conservative Jews who were going to drive on Shabbat regardless of whether they received permission." The same goes for the dietary laws. Even if they keep kosher in the home, there's a good likelihood that the Conservative Jews eat treif outside, the more irreverent debating whether consuming milk with shrimp is permissible. Minus the pilpul, their situation is not much different from that of the Goldsteins back in Uzhhorod.[6]

Clearly, the decline in numbers has little to do with the attitude towards halakhah. When the external pressures on the group have abated, and when halakhic ways have been funnelled into the major holidays and festivals, the influence of the surrounding culture is felt unbuffered. At some point, the line of demarcation to the non-Jewish side is breached across a wide front.

A re-energized form of halakhah would seem to be indicated. Obviously, one can't have this simply because one wants it. There may be no charging stations outside the Orthodox *eruv*.

Defeatism here is alarmist. I'll get to that. The point of immediate record is that Gordis is no halakhic revivalist. His ulterior motive in this regard is, again, that the cleaner the sweep, the better for his proposal.

It serves Gordis's purpose to toe-tag Conservatism. Could it have done better? Gordis's fuzziness becomes clear as soon as his proposal is quoted. The movement's leaders, he argues, should have developed the idea that the identity of men and women is a matter not of punctual self-definition, but of links extending backward to forebears, outward to community, and forward to progeny. No Jew is an island, so to speak.

Gordis approvingly quotes two modern thinkers. Here's his excerpt from Charles Taylor's *The Ethics of Authenticity* (40–1):

> [W]hat is self-defeating in modes of contemporary culture [is that they] *shut out* history and the bonds of solidarity ... I can define my identity only against the background of things that matter ... Only if I exist in a world in which history, or the demands of nature, or the needs of my fellow human beings, or the duties of citizenship, or the call of God, or something else of this order *matters* crucially, can I define an identity for myself that is not trivial.

And here are a few lines from Michael Sandel's *Liberalism and the Limits of Justice* (179):

> We cannot regard ourselves as independent ... without ... understanding ourselves as the particular persons we are – as members of this family or community or nation or people, as bearers of this history, as sons and daughters of that revolution, as citizens of this republic ... For to have character is to know that I move in a history I neither summon nor command, which carries consequences none the less for my choices and conduct. It draws me closer to some and more distant from others; it makes some aims more appropriate, others less so.

Gordis effuses:

> Arguments such as those would have put the most human, most self-defining, most existentially significant questions of human life at the centre of Conservative Jewish discourse, and the result might well have been a very different prognosis for the only movement that was primed to raise these questions. It is true that young [Jewish] Americans might still have opted for triviality; but they might also have returned to something less vacuous as they grew older and wiser.

Opposing the view that the bowling team is an accurate model of supra-personal association, the quoted thinkers toe the "conservative" line. Professional

philosophers both, their criticism of the idea of an autonomous chooser isn't
political. The liberal view, they hold, distorts the reality of the matter.

What does Athens have to do with Jerusalem? Taylor, a Catholic, isn't defending Jewish identity. And despite Gordis's "a Jewish intellectual," neither is Sandel. Attend here to "young Americans." Gordis's typing fingers sense that there
is nothing essentially Jewish about the answers to the existentially significant
questions. In any case, "young [Jewish] Americans" doesn't convert with "young
[Jewish] people." "I am an American … and go at things as I have taught myself,
free-style, and will make the record in my own way."

Gordis sounds like Krishna of *The Bhagavad-Gita*, working to persuade the
wavering Arjunas of *his* audience to cleave to the tradition. "The Jewish way
has a long history. The longevity attests that it satisfies and is a meaningful way.
Cleave to it because it works."

If people, uncoerced, live the Jewish way, it satisfies them. About "meaningful" we are however given only the circular "It has given meaning to the lives of
your forebears." Pointing to *their* long history, Christians could argue that theirs
is a better tool for coping with the reality of which the Jews' historical experience is the proof. What could Gordis say to gainsay Augustine's reflections on
the inexpungibility of sin, reflections linked only loosely to theological sticking
points with Judaism?

Why does Gordis think that implementing his recommendations would be
worth the effort? Maybe it's past time to join the men and the woman in Pew's
"Portrait."

Kwall's focus is the threat that intermarriage poses "down the road" to Jewish survival. The Conservative movement, she argues, should resist the kind of
outreach to non-Jews (non-Jewish spouses of Jews) that typifies Reform, from
which Conservatism is, she says, becoming increasingly hard to differentiate.
So where Gordis's view is "Do it because it's what's been done by your forebears,
which shows that it's satisfying," Kwall's is "Do it lest there be no you."

Kwall's valediction (35) is a clarion call:

> The [Conservative] movement should refrain from attempting to widen a tent that
> is already losing its shape and structure. Instead, it should commit itself to a col-
> lective effort to develop a stronger, distinct, religious identity based on what it can
> legitimately claim as its unique legacy. Such a path may not result in an explo-
> sion of new adherents, but it will maintain Conservative Judaism's distinct defini-
> tion – and chart a course away from its self-destruction.

"Unique legacy"? Since Kwall is contrasting Conservatism and Reform, it's got
to be halakhism. The label "Conservatism," after all, connotes the selective conservation of tradition, conservation minus the transcendental twaddle. But this
swings us round in a circle.

The basis of halakhah, the Orthodox claim, is God. This is stated plainly by several who respond to Gordis's "Requiem." Here are the words of Joshua:

> Orthodox Jews – at least the thinking ones – observe halakhah because that is what God has commanded and what God wants from them. Then the unthinking ones follow because they are born into a lifestyle. I attended [the Jewish Theological Seminary], Ramah, etc. – there is virtually no talk [in these locales] about God at all, not to mention what He/She wants from us. If the Torah is from man, and [Talmud and its offshoots are only reflections] of the needs of rabbis of the time, then as Gordis states, there are no expectations and halakhah at best has a vote but not a veto.[7]

And here is Charles Hoffman's intervention:

> The reason for the observance of mitzvoth is that [Jews] were commanded [to do so] by God.

Tradition alone, the Reconstructionist substitute for theology, proved (Hoffman goes on to say) ineffective as a basis for devotion. Why observe, save out of politesse, or inertia, if it's only a customary form?

What Joshua states about the JTS, Camp Ramah, and so on bears directly, and negatively, on Kwall, who points to reduced intermarriage and continued participation in traditional ritual among attendees. The more one socializes with Jews, the more one is apt to marry a Jew and abide by Jewish practices. Big surprise!

When all is said and done, the position is this: be a (Conservative) Jew for the sake of being a Jew. There is no positive core, nothing to take up from "God wants and commands it."

Here is Kwall, on the sabbath (35):

> Committed Conservative Jews, regardless of whether they drive or use electricity on Shabbat, have always appreciated the benefits of keeping its 25 hours holy. Such benefits were emphasized by Rabbi Ben Zion Bokser, who wrote a strong minority opinion to the *Responsum* emphasizing the importance of a Shabbat experience grounded in home and quality family time. In language that is still remarkably relevant today, Bokser spoke of the importance of Shabbat as freedom from machines and modern life's complexities. His opinion did not parse the halakhah but rather presented a sociological and psychological argument for why a normative, traditional Shabbat experience matters.
>
> Conservative … leaders should follow Bokser's lead. They should focus on developing, communicating, and selling to their membership a set of ritual norms of observance currently being practiced by the movement's most dedicated Jews. An emphasis on thicker forms of traditional practice will provide the best path not

only for retaining the core but also for reclaiming other traditional Jews who feel that Conservative Judaism has lost its footing.

Kwall says "keep … holy." The religious term *par excellence* has been diluted to "salubrious (in)activity."

The seventh day rest as Judaism's seventh inning stretch. Verily, *Hamlet* without the Prince! What sociological and/or psychological facts does kashrut honour? How are men and women who do not live by the dietary regulations less good people? The Jews among them might be less good Jews. But isn't that the issue? No one gets merit points for being a good bowler; or, for that matter, a good boxer.

Kwall's approval of this I find astonishing. How does a thicker praxis do more than defer and/or distract?

Getting Back to Trinity

On an outing in the Cambridgeshire countryside, Bertrand Russell takes a wrong turn. "You've lost your way?" asks an old-timer whom he approaches. "Yes," says Russell." "You're bicycling?" "Yes." "You're from Cambridge?" "Yes." With a shrug, the man resumes poking in his plot. "All questions and no answers," said Russell when, in didactic mode, he cited the encounter, "is not much help."

Gordis and Kwall differ only cosmetically. The only idea of transcendence on which they can call is horizontal: outwards to other men and women, backward to the past, ahead to the future. Orthodoxy's vertical transcendence, the God–halakhah link that Joshua and Charles Hoffman mention, makes no sense to them.

I'll now turn the history that Gordis and Kwall use to attack Orthodoxy against them; I'll do so while also criticizing the rabbinic view.

What can one say, from a historical vantage point, about the vast (and ongoing) elaboration of the sketchy practical guidelines in core Scripture? Rabbinic Judaism has its basis not only in the Torah but also in Pharisaic thought of the late Second Temple period. At that time, the land that had been promised to the children of Israel in the Torah was compromised. Also, schism threatened the community. How better to quell the dissension in order that the external pressures be resisted than by extending the ordinances so as to leave no area of life about which God is indifferent? Given this Pharisaic parentage, halakhah's inward focus and rigidity are to be expected.[8]

A second such factor is as significant. Usually, the Romans tolerated the religions of the subjugated peoples. An enlightened multiculturalism? Nothing of the kind. Rather, the belief-systems were, usually, of the same type as theirs. In Judea, the attitude was tested. Regarding the non-pagan character of their religion the hands of the Jewish authorities were tied. But to some degree they were able to assuage the worry of their conquerors. The yoke of the practices was sure to make Judaism a hard sell. Also, the genealogical condition on membership served to limit expansion.[9] The inexportability had long-term effects; Judaism's footprint remained small. Should Judaism's spokespeople through the ages be priding themselves on not having a Paul of their own? One can however appreciate the situational reasons for curtailing outreach.

Halakhah as rabbinic Judaism knows it is therefore a clamp on schismatic forces in the late Second Temple period; a mollifier, also, of the Romans. This history is a basis for distinguishing between the instrumental function of halakhah, which concerns the situation of a specific group of men and women, and a primary, non-instrumental one plugged into the general human condition.

The Bible's story about itself represents the new way of being coming to be, all of a sudden, with Abraham. Are there reasons for its arising when and where it does? One imagines so. But it can't be concluded that these determine the way's identity. Presumably, situational factors explain the emergence of mathematical means of expression. Yet even if the census-taker or the taxman is behind it, mathematics is its own thing.

The idea behind the Bible is a philosophical one. *Paganism doesn't do justice to human nature; its conceptualization is abstracted from a unified physical whole of reciprocally dependent parts.* God's not being a nature deity is the Bibleists' way of saying that the conceptualization is a bed of Procrustes with regard to men and women.

Nature is a system. Men and women live in nature. No more does that make them parts of the system than living in your house makes you a door. People are separate – from nature and from one another. This being the view, it explains why, having described the creation of humankind in Chapter 1 of Genesis, the writers/thinkers proceed to describe the making of a single person in Genesis 2.

The core idea of the Bible is the separateness of persons. The protection of this separateness in thought and through practice is required of beneficiaries of God's breath of life. Its protection is, if you will, what God wants and what God's Commandments are there to protect. The Bible is the charter of individualism, and in this regard it qualifies as liberal.

To confirm, a more technical point of interpretation. Genesis 1:27: "So God created the man [ha-adam] in his image; in the image of God he created him ['oto' – third person singular objective]; male and female he created them ['otam' – third person plural objective]." A recurring absurdity in biblical commentary is the claim, based on the pronominal shift from singular "him" to plural "them," that God creates a being at once male and female.[10] The reference of "the man" and of "him" is to the species. "Them" refers to the members of the species. It's therefore best to render "him" as "it." In Genesis 1, the Bible is speaking biologically. The human species is a species among species, and species have two sexes. In Genesis 2, a particular man – the word is also "ha-adam" – is created before a woman. Biologically, this is absurd. Genesis 2 isn't speaking biologically.

The Bible is the charter of individualism. "I am the Lord your God ...; you shall have no other gods before me" means "Each of you (like God) is one: a separate entity. To see your life in collectivist terms is to elevate other gods." It's not that these are not gods. It's that they are not gods of the addressees of "you."

Examination of many of the core practices confirms that halakhah is designed to actualize Abraham's insight. Recall the proportionality: "sabbath : time :: the first person : matter." The left-hand terms are set apart from nature. I quoted Jesus's justification for sabbath non-observance. "My father is still working" (John 5:17). Despite missing the ontology behind the day of rest, Jesus is closer to the truth than is Kwall, whose Wordsworthian comment about the benefits of the twenty-five hours misses the point. If responding to the needs of others conflicts with the halakhic letter, the letter should be returned to sender. What Joshua and Charles Hoffman say about sabbath observance applies to helping the needy traveller. "God wants it." God wants it not because he is working on the sabbath but because he isn't.

There is, then, a halakhic way outside the *eruv* of Orthodoxy, a way that should be compelling to all because of its philosophical basis. It's a way that requires the wayfarers to understand that what they're doing they're doing because of what they are. If anything, this involves thinning out the practices incumbent on Jews according to Orthodoxy, many of which are linked not to the being of men and women but to where some men and women happened, at a point in their history, to be.

I said about the Goldsteins that, like the smokers and eaters of the vignette, they honoured Judaism as much in the breach as in the observance. In deviating from the practices they knew all about, they were emulating the first man and the first woman, who in departing from God's instructions gave practical expression to the breath of life that vivifies them; to their not being, as all other creatures are, no more than parts of nature.

11

God Loves You, Christopher Hitchens

Birtwhistle's Bet

A number of fixtures reposed amid the welter of the common room at the Oxford college to which I was attached in my graduate student days. Prominent was a tombstone-like notebook between whose marbled boards wagers that the collegians contracted were set out. Of the wagers that crowded the pages, one laid down a long-term deposit in my memory bank. In a break with protocol, the party who accepted the bet didn't attend Balliol. More unusually still, this party, though referred to on the university's crest, wasn't even an Oxford matriculant. Here's what the proposer, an undergraduate named John Birtwhistle, had inscribed. "I bet you, God,  that you do not exist." The stakes were high; Birtwhistle was hazarding his soul. A brown-edged hole of the sort that the literal-minded would attribute to the business end of a lit cigarette signalled the second party's contracting in. These words were affixed: "God, his mark."

In *these* pages I place a side bet against the position of the flesh-and-blood punter. The immediate target of my wager is as luck would have it another Balliol undergraduate, as he then was, who, until his untimely passing on a dark, cold day in 2011, was almost as present in the English-language media as on Augustine's formulation God Almighty is present in the universe: a circle whose centre is everywhere and whose circumference is nowhere. Another remembrance from that past time serves well by way of making acquaintance.

I'm in the common room, pouring a cup of coffee. I answer the phone. The voice asks for Christopher Hitchens. Hitchens, who has a spot in my consciousness only because of the Pams and Tessas that he parades through the quad, is sitting in one of the alcoves with several of his coevals. A mixture of plummy and nasal tones, punctuated by eruptions of chimp-like laughter, emanates from the klatch. Hearing his name, Hitchens strides across and, without a word of thanks, takes the receiver. One more, this, in the string of what have come to be known in my circle – a circle whose circumference is not far from its quite localized centre – as the cuttings of Glouberman.

Does this display of patristic erudition elicit a chuckle? I hope so. Otherwise, what function would it serve? Excepting the handful who, fidgeting in the waiting room of a Ph.D. (ABD), D.D.S., self-administer the lines as inky chloroform, readers will know all about Christopher Hitchens. Hitchens's success as a public intellectual was Anselmian: than which greater is scarce conceivable. The rare week without his mournful visage and gravelly sourness on this or that late-night TV panel, the rarer one without a few hundred pungent words in one or another of the larger organs of the right-leaning press. Hitchens was a contrarian. To a fault. God-likeness affected him like a poke in the eye. As for me, I too have spent a career talking truth (as I see it) to power. But my targets, being long defunct, are in no condition to talk back. For I plod the academic straight-and-narrow. The remote chance of the limelight snuffed out for the graves of academe? Hitchens took the call from outside the ivied walls and answered it, did so abundantly. The cuttings of Hitchens would constitute a veritable ziggurat.

Though the paths that briefly crossed in those Arcadian days might never have intersected again after the matriculants of the late sixties creeped their last to tutors' rooms and lecture halls, a few months prior to his death I had occasion to read Hitchens's bestseller *god Is Not Great* (2007), and this minion of the Owl of Minerva did, I found, give two hoots about the book. One of them is appreciative. The other, which it is the primary object of this appreciation of the man to tweet, is critical. Here, in brief, is an orchestration of the two.

In having his own go at the Book of Mormon, Hitchens quotes Mark Twain's squib on the channellings from (so John Smith claimed) the angelic bandwidth: "chloroform in print." While insults often spatter the hurler, Hitchens's work, like Samuel Clemens's, is more mimicked than mocked. But although *god Is Not Great* is the farthest thing from literary $CHCl_3$, the Book of Hitchens can be likened to another substance that enjoyed a career as an anesthetic: N_2O, known as "laughing gas." Hitchens would so far not necessarily have objected to this twist on Twain. His project was after all to cleanse the system of a poison that, in his judgment, causes it to sicken, and to the task he brought his surgical wit. (The book is subtitled "How Religion Poisons Everything.") The fact is, though, that rather than detoxify, the laughing gas tranquillizes the reader while, the Hippocratic intentions notwithstanding, healthy tissue is excised. The patient leaves Hitchens's hyperbolic chamber one wisdom tooth to the bad.

This doctor synthesizes an antidote: NO_2CH.

Canis familiaris

god Is Not Great is thick with references to the gods of the Western philosophical pantheon: Plato, Aristotle, Cicero, Ockham, Bacon, Hume, Kant. Also much in evidence are more recent aspirants to philosophical apotheosis: Bertrand Russell, A.J. Ayer, Daniel Dennett. Hitchens, who went down from Oxford with a third-class degree, denied, as he therefore had to, that he was an A-student. (In our day, a "third" was said to be preferable to a "second" – the conferral of the latter tantamount to a stamping of "Plodder (Oxon.)" on one's résumé. For evincing lukewarm commitment to dissipation, the former was however rated below the fourth-class degree. Unless money made this immaterial, it was best – so beginning undergraduates were cautioned – not to mess with Messers In-Between.) Not only did Hitchens have a broad knowledge of philosophy's past, but, impressively for one so active in public affairs, he was also plugged into the live outlets in the inner sanctums of regal intellection. It therefore matches the texture of the book for me to couple my largest critical point to an analogy that, in the *Republic*, Plato puts into the mouth of his Hitchensian spokesperson, doubly so because in offering it Plato is uncorking his small vial of NO_2. Indeed, it is triply in keeping, since at issue is the basic issue of philosophical anthropology: man's nature.

The dog's nature, Socrates states, is philosophical; it's a true lover of wisdom. Towards people the dog behaves on the basis of its knowledge of them. Gentle with friends, the dog is wary of strangers. Enemies? Bared teeth and snarls.

Since with respect to the present issue I, despite high regard for the man, am no friend of the man's ideas, couldn't Hitchens have cited his comportment in the common room to attest an admirably doggy nature? The truth is that where it really counts Hitchens was insufficiently canine. He bared his incisors at the personage who in the matter of man's nature was his greatest friend. With respect to the parts of the book that interest me, the parts that address the Hebrew Scriptures, this confusion undermines the argument.

Though he didn't know it, Hitchens was of the party of the deity of the Hebrew Bible. ("God" should hereafter be read as the proper name of this deity – the deity also denominated "Jehovah" or "Yahweh.") As payment for checking disbelief at the porter's lodge, the reader will require some explanation of how Hitchens came *mutatis mutandis* to do in the present regard what Balliol undergraduates were wont in pre-coed days to do when in their cups: micturate on Trinity's wall. (See Google under "Gordouli.") The short answer is that he read the biblical text as if it were a contribution to current debate. It was to him as if those behind the Bible were standing opposite in the Oxford Union, taking the anti-Birtwhistle side of the resolution while he defended Gaunilo from the charge of being a fool. This, to quote the philosopher Bernard Williams, another Balliol matriculant, is like "a nightmare … in which one met a man who insisted on translating the Greek word for trireme as 'steamship' and then complained that the Greeks had a defective conception of a steamship."

Hitchens approached the biblical text as being pro- what he was anti-. To Hitchens it was axiomatic that the Bible is the charter document of the infamous thing on which he was doing a Voltaire. Two major adjustments are needed so that truth will out. The Bible has to be read in context. Modern secular thought must therefore be kept out of the mix. Allegedly dialectical appropriations of the Bible by post-biblical creeds and religious traditions must not be taken as gospel.

A Con-Text in Context

Like the waters, upper and lower, interpreters divide on whether the biblical narrative begins with an act of creation *ex nihilo*. By the lights of those who say yea, the absolute beginning is "Let there be light" (Genesis 1:3). The nay-sayers maintain that God's creative vocalization is hurled against a pre-existent chaos – the waste and void of Genesis 1:1 – and comes back spattered, so that God must further "separate … the light from the dark" (4). Although, theologically speaking, a lot hangs on how one jumps, the operative point for here is that while the Bible's opening words are the first printed words (the Bible being the first major piece that Gutenberg pressed), the Bible itself is not the first word. It's injected into an environment in which religious institutions and attitudes are already alive and kicking. Too, the Bible is, in this environment, revolutionary. "I am the Lord your God …; you shall have no other gods before me." Those behind the Bible are, like Hitchens, contrarians. The substance of the biblical revolution can be encapsulated in a word: monotheism. "Let there be light" might indeed be understood as a request to illuminate what those behind the Bible regard as creedal darkness. Nearly enough, the motto on Oxford's crest: "Dominus Illuminatio Mea." In the Genesis narrative, God proceeds to separate the light from the dark. From this point of view, the meaning is that enlightenment creeps in like the dawn. God will have to shout "Order!" some more before the chaos abates.

The men and women the Bible addresses are nothing like visitors from a distant land plunked down in front of the shelves of breakfast cereals. The addressees either subscribe to the other gods or are hesitant about God's goods. The character called "God," a character that many are meeting for the first time, is telling them they must cancel the subscription and master the uncertainty.

Two episodes in the Bible give a feel for the range of the audience. The first finds the children of Israel at Mount Sinai. In this episode Moses is, as we all know, Charlton Heston. The other episode, after Jeroboam's Brexit, concerns the inhabitants of the northern entity, Israel. The star in this case, Elijah, takes *his* cue from Jim Morrison. At the foot of Mount Sinai we have a group that has initialled the contract but whose members are now being asked to sign an irrevocability clause. On Mount Carmel, the group consists of dissidents and fence-sitters all of whom are being romanced by the opposition. In neither case are the members of the target audience innocent of the other gods.

The text, as this confirms, is directed to men and women who are in some way torn. Latter-day readers, unless they appreciate the fact and budget for it, are like motorists trying to start their vehicles guided by a superannuated manual. "Rotate the crank clockwise."

In *god Is Not Great*, Hitchens applauds the idea that the manual's words are dead letters today. But my meaning in asserting their irrelevance is not his. I mean that those directly associated with the Bible would be shocked to discover that any among us are still hanging on every jot, as we would be shocked to see a person approaching the BMW crank in hand.

The Bible addresses its audience stridently. Sometimes, "or else" can be felt in its words. It's not from a motive of personal profit that the character called "God" takes exception to the digging in of heels. At issue is how the addressees think of themselves. The Bible puts this by saying that "it will go well" (Deuteronomy 6:3) with those who take the pledge. Non-signatories are out of touch with their natures and their places. This already explains why the benign *Canis familiaris* should appear the fearsome *Canis lupus*. The members of the audience either have not yet been domesticated to the God House or are wary about entering. Under the circumstances the soft sell would be a marketer's blunder. Under the circumstances *then*. *Our* circumstances are *now*. *We* might be wearing the T-shirt and harmonizing around the campfire.

The Bible is attacking a way of living and the associated way of thinking at whose core lies the worship of other gods. For being on the attack here, the Bible is *anti*-religious. Agreed, this "anti-religious" is thin stuff. An anti-Christian may be pro-Islam. My own view is the stronger one. But even on the weaker view, distinctions that Hitchens does not make seem necessary.

Ockham All Ye Faithful

Hitchens, in the days of his youth, called London home. Thereafter becoming, as the Oxford British were wont to put it, a Yank, he hung his hat inside the Beltway. He was, then, very much a man of capitals. But Hitchens's title slights a capital. The typographical departure in the case of "Dominus" from Hitchens's choices of domicile is, it turns out, philosophically ill-advised.

God is telling the members of the audience, negatively, that they should stop putting other gods first, and positively, that they should accept him. In the words "stop putting other gods first" we begin to see that his titular provocation spells trouble for Hitchens, trouble with a capital "T."

The lower-case letter "g" of the first word of Hitchens's title draws attention to itself. It's an orthographical expression of disdain for the main fixture amid the theological welter – with an extra kick at the Qur'an. Hitchens's wit is generally on the mark. But in this instance he is, as the greatest of Brits puts it, hoist with his own petard.

The upper case "g" in "God" is, it turns out, not otiose. Lowering the case to score a point, Hitchens scores an own goal. A core claim of his is that anything the theological *explanans* is called upon to do can be done better in less problematic terms. Ockham's razor therefore instructs us to shave off the theology. Hitchens is mistaken about this. He overlooks an option that falls between the transcendent and the natural.

A distinction needs to be observed between the proper name "God" and the common noun "god." The claim expressed by "Zeus is God" is false. Obama is not Bush, and Zeus is not God. Nor is Zeus god. Like "George is man," the sentence "Zeus is god" is ill-formed. Zeus is *a* god; that is, "Zeus is a god," a classificatory predication like "George is a man," is true. The biblical god is God. That is: "The biblical god is God" is an identity statement, like "The man in the beret is Sartre." A German literary type might write: "Thomas Mann ist ein Mann."

"God" is the biblical deity's proper name. In written English, when it starts a sentence a common noun's first letter is capitalized. Isn't this asking for trouble? Fear about mistaking a common noun for a proper name is alarmist. Unless enclosed by quotation marks, common nouns in subject position are always prefixed by "the," "a," "some," "eight," and so on. Poetic licence apart, "Dog barks" is ill-formed. Should the sentence read "Dogs bark," the subject term wouldn't be taken as a plural form of a proper name. The exceptions prove the rule. *Brideshead Revisited* features a character named "Boy Mulcaster." And the English pop scene presents Boy George and Del Boy Trotter. "Boys of the U.K."

What is the point of this, as it may seem, grammar tutorial? Once we recognize that each of Zeus, Isis, Allah, Shiva, and Baal is a god, we are compelled to seek clarification. Who does Hitchens's title diminish? All gods? This god? That god? The title is an obstacle to making distinctions that might need making.

To prevent confusion, a finer classificatory system would help. Let "deity" serve as the large pigeonhole for religious attitudes such as worship, reverence, awe, and for intended sacramental activities such as prayer, sacrifice, and self-denial. The Greek gods, then, are deities. Cleaving to how "god" is used, let us also say that these objects are gods. God of the Hebrew Bible and Allah of the Qur'an are deities. On this new taxonomy, they are *not* gods. What are they? For the meantime, they are non-god deities.

Where does Hitchens stand? His title is "god is not Great." Is "god" synonymous with "deity" in the finer taxonomy? On the basis that he is opposed to the non-god deity of Judaism, to the Christian non-god deity, and to the non-god deity of Islam, Hitchens's defenders will complain that I am hairsplitting. Although they are right about what Hitchens thinks, the defenders are wrong about the truth. Once we get clearer on the classifications, strange reversals and inversions occur. In one aspect Hitchens approves gods. But it turns out that he does not know what such approval implies. When the ignorance is cleared up, it turns out that he approves not gods but God of the Bible.

It turns out that, for Hitchens, God *is* great.

"I am the Lord your God"

"For the greater part of human existence ... th[e] option [of rejecting god-worship] did not really exist" (67). Doesn't it follow that even if the men and women behind a piece of writing that deals with matters of worship are trying to extinguish the reverential attitude, the product will be couched in terms of the numinous? In politics both inside and outside the Beltway, professed atheists rarely end up among the elect. For that reason, we suspect many candidates for office in America of decoy devotion. That is one of two points. The other is more specific. Since God is enjoining the Israelites to defect from the other gods, it is important to determine what God objects to about their erstwhile creedal ways. Like a parody of an Old Testament prophet, Hitchens just blows his top.

Here are a few representative lines (98–9) from Hitchens's gloss on a core passage of the Hebrew Scriptures.

> The first three [of the Ten Commandments] are all variations of the same one, in which god insists on his own primacy and exclusivity, forbids the making of graven images, and prohibits the taking of his name in vain. This prolonged throat-clearing is accompanied by some very serious admonitions, including a dire warning that the sins of the fathers will be visited on their children.

After bolting through the remaining ordinances, Hichens pronounces (99):

> It would be harder to find an easier proof that religion is man-made. There is, first, the monarchical growling about respect and fear, accompanied by a stern reminder of omnipotence and limitless revenge, of the sort with which a Babylonian or Assyrian emperor might have ordered the scribes to begin a proclamation. There is then a sharp reminder to keep working and only to relax when the absolutist says so.

The first lines of the Commandments are not throat-clearing. Nor, unless in the grip of some *idée fixe*, could one characterize what is written as a threat. Like the preamble of the American Declaration of Independence, the lines assert the principle that underpins the rest. The principle we have encountered, at least in name: monotheism. What's in the name?

It's not only that God, the deity of monotheism, wants fealty. It's that there is but one deity. Fealty to one deity is wanted. Missing this is missing the point. But what's so important about one? What *is* the point?

An examination of Genesis 2:16–17 will point us in the right direction. Here are the words, voiced by the same speaker as "I am the Lord your God." "You may freely eat of every tree of the garden; but of the tree of the knowledge of good and evil you shall not eat, for in the day that you shall eat of it you shall die." Observe that the prohibition is conditional. "Do not eat, lest you die." Many take the latter clause as rhetorical. "You'd have to pay me a million dollars ..." is a way of saying "I won't do it, period." This is an error. The issue for the recipient is whether they want the knowledge enough to die with the consequences.

Observe, too, that this isn't the material conditional of propositional logic. The consequent connects internally to the antecedent. "Do not go into the desert; in the day that you go there you shall be without access to rivers and to rainfall." Having no reliable natural sources of water is not a sanction for following Doughty. So it's more like "You'll have more than 3 if you add 2 and 2" than like "If you add 2 and 2, you'll avoid the ignominy of a third." Being a knower, that is, is (=) being subject to death.

The purport of this last equation is obscure. Leaving it as a teaser, I turn to the issue of context.

The assertion of God's unique status as deity is made in the frame of creedal systems that enjoin worship of a pantheon. Because Hitchens handles "deity" and "god" interchangeably, to him the distinction between monotheism and polytheism is angels on pinheads. If throat-clearing is what we have here, what mattereth it if a soloist or a choir hawks into the spittoon? Whenever he speaks for the group that he loosely controls, Zeus could say: "Mortals, obey us." That, early in the *Iliad*, is what Athena says. "Obey us both," she declares to Achilles. The plural reference is not regal. Athena is also referring to Hera.

The same goes for another connection that the Bible states. Both enunciations of the Commandments refer to the liberation from Egypt. "I am the Lord your God, who brought you out of the land of Egypt, out of the house of slavery; you shall have no other gods before me." What's the removal of the chains to do with the worship of God? Eye peeled for the sneer of cold command, Hitchens has his answer at the ready. But mightn't the liberation from bondage, at a more abstract level, be liberation from the wrong sort of worship? The Bible proceeds: "You must ... do as the Lord your God has commanded you; ... so that you may live, and that it may go well with you, and that you may live long in the land that you are to possess" (Deuteronomy 5:32–33). Being enslaved is the same as (=) not worshipping God. To follow the Lord is to be outside the borders of Egypt.

Taking guidance from the points about Genesis 2:16–17, the relevant implications are, we see, these. "I am the Lord your God" states a condition on the remaining Commandments. The rewards of compliance are not external to the compliance.

Though I am not defending in full the readings that I furnish, I do want to show that the idea of wages' being internal – being out of the state of Egypt is [=] being in a liberated state – is a constant in the Bible.

Curses!

After the fratricide, God curses Cain to a life of wandering. "You will be a fugitive and a wanderer on the earth" (4:12). As a result of Ham's having witnessed Noah's nakedness, "cursed be Canaan [the progeny of Ham]; lowest of slaves shall he be to his brothers" (9:25). Although the maledictions are enunciated after the transgressions, both can easily be reformulated. "If you kill Abel, you will wander." "Eye your father's nakedness, and enslavement awaits." The logic is as in Eden: to kill Abel is (=) to wander; to see Noah's nakedness is (=) to be a slave. Also, each of the consequences is, again as in Eden, internal.

The curse meted out to Cain is wandering. A wandering farmer? Only appreciate that Cain's killing of Abel dramatizes the shift to agriculture, and everything falls into place. Having left the tried and tested, men and women are in the dark as to whether the superseding *modus vivendi* will be viable. God had said to Cain (4:7): "If you do well, will you not be accepted?" Whether the travellers of the new way will prosper is up in the air. That's the meaning of Cain's vagabondage. No sooner is Cain cursed than he settles in the land of Nod. "Nod" in Hebrew is cognate with "wander." Cain's settled condition is unsettled. With progress *per se* the Bible has no beef. In this instance the Bible isn't advising the beating of ploughshares into crooks. Rather, it's flashing a yellow light about departing well-travelled ways, as in Eden the inhabitants were warned about straying from the garden paths to which their birthday suits suited them. Should agriculture have supplanted shepherding? The problem with Cain isn't the farming. It's "am I my brother's keeper?" The farm is Abel's cemetery. Just so, when we began purchasing milk at the supermarket, an obligation fell upon us to reintegrate the laid-off home deliverers. Otherwise, God's indictment of Cain will condemn us. "Your brother's blood is crying out from the ground." "Brother, can you spare a dime?"

The Bible admires gumption. Abraham, a biblical paragon, puts his native land in the rearview. The Bible knows that not all are made of stuff so stern. In Isaac, the Bible presents a character who, though sprung from God's hand-picked Israelite progenitors, never ventures far from the homestead. Both Abraham and Jacob trek in times of trouble to Egypt; Isaac doesn't depart the borders of Canaan. Abraham finds a partner for Isaac, as God does for Adam. Jacob makes his own match. Isaac stands to his father as Adam and Eve in the garden stand to Adam and Eve after they exit. The Bible tolerates Isaac. Abraham his father and Jacob his son, both pressed harder by life, get a better press.

As for Ham: the slavery spoken of explains itself once we understand that the father's nakedness is the principle of creation. Ham's specialty is city-building. If he, privy to the principle, becomes the postdiluvian city-father as Noah becomes the postdiluvian father of all mankind, he is apt to be the slave of his erection. Not only will he work from sunup to sundown. He'll also have to clock in for a nightshift. The city is so much a departure for the Bible as to constitute an ongoing problem.

The story of Ham continues the story of Cain. The move to city-dwelling (Cain's son Enoch, and Ham) tracks the move from gathering (Eden) to shepherding (Abel) to agriculture (Cain). The Bible guides the reader by the hand. Cain himself is represented as the first city-builder – see Genesis 4:17. The curse is issued not to Ham but to Ham's son Canaan. Also, as in the case of Cain, the "punishment" of Canaan fits the crime.

From this sample we come to appreciate the Bible's fine patterning. The Commandments takes on a new look. It's not that God requires obedience. It's that not obeying the Commandments is the same as (=) not accepting God. To accept the other gods is to lose the morality that the Commandments codify.

Deus lupus and *Deus familiaris*

"By the dog of Egypt." So Socrates frequently exclaims. One can live in Egypt, with the dog-like Anubis, or in the Promised Land, worshipping God. Why is worship of the Philistine Dagon slavery?

Like the deity whose image and likeness they are said to share, men and women are not submerged in nature. That, I mean, is how adherents to the biblical belief-system conceive themselves. As for men and women who worship other gods, they conceive themselves as parts of the natural realm. *Their deities are bound up in the way of identity with nature. Poseidon *is* the waves. In *his* nature, God is separate from nature. He *rules* the waves. A corollary of the theological difference is the Bible's ascription of "dominion" (Genesis 1:26) to men and women alone. Those who advance the claim of dominion, like those who receive it, are conscious of their puniness. The ascription's meaning is illuminated by the representation of God as outside nature. Men and women are not fully at home within the natural world. *Their domain is in part extra-natural.*

To be in Egypt, to be enslaved, is to think of oneself along pagan lines. Moses, in Egypt, and Elijah, on the Carmel, are both working to liberate their charges from the mistaken self-image – an enterprise of philosophical anthropology.

Obviously, one can't exit nature simply by writing a scripture in which one is represented as breaking free. Which brings me to the deepest point, about monotheism.

The biblical deity is independent of nature. Furthermore, God is one. The Bible takes each person to be an autonomous object, not, as are the birds and the beasts, parts of the natural system. God, the deity in whose image we men and women are made, is one. The one-ness is understood to be of our essence. The claim of dominion is the claim that each man and each woman, for being a particular, stands in a skewed relation to nature.

Nature is a system. How do we men and women, separate from the system, come to be? The Bible's answer is that each of us is inspired with God's breath of life. Monotheism transposes into a theological register this theme of anthropology: each of us is a square peg in the natural system. God, *qua* one, isn't just one more deity; each of us, for the same reason, isn't just one more creature. If particulars do not fit into the round holes because of their one-ness, it makes good sense to represent them as deriving from an extra-natural square that is one.

As to morality: "good" is the sole evaluative word applied in Genesis 1 to the creation. "Bad" first appears in Genesis 2. The implication is that without particulars, there is no morality. That is why "I am the Lord your God &c." heads the Commandments. Summer does not steal from spring. Spring does not take back from winter the spoils of a victory over fall. We have a system in which some parts are treated as if they were independent. Like the Cheshire Cat's smile, they can be singled out. But they are not independent. Killing in the moral sense is unknown in nature, and not because nature involves no higher consciousness. The death of an antelope in the jaws of a lion is good for both lion and antelope – on the species level and from the standpoint of the whole.

The beginning of the Commandments is not throat-clearing. Nor is it a threat about the wages of non-compliance. Nor yet is it a demand of payment for services. It is the statement of the condition for morality. To be submerged in nature is (=) to lose morality. This is not to say that pagans must murder, thieve, and lie. It is to say that the pagan system of thinking has at best a prudential basis for eschewing such modes of conduct.

After making one new point, I will end, as the Commandments require, by redeeming several promises.

Sacrifice is central in the pagan context. The deities are parts of nature. Ricocheting around the natural world like pinballs, men and women strive to line up with the forces that have the power to assist them and to tilt in a favourable way the forces that otherwise would crush them. Sacrifice is in this regard like seeding the clouds. But sacrifice (effective or not) makes no such sense in the biblical context. Getting God to do one's bidding is the same as getting another person to do so. Unlike the wind and the rain, God can understand a request. Petitionary prayer therefore is, conceptually, intelligible in the biblical context. If such prayerful supplication is futile, that's not because praying to God is talking to the wall.

"Isn't sacrifice an important sacrament of *biblical* faith?" The Bible-writers view the activity as dangerous. Grafted on from an alien branch of the tree of religion, might it not if not severely cut back bear forbidden fruit? Maimonides (*Guide for the Perplexed*, vol. 3, ch. 32) sees a compromise. The Israelites in Egypt were so taken with the practice that God, anticipating a bad reaction to "Thou shalt not," assigned them the rites as a sop. And indeed, when we examine how sacrificial activity is described in the interior books of the Torah, the intention, it certainly seems, is to suck it clean of what pagans look to it for.

Hitchens misses the point of the sabbath. God is not part of nature. Sabbath observance is recognition, through practice, of this fact of ontology. To observe the sabbath is to separate oneself from nature, which, as a unitary system, never rests. Observance is thus internally linked with the presupposition of morality.

Paganism, it will be appreciated, is proto-natural science. Here is the final minute from Steven Weinberg's book *The First Three Minutes*, which Hitchens recommends as a substitute for the early chapters of Genesis:

> Men and women are not content to comfort themselves with tales of gods and giants, or to confine their thoughts to the daily affairs of life; they also build telescopes and satellites and accelerators, and sit at their desk[s] for endless hours working out the meaning of the data they gather. The effort to understand the universe is one of the very few things that lifts human life a little above the level of farce, and gives it some of the grace of tragedy.

How many Nobel Laureates does it take to make a bunch of serious errors? Science has a pre-history. Many of the tales of gods and giants to which Weinberg condescends are part of his own tradition. I explained that pagan religions are central to this pre-history. It is no accident that science arose in pagan Greece. Weinberg is blind to the gods and giants on whose shoulders he is standing. Also, the Bible's account of origins is not, expressly not, part of this tradition. Accordingly, the Bible must not be read as offering an account of the origins of the physical universe competitive with the Big Bang account, the Steady State account, or any other account that has its genesis in the reflectoria of scientific cosmology. The Bible is focused tightly on human reality. God and men and women are, to one another, familiars. The Bible's first relevant minutes are the minutes in which particular men and particular women appear. These are as near to the end of creation as possible: in the afternoon of the sixth and final day. Given the grid, this approximates well the percentage of the lifespan of the physical world that is human history. The origin of the physical world is not the Bible's issue. It is backdrop.

The claim that human life is farcical is not unexpected from the tradition that paganism began – though I have to wonder what Weinberg does when he rises from the endless hours searching for meaning and returns to the farcical doings of his wife and kids at home. For men and women are in that tradition jumped-up elements of nature. Can Weinberg believe what he is saying?

Hitchens counted Weinberg a friend. But by climbing onto Weinberg's wagon Hitchens betrayed his humanist impulse. Passionate about human beings' doing well, he battled tirelessly against (as he perceived them) deterrents. However much his trademark stridency irritated, for the strength and constancy of the impulse Hitchens merits admiration. His heart was in the right place. God, then, is Hitchens's friend. It's not only that God's heart is in the same place. It's that that heart, and that place, are outside nature, as is the biblical deity.

Having breathed into us his life-breath, God never regards our activities as far-cical. Does God delight in them? He does. Do they ignite his anger? Often. Indifferent? Never. Hitchens didn't notice what was staring him in the face: his own God-likeness. Like Weinberg, the pagan gods are self-absorbed. Busy doing their thing, they do not care. Nature does not care. The Bible's view, then, is that given what we are we are bound to care for one another. Once we understand *why* caring makes sense at home, we see that it is incumbent on us to reverse Cain's "am I." This view the Bible develops through a story in which God is the major character.

John Birtwhistle, the bet-maker of the Balliol common room, thought of himself as a human being. He therefore loses the bet. In a twist on Faust, winning the bet is (=) losing one's human soul.

Hitchens died a public death, writing about his condition, about mortality, until the end. He did not cease being active in the political arena because of the ravages, though we would have forgiven him despite our loss had he gone silent. Hitchens's performance is ratified by Scripture and indeed provides a model for those who guide themselves by it.

That apparently most despondent of biblical texts, Ecclesiastes, contains an admonition against despondency (12:1):

> Remember your creator in the days of your youth, before the days of trouble come, and the years draw near when you will say "I have no pleasure in them."

Are the final verses of this final chapter an inconsequent add-on, a refusal to face the facts earlier stated? Here is the penultimate verse (12:13).

The end of the matter; all has been heard. Fear God, and keep his Commandments, for that is the whole duty of everyone.

In fact, 12:1 and 12:13 are a fit. In (non-human) nature all that we have is recycling. "All streams run to the sea, but the sea is not full" (1:7). The life of a person is the life of an entity that isn't entirely part of nature. That is why it is terminating. To keep God's Commandments is to retain one's duty towards oneself qua inspired with God's breath. Though he did not explicitly know it, Hitchens remembered God when the days of trouble came. Remarkable in many ways as he was, he even appears to have had some pleasure in those days.

12

Jerry and Jewry:
Ethnicity and Humanity in G.A. Cohen

Jews are associated with liberalism in the way the French are with wine: it is considered native to the region.

– Ruth Wisse (2001, 21)

Jewish Identity: Two Questions

Gerald A. Cohen, one of the few philosophers of international renown to whom the label "MADE IN CANADA / FAIT AU CANADA" sticks, burst onto the scene in 1978 with *Karl Marx's Theory of History: A Defence*, the founding work of analytical Marxism. In the post-Marxist phase of his career, Cohen staked out a non-liberal position in normative political philosophy.

A native of Montreal, Cohen ("Jerry" to colleagues and friends alike) studied philosophy at McGill University and went on to graduate work at Oxford. From 1985 to 2008, he held Oxford's Chichele Professorship of Social and Political Theory, a position the more prestigious because of the earlier incumbency of Sir Isaiah Berlin.

Throughout his life, Cohen identified as Jewish – "very Jewish," he states (20) in the autobiographical chapter of *If You're an Egalitarian, How Come You're So Rich?* But in his earlier years he was, as a Marxist, critical of the bourgeois, Zionist, religion-friendly types who set the tone in the Montreal community. The attitude went beyond thought and talk. Cohen even distanced himself socially from the young men and women, sons and daughters of the tone-setters, who constituted the bulk of McGill's sizeable Jewish student body.[1] Although Cohen eventually broke with Marxism, he remained opposed to the bourgeois, Zionist, moderately religious constellation.

Cohen's reflections on Judaism and on Jewish life raise *the* question of this chapter. *What does the application of "Jew" to a person mean?* Cohen's lifelong anti-liberalism provokes a more specific question. *Is a person's identity as a Jew linked otherwise than statistically to liberal values?*

Imagining the End

At the end of the mentioned chapter of *If You're an Egalitarian*, Cohen muses about *his* end (40):

> I sometimes imagine myself, as my death creeps up on me, reciting the "Shema Yisrael," which is the prayer to be said when dying, and which runs: "Hear, O Israel! The Lord is our God, the Lord is one." I don't know whether this is just an idle fantasy on my part, or something deeper. If it is deeper, then the desire it expresses is not to pay final homage to the God of the Old Testament, whom I find unattractive, but to solidarize with my forebears, from Canaan to Kishinev, from Belsen to Brooklyn. (40)

In regard to uncompleted projects that were important to the departed (in 2009, at the age of sixty-eight, Cohen succumbed to a stroke), those who sorrow at their passing should if possible render them the service. Recite the Shema for Cohen we cannot. The uncertainty that he expresses we *can* try to clear up.

In imagining himself reciting the Shema, Cohen does not think it would be inconsistent for him to imagine the imagined person endorsing the philosophical position on the nature of men and women that he, Cohen, endorses. Not that Cohen has concluded compatibility after deliberating. For it's in the context of describing an unusual Jewish upbringing in postwar Montreal that he does his imagining. "Given my *personal* background, can I perform this act, an act closely associated with the Jewish faith?"

Cohen the situated person is not so easily quarantined from Cohen the philosopher. As I see it, the philosophical position renders the recitation of the Shema problematic for the person. Cohen's disbelief in God (I hasten to add) has nothing to do with it.

"Who is a Jew?" One who can meaningfully recite the Shema.[2] In asking whether the idea of his meaningfully reciting the Shema isn't a fantasy, Cohen is asking whether he is a Jew.

The performance of the act that Cohen imagines marks a person as a Jew. To assert God's status as *our* deity is to accept the Bible's conception of the nature of men and women. For advancing the conception, the Bible is the revolutionary document that it is.[3] Clearing up Cohen's doubts will therefore shed light on the issue of the greatest moment in the Jewish world, and of great moment outside that world too.

Solidarity: Us and Them

Cohen sets reciting the Shema in a worshipful frame of mind apart from reciting it as an expression of solidarity with fellow Jews. The first – "to pay final homage to the God of the Old Testament"[4] – he would decline. The second – "to solidarize with my forebears" – appeals to him.

When he refers to the Shema, Cohen isn't referring to a sentence in an ancient Semitic language that is Greek to him. He is referring to the biblical creedal declaration whose meaning he accurately articulates. Obviously, Cohen thinks that expressing solidarity is more than a use to which the Shema can be put.

"Our God" figures in the Shema. In reciting the Shema, the person *is* linking to a group. Which group? The group comprised of men and women who (can) meaningfully recite it. In this regard the prayer resembles "O Canada," "The Star-Spangled Banner," "Hatikvah": "*our* home and native land"; "what so proudly *we* hailed"; "to be a free people in *our* land."

Cohen's recitation would, he tells us, be an expression of solidarity with other Jews. The fact is, though, that not all inhabitants of Canaan or of Kishinev or of Brooklyn were/are Jews. Non-Jews too perished in Belsen. On what grounds, then, are the objects of Cohen's solidarizing characterized as Jews? "Because *they* express solidarity with other Jews" is worse than uninformative. The words of the protagonist of the Bible's Book of Ruth, a Moabite, voice an outsider's decision to join: "your people shall be my people, and your God my God" (1:16). The solidarizing is however compatible with remaining outside. If you don't pack your bags and depart *your* Moab, is your expression of solidarity with the factory workers of Bangladesh hypocritical?

"Fellow" in the first sentence of this section is problematic for Cohen; so is "other" in the first sentence of the paragraph just concluded. It's possible to express solidarity with Jews without expressing solidarity with *other* Jews. Nor must the solidarity be expressed with *fellow* Jews. Intending thereby to express solidarity, Cohen imagines himself reciting the Shema. He imagines that he does the imagining from a position inside the group. Cohen's inability to recite the Shema otherwise than as an expression of solidarity excludes him from the circle. That's my thesis. To be included, one must be able meaningfully to recite the Shema in a fuller sense. *Some* of the axis of worship has to be engaged. "What part?" Cohen asserts (20) that he is "cut off from the Jewish religion." I agree that this in and of itself isn't what bars the door. The inaccessibility of the prayer's operative part is what does it.

Fictional Assistance

Bernard Malamud's *The Assistant* furnishes a parallel from the shelves of fiction that supplies structure to this judgment of exclusion.

Having pistol-whipped a Jewish storekeeper, Frank Alpine finds himself ridden with guilt. To counter the paralysing effect, he casts in his lot with the victim. Apprenticing himself to the man, he eventually enters fully into the storekeeper's life of reversals and disappointments. Fully. Alpine submits himself to the physical procedure that being a Jew requires.

Is Alpine, at the end, a Jew? Ruth Wisse (2001, 16) characterizes the identity that Alpine takes on as Christian. This she does *in spite of what she understands Malamud himself to hold.* "In … *The Assistant*, a troubled Italian boy finds his spiritual father in a Jewish shopkeeper who interprets Judaism as an ethnic form of Christianity and says to his disciple 'I suffer for you.'"

Here is my reasoning for the same conclusion.

Christ, according to Christians, redeems the world's otherwise irredeemable sin. Racked by feelings of guilt, Christians identify with the redemptive act, the crucifixion. Suffering is after all what *they* deserve. From the Jewish perspective, human choice causes sin. Guilt and suffering (the concomitants of sin, as Alpine's case illustrates) aren't woven into the pattern of the creation.[5] From this perspective, the practical imperative is to eliminate the conditions in which sinful behaviour occurs. A hand is to be extended to the transgressor. Christians extend a hand too, but since their view is that we're all sinners, this is an act of *commiseration*. It's objectionable to tolerate suffering in someone else's life, outrageous to invite it into that place, and satanic to welcome it there. Yet from the Christian vantage point there is nothing objectionable in adherents seeking out trials of adherence. "Anyone whose faith is healthy … actively crave[s] instances in which that faith might be tested."[6] Asceticism is therefore an ideal, non-enactment of which aggravates in many their sense of personal unworthiness. In the Jewish frame, hair shirts, beds of nails, vows of silence, are discouraged. Backing, cultural and/or theological, is lacking for abnegations and penances. Life is not a pilgrimage; life's way is not a way of dolors.[7]

Malamud's assistant not only assists a person in pain. Having caused pain, he invites it into his own life.

The imagery resists a foot-of-Sinai construction. Alpine is accepting Calvary. Agreed, it's a stretch to figure the circumciser's clamp and scalpel as instruments of reform. But it's even harder to liken them to the cross and its nails.

Malamud, referring to the formalities of conversion, writes that Alpine becomes a Jew "after Passover." It's the wrong red-letter day. Easter is what it is.

Interpreting Cohen's autobiographical story is like interpreting Malamud's novel. When we first encounter Cohen, he is day to Alpine's night. Bearer of the most Jewish of surnames, Cohen speaks the language of Eastern European Jewry. Many Jews are friends and companions. "If it quacks like a duck?" Yet it may turn out that Cohen's Cohen, like Malamud's Alpine, is a bird of a different feather.

Three Terms, Not Two

Cohen distinguishes reciting the Shema as an expression of solidarity from reciting it with its core meaning: at first sight, and in Cohen's view, it is the (worshipful) acceptance of God. Cohen thinks himself entitled to "fellow" and "other." This begs the question against those who hold essential to status as a Jew the Shema's recitation in the second sense. To be sure, the proposition that it is essential in this sense isn't self-evident. But the argument for it hasn't yet been set out.

Cohen never questions his entitlement to "fellow" and "other." Here is the start of the autobiographical chapter: "I consider myself Jewish. But I do not believe in the God of the Old Testament. Some people, more especially some gentiles, find that strange. One purpose of what follows is to demonstrate how one might be very Jewish, yet cut off from the Jewish religion" (20).

What Cohen needs to demonstrate isn't what he says that he is undertaking to demonstrate. The two terms available to him aren't enough for doing the job.

An adherent to Christianity is a Christian. We can also say: "is Christian." An adherent to Judaism is ... what? One would naturally fill the blank with: "a Jew." Cohen was quoted to the effect that one might be Jewish without adhering to the Jewish religion. Doesn't this imply that a Jewish person might not be a Jew? "Isn't a person who is Jewish (*ipso facto*) a Jew?" The terminology stands in the way of answering negatively. Still, the three terms present here, "adherent to Judaism," "Jew," "person who is Jewish," can be arranged so as to leave at least verbal room for the response.[8]

Is Cohen an adherent to Judaism? He doesn't believe in God, nor does he feel guilty in breaking with the forms incumbent on adherents. Is Cohen Jewish? On his understanding, which I share, being Jewish is a broad cultural matter. In this respect, Cohen qualifies.

Being Jewish is a graduated thing. The cultural features might be salient; they might be recessive. What about being a Jew? My *Sprachgefühl* inclines me to resist the scale. If so, to be a Jew isn't the same as to be Jewish. But being a Jew isn't the same, either, as being an adherent to Judaism, which also has a binary logic.

Is Cohen a Jew? That's the question. Cohen says that he is. He says it because he allows – or, better, doesn't disallow – two-way traffic between "X is Jewish" and "X is a Jew." Being Jewish and being a Jew are not however linked so as to license the conversion.

Being an adherent to Judaism and being a Jew aren't the same. But neither is being a Jew the same as being Jewish. My thesis is that a Jew is one who can, meaningfully, recite the Shema. Meaningfully to recite the Shema one must accept part of what it is to be an adherent to Judaism. Which part? The part connected to the Shema.

If a non-believer can meaningfully recite the Shema, the reference to God is a way of saying something about men and women. Reflecting on their position in the world, men and women find that they do not fit seamlessly with the rocks and stones and trees. In portraying them as they do, the writers/thinkers are *indicating that*, not *explaining why*, they cannot be fully naturalized. The act of respiration is the writers'/thinkers' way of saying that men and women cannot be fully naturalized.

Cohen's Context

Jewish people like Cohen were a tiny fraction in Montreal during his formative years. The majority? Middle-class, Zionist, religion-friendly.

Because of the historical experiences and political circumstances of Montreal's non-Jewish population, the daily lives and modes of social organization of this majority group had many distinctive features. Once the causation of the features is understood, the life of Jewish people in Montreal is seen however to be typical enough of Jewish experience in urban North America.

The modes of institutional organization, the aspirations, the politics of the members of the group: all these reflected a broadly liberal outlook. To be sure, many outside the Jewish circle were like-minded. But for those within the circle, the outlook had a significant basis in what it is to be a Jew. I'll take up this point after commenting on several relevant characteristics of Jewish life in Montreal in Cohen's day.

Typically, Jewish Montrealers aspired to middle-class status. "Proletarian" would have been absurd as a characterization of those who made their living on the shop floors.[9] For the most part, those of lesser means participated alongside their better-heeled brethren in the life of the community. In absolute terms, the Jewish population was large. This wasn't therefore because their numbers couldn't have sustained separate institutions.[10]

A strain of leftism suffused the Montreal Jewish community. But like dye in water, it coloured all levels. And it did not originate in North America.

The older population of Jewish people in the 1940s and 1950s consisted largely of immigrants who landed in the 1920s and the 1930s. It was not uncommon for unassimilated non-religious Jewish youth in the countries of origin to belong to leftist or left-leaning Zionist organizations. The affiliation travelled to the New World. It had an appeal to the (usually younger) middle-class men and women in whom a streak of romanticism ran. Otherwise, it had little effect on middle-class existence.[11]

As is usual in Jewish communities, the community was strong in social organizations. *Ça va sans dire*: wealth redistribution was no part of their mandate.

A mild religious affiliation was typical of the Jewish Montrealer, as was an interest in parochial schooling. The breadth of the affiliation, and the degree of influence of the interest on personal choices, had a partly external source, social in the first case, institutional in the second.

Like much in Quebec's public sphere, the school system was structured along confessional lines. With rare exceptions, Jewish students who enrolled in Montreal's public system attended schools overseen by the city's Protestant School Board.

Neither Catholic nor Protestant elements in Montreal were friendly to the Jewish inhabitants. Protestants implemented exclusionary practices of the gentleman's agreement variety; Catholics did not shrink from overt anti-Semitism. The pressure to found separate institutions is under the circumstances no wonder.

As one would therefore expect, Jewish schooling wasn't primarily an expression of religiosity. In the parochial schools to which the middle-class sent their sons and daughters, attitudes towards Judaism varied. Despite its name, even in the Talmud Torah system the attitude was relaxed.[12] Similar remarks apply, *mutatis mutandis*, both to the organized forms of religiosity, as attests the failure of the Reform strain of Judaism in Montreal to attract members of Orthodox Synagogues, and to the Zionist element.[13]

Rather than lengthen this somewhat desultory list, I'll make my large point and move on.

Beneath the differences among Jewish people of cuisine, dress, aesthetic taste, degrees of religiosity, and so forth, are a few stable values: respect for learning; emphasis on family; commitment to institutions that offer relief to the less fortunate; moderation in the use of intoxicants. These are central for middle-class men and women. My claim is that their basis is in the inherited culture, not in the thought of the two Johns, Locke and Stuart Mill. It would be laughable to represent the founders of Jewish thought and life – Abraham, Moses, and/or the thinkers who write their lines – as liberals in the political sense. The operative element is a view of the person as an autonomous agent, a view that is at the heart of the Bible.[14]

Each of the listed values is a means of strengthening the integrity of the self. Learning enhances effectiveness as an agent. Ecstatic states blur the boundaries of the self. Excessive assistance eats away at autonomy and saps vitality. The supportive family is the supra-personal social environment in which the individual stands the best chance of developing.

Given Cohen's disaffection with the values of Jewish people in Montreal, it's plain, then, that the idea of Jewishness informing his (true) self-description runs tangential to philosophical questions of human nature.

Cohen, born in 1941, matriculated at Oxford in 1961. The years are significant from a Jewish perspective. The early 1960s were a short decade and a half after the war. If during his first years in England Cohen was at all alive to the recent experience of the Jews of Europe, there is no sign of it.[15] The shift of consciousness occurred in 1967, when, as it initially seemed, the State of Israel hung in the balance. The strength of Cohen's emotional reaction took him by surprise. Not that the events sparked the Zionism that he had from early on repudiated. What welled up was, rather, the sense that the men and women under existential threat were his brethren.[16] Whatever this sense of connectedness amounted to, it couldn't have been like Ruth's with Naomi. Ruth's has to do with the biblical declaration that the Lord is one.

An Unattractive God?

"The God of the Old Testament" Cohen (40) finds "unattractive." From the word "unattractive," the reader would guess that the sources of the revulsion are the irascibility, the long memory for slights, and so forth. "I the Lord your God am a jealous God, punishing children for the iniquity of parents, to the third and fourth generation of those who reject me" (Exodus 20:5).[17] Cohen has something else in mind. "According to Hegel, the Jewish conception of a God set over and against men is a primitive one" (84). The exposition continues – and this now is Cohen speaking for himself: "The advent of Christianity signifies great progress, for it brings the realization that God, to *be* God, must express Himself in a world, and in a world of men, of finite spirits." *This* is why he finds the God of (what he repeatedly calls) the Old Testament unattractive.

Pace Cohen, as I'll explain in a moment, a clear sense exists in which the deity of the Tanakh is (1) present in the world of finite men, and (2) present in that finitude. This finite presentness is, indeed, crucial to the Shema.

Cohen's upbringing substituted Hegel for Hebrew and replaced Moses with Marx. His social environment and intellectual formation disadvantaged him, then, to understand the Shema. "Didn't Cohen make the trek from scientific history to normative political theory?" His philosophical thinking about Jews and Judaism continued however to be influenced by Hegel and Marx. Strip off the dialectical element, and the mature philosophical anthropology is revealed to be much the same as Cohen's in his earlier years.

Hegel's complaint about "the Jewish conception of God" (I move on now to substance) perpetuates a misunderstanding.[18] Jewish thought disallows God's presence in the world in the Christian way. The fact remains, however, that God, according to the Hebrew Scriptures, does enter into the world of finite men and women. *In creating the first man, God puts something of himself into the (finite) creature; something that gets transmitted to the first woman, and through the couple to each and every one of us.* Not that we alone among living things are *God's* creatures. But into us, and into us alone, God has breathed the breath, his breath, of life.

Cohen quotes Genesis 1:26–7. Acknowledging that the verses are not easy, he asserts, with mild inconsequentiality therefore, that "surely [they] mean … at least three things" (82). One, Cohen says, is this. "[God] did not produce a perfect replica of himself in creating man: the metaphor of the 'image' conveys that man is not on a par with God" (ibid.). Not on a par? What, then, about Genesis 5:3? "When Adam had lived one hundred and thirty years, he became the father of a son in his likeness, according to his image, and named him Seth." Like father, like son. So verses 26 and 27 arguably do not mean what Cohen says. In fact, God isn't even described as creating man in Genesis 1. The verb in 1:26–7 differs from the verb in 1:1. The NRSV renders the earlier verb "create," the later one "make."

Cohen is an acute analyst. That the sentence from page 82 is illogical tells of muddle. In Genesis 1, God makes mankind, not a man. Observe the pronoun "them" in verse 27. A replica of God cannot be a kind; it has to be, like God, a non-general thing.

To determine whether Hegel has a point, a proper sense is needed of God's presence in the Tanakh. Lacking such a sense, Cohen is in no position to understand the Shema's meaning – surely a precondition for meaningfully reciting (or declining to recite) it.

God of Abraham: A Lighter Look at the Shema

Chapter 7 of *If You're an Egalitarian* consists of one paragraph. Cohen explains to readers that in this portion of his presentation – the book is based on the 1996 Gifford Lectures – he invited the audience to join in singing a few popular songs that give a light perspective on "how bad things can be good" (116). I've dealt with the Shema in earlier chapters. Taking my cue from Cohen's performance, I shall, in this section, use a poem to make the point. Fortuitously, the point is that what we regard as the worst thing isn't as bad as it seems.

The link with death is internal to the Shema's meaning. In words resembling the Shema's, Ruth makes the link. The treatment of mortality in the opening chapters of Genesis disturbs many who read the Bible. If, as Christian exegesis holds, we men and women are at fault for what befalls us, what's the point of reciting "God is our God" in its connection? If, contrariwise, death is inevitable because of God, wouldn't it make more sense to say that we declare our faith *in spite of that*?

Pace the Christian line, the Bible's view is that death awaits us because of what we are, not because of what we do and/or what our forebears did, and that we could not have been created differently. Thankfulness is due because our existences have positive value.[19] If the price for not dying is not existing, would you pay?

In Philip Larkin's "The Trees," the poet reacts with anguish at the trees coming into leaf:

> Is it that they are born again
> And we grow old?

A negative answer is given.

> No, they die too

The tree brings forth new leaves each spring, while the hair that we lose isn't replaced. Appearances notwithstanding, there is parity. Hair loss might be used to calibrate the chronology of a person; for trees, we count "the rings of grain." Is the poet consoled?

As the Bible sees it, appearances are closer to reality than Larkin's poem allows. Consider verses 5–7 from Chapter 1 of Ecclesiastes:

> The sun rises and the sun goes down,
>   and hurries to the place where it rises.
>
> The wind blows to the south,
>   and goes around to the north;
> round and round goes the wind,
>   and on its circuits the wind returns.
>
> All streams run to the sea,
>   but the sea is not full;
> to the place where the streams flow,
>   there they continue to flow.

Extra-human nature is a perpetual cycle of exchange of matter and energy. An accurate conceptualization figures the tree as one part of an interconnected whole, the forest, and the forest as bound up with the natural system. Extra-human nature whirls round and round, a system of exchanges that sometimes, for long periods, is, like a forest, in balance.[20]

Ecclesiastes's assertion that the sun shines on the nothing new is a fine piece of analysis. The analysis does not however apply to men and women. The man's creation in Genesis 2 is a genuine beginning. It's surprising that commentators miss this. Genesis 1 is full of "good." In Genesis 2, God says that it is "no good" that the man should be alone.

This is explanatory of the Shema. Our existence is of beings that really begin and that really end. In Larkin's view, the tree's annual renewal offers a model for coping with the inevitable. "Begin afresh, afresh, afresh." The Bible's more philosophical position is that it's our mortality that marks us as special among creatures. Because we die, we live too – in a way that a tree cannot.[21] The Bible would characterize Larkin's prescription for the initial despondency as an opiate. "The Trees" is a deathless poem, though.

Both predicate terms in the Shema are theoretically active. God is *our God* in a way that God is not the deity of trees. God is *one* in the sense that God is responsible for our genuine entity-hood. That entity-hood resists the principles that govern the system to which the trees belong.

Why, then, according to the Bible, do we die? *Because we are not just parts of nature.* Like God, we are extra-natural: we in part, God wholly. And God is responsible (in the biblical narrative) for our status.[22]

We appreciate now why recitation of the Shema is appropriate for the dying; and why, were that possible, for the newborn too. The real beginning that is birth; the real ending that is death; these are in the world because (in a sense) of God. God's breath of life is the kiss of death. Is it a blessing to the tree that it doesn't die? Ecclesiastes comes close to Sartrean nausea at the condition.

The Shema is theologically attired philosophical anthropology. "The Lord is our God" asserts that paganism is mistaken: "Baal is not our god," "Marduk is not our god," "Zeus is not our god." "The Lord is one" identifies *why* the worship of the other gods is objected to. Underpinning the worship is a mistaken self-understanding. Men and women are separate from nature in their mode of being. Each of them is, in a word, *one*, as is God, according to the Shema. As to the issue of death: each of us does end. The one-ness is a precondition. An expression of the acceptance of God as "our God" is appropriate to that limited experience.

The Bible's Conception of History and Cohen's

Socialism and liberalism are in agreement on basic human nature. Communism, contrasting with both, extends to us the system-character of the natural realm. What I said above of the natural case is what Marxists say in the social/historical sphere. The shift from the class-ridden to the class-free is like the metamorphosis of a grub.

The long story is too long for this chapter. I'll conclude by contrasting the biblical view and the Marxist one at one point on which, on the Marxist side, Cohen comments critically. Then I'll identify what it is in Cohen the normative political theorist that, despite his departure from the Marxist fold, is at odds with the Shema.

In Chapter 3 of his book, "The Development of Socialism from Utopia to Science," Cohen exposes (in both senses) the Marxist position that the shift in ideas about society is a function of shifts in the modes of production. It follows that ideas critical of the extant economic arrangements do not emerge until the productive modes cease to suit the needs that up to that time they satisfied. The claim is then made that the means for transforming the modes so that in their new form they suit the new needs will emerge from within the circumstances of breakdown. Cohen points out an ambiguity in "no longer suited." The phrase can mean "unsuited" in an absolute sense. In this sense, a mode can be "no longer suited" without a replacement being available. "If, on the other hand, 'no longer suited' means 'less well suited than some other mode,' then, by definition, a superior mode is possible. But," Cohen concludes (56), "on this comparative understanding of 'no longer suited,' a mode could now be awful, yet *not* 'no longer suited,' since it might be true that nothing better than it is now feasible."

The Bible considers shifts in modes of production. Also, it provides a template for thinking about socio-economic change. The episode of Cain and Abel sees farming supplant shepherding. The rooting out of shepherding, one might think, is inevitable. Population size could however be restricted. How does the normative voice of the Bible react to Cain's fallen countenance? "If you do well, will you not be accepted?" (Genesis 4:6). In other words: "Perhaps in the future your sacrifice will be found pleasing." Then again, perhaps not.

There's no sense of inevitability here. Even when the pressure for change seems irresistible, acceptance of the outcome is not assured.[23] Two requirements, both anchored in what the Bible understands to be basic human nature, have to be met. Those who are superseded must be reintegrated. NO ONE LEFT BEHIND. *That* identifies what is wrong with Cain: the insouciance of "am I my brother's keeper?" No such change can be accepted if human flourishing gets compromised. NOT EVERYTHING GOES. Both requirements are anchored in the Bible's claim that what counts is the life of each person, a claim whose theological expression is God's breathing his life into the first person.[24]

God, then, *pace* Hegel, does express an ideal valid among us finite actors: the intrinsic value of the particular person. This is the principle of the Bible's normative position in politics – about what is just. The position the Bible endorses, then, is individualistic in ontology and liberal in attitude. What is acceptable down here, and what will "be accepted" by the biblical character called "God," has got to respect the integrity of the particular person.

The working-class men and women in Cohen's Montreal who identified themselves as Jews (not only as Jewish) would have agreed; the more so once the theological note is muted.

Consider Cohen's remark about God's presence in the world of finite spirits. God, he is saying, is an ideal for men and women, an ideal for them to realize as best they can in their lives. This is a view alien to the Tanakh. God is present in that each of us is a particular. Our lives, of the God-type, are our own. We try to figure out what to do with the particular entity-hood of ours; how comport ourselves as family members; how arrange our communal affairs; how do politics. The way of a Jew is to come up with *modi vivendi* that, both with regard to our personal conduct, and with regard to our social and political lives, respect the separate entity-hood. Not to do so is to infringe our Godliness. The *modi vivendi* acknowledge, in practical terms, what the Bible dramatizes as God's breath of life in us.

Also, the *modi vivendi* aren't implementations of a divine plan. There isn't any such plan, only negotiable ideas about how to live – ideas informed by the non-negotiable idea of what we are. A person who claims to have access to such a plan is a false prophet.[25]

With all this, Cohen's early communitarian views don't sort. His later political philosophy, *luck egalitarianism*, also infringes our Godliness. Unquestionably, *how* each of us is is a function of contingencies and accidents (in short: luck) for which no credit is due us and no blame. That does not mean that the same is true for *what* each of us is, unless by that you mean that we might not have been born. What we are is a function of God; that is a necessity. Cohen's way sinks the *what* into the *how*. Godless ways of thinking result.

It's a wake-up call to a reconsideration of the Bible to observe that the mortality of men and women is in its view anchored in God's extra-natural status. Men and women are finite sharers of that status. Mortality is the temporal aspect of finitude.

If that which is essential to being a Jew is available to any, it is available to all. Many take the essential condition as granted. For these, no act of conversion is necessary.[26] What many of these many do not appreciate is that the view comes out of the biblical context. As to the Shema's being heard only where adherents to Judaism congregate, the reason is, arguably, a historical one that does not stand in the way of generalizing the creedal declaration. At the start of his mission, in Beer-sheba, Abraham addressed all available ears – which are represented as few in number. Finding the wider world cool to his message, Abraham turned inwards. In the shade of his tamarisk tree, the tree of distinctively human life, only Abraham's kin, and a few who, like Ruth, chose to shelter there, were to be found at the start.[27] Being a Jew came thereby to be associated with living according to the complex system of practice that makes one an adherent to Judaism.

Appendix: Jewish Philosophy and the Jewish Philosophers

The deity of the Bible, God, is the principle of particularity. The one-ness stated in the Shema is a theologically couched assertion of the thesis that each person is a separate entity. Monotheism thus has to do at heart with philosophical anthropology.[28] The most important scene in the Bible is the Genesis 2 scene depicting the creation of the first man. This is the Bible's representation, in the genetic terms that the formulators default to, of the separateness from the natural world of what would elsewise be a piece of it. The Shema asserts that God is the principle behind men and women. The meaning is that men and women, in their one-ness, resist capture by natural principles. While constantly affected by and in interaction with it, the man's identity is not a function of the system. As God is outside nature, so, *mutatis mutandis,* are each man and each woman.

Isn't this, *pace* Cohen, an expression of God's presence in the world of men and women; of, indeed, God's presence in their finitude?[29] The target of the biblical thinkers is, metaphysically, of the same genus as Cohen's ideology. In paganism, the individual is sunk in nature and its laws, in Marxism, in class and its dialectical principles. Both positions are anti-humanist.

Although I won't develop the links here, I will connect my reading of the Shema with the positions of modern Jewish thinkers who operate in a philosophical mode. As I see it, they are out of touch with the core expression of the issue.

Jewish thinkers down the ages who hanker after philosophy typically call upon Greek-based philosophical sources to work out the principles of the biblical worldview. The Bible *is*, I counter, a philosophical work; although the philosophy, not exposed in the mode of argumentation, doesn't look the part to the men and women within the ivied walls.

I developed the critique of Cohen in biblical terms. The critique's core is philosophical anthropology. The position taken explains the meaning of the Shema. The critique is possible because the Bible has a philosophy of its own. Unless you operate on the philosophical level, you cannot without appeal to elsewhere have a position in philosophical anything.

To elsewhere the Jewish philosophers appeal. Levinas speaks, correctly, of "a principle ... about which Greece [knows] nothing" (1998, 201). Then, incorrectly, he adds: "Jewish particularity still awaits its philosophy." Thus the need for Jewish thinkers "to express [it] in Greek." The Bible contains a philosophical position, not just a series of thoughts receptive to philosophical development.

The criticism that applies to Levinas applies to Philo, to Maimonides, to Hermann Cohen. Jewish thinkers must learn, as philosophers, to speak Hebrew. Their reverence for *the* philosophers raises a pointed question. To what extent are their positions Jewish?

Let's stick with Levinas's position. Its heart is an elemental face-to-face encounter in which the other's need commands a response that one's own need cannot modify. This is ethical bedrock.[30] Levinas is insistent that the elemental encounter occurs on a level beneath the level of generalizations like "Do unto others," of which "Why?" can be asked.

Is the position a Jewish one? I think not. Not that the position cannot be motivated from within Jewish experience. The Holocaust, which Levinas experienced, is an obvious springboard. Think of the reaction of an Allied soldier upon first encountering a concentration camp inmate. The response would be as Levinas says: assist immediately, assist unqualifiedly.

What about (Leviticus 19:18) "love your neighbour as yourself"? On Levinas's gloss the imperative conforms with his philosophy. "Love your neighbour; he is yourself" (1998, 90). Levinas wants to deny that the Bible's position is based on self-love. But to say that I must love myself differs from saying that I am self-interested. The obligation to love myself may be based on the fact that I am a person, a self, and that people, selves, have intrinsic value.

There is a non-apocalyptic environment outside the palliative care unit in which what Levinas says grips. The child in the nursery requires us, period. But the biblical story most closely mirroring the circumstance, the story of the garden of Genesis 2, shows God testing the man and the woman, who are figured as children. If it seems that the Bible thinks it okay to set children up for a fall, this is only because several balls are being juggled. That the episode holds innocents to an impossible standard signals how biblically normative the idea of the autonomy of the person is.

"Thus you shall say to [the Israelites]," God instructs Moses, "I AM has sent me to you." The Bible's thrust is to secure the position of the particular, whose self-identification is the same. Leviticus 19 contains something that Levinas omits.

> ... you shall love your neighbour as yourself: I am the Lord.

The end is not an appeal to authority. It's an appeal to the ontological basis. God, as I said, is the principle of particularity. Not "it is," but "I AM."

The love of which the Bible is the wisdom is tough love.

13

"O God, O Montreal!"[1]:
Charles Taylor and Turbocharged Humanism

Ideology and Geography

The mountain from which Montreal derives its name dominates the island that the city occupies. The positions on religion of the three Montreal natives encountered in these pages connect to Mount Royal's three peaks – each to a different peak. Charles Taylor's academic home at McGill University situates him on the south slope of Colline de la Croix, named from the monument that was raised on its highest point in the early days of French settlement. The foot of the cross's current version is the very site for the devout Catholic. Jerry Cohen's formative years were spent in the neighbourhood on the plateau to the east of Colline d'Outremont. In this "working-class Jewish part of Montreal" (Cohen 2000, 11) memorialized by Mordecai Richler, Cohen acquired the attitude towards religious belief that appertains to Marxism. Affiliated to the liberal and humanistic strain of their religion that prevailed among the Jews who constituted a significant percentage of the middle-class area's inhabitants, the author lived his early years a short hike north of Westmount Summit, halfway between two shrines to which the faithful made pilgrimages to sustain body and soul: the outsize sphere of Gibeau Orange Julep on Décarie Boulevard and, on Queen Mary Road, the pile of St Joseph's Oratory topped by its massive cupola.[2]

Three Montrealers, three philosophers, three areas of the city each at the base of a different one of the three peaks, three philosophy-informed views of the locus of value in the lives of men and women: transcendent, socio-economic, humanistic.[3]

In "Jerry and Jewry," I advocated for the position on belief beneath Westmount Summit against that of the area that Colline d'Outremont overlooks.

Here I critically examine the position in the lee of Colline de la Croix. The irony won't be lost. On the earlier occasion the charter of the Jewish people was turned against a person who considered himself very Jewish. The present critical target is a Catholic whose faith has a Mosaic basis. Had my arguments about the Bible persuaded Cohen that his philosophical commitments bar recitation of the Shema, he would, I imagine, ruefully have shrugged. Taylor cannot so easily finesse failure to appreciate the Bible's philosophy.

Taylor on Secularism

The target of Taylor's *A Secular Age* is *exclusive humanism*, a position that he links in the way of identity with Western (non-absurdist) anti-theism. Who are the exclusive humanists? The men and women who hold that value for men and women lies within the circuit of the human.

Many in our midst declare themselves exclusive humanists. The higher of profile – for example Christopher Hitchens – emphasize with crusading fervour that their natures, duties, and destinies are understood without reference to God.

Taylor's thesis, worked out through an enquiry into the emergence of the modern secular cultural ensemble, can be capsuled thus. (1) Modern secularism carries in it more than a trace residue of the explicitly religious way of thinking that it supersedes. (2) The carry-over is essential to the ensemble's identity. The combination of (1) and (2) means that modern secularism is not exclusively humanistic. As Taylor sees it, many who profess exclusive humanism, even perhaps the majority, are exclusive humanists in name alone.

As *I* see it, Judeo-Christianity, in its teachings about men and women, is a humanism. Sufficiently unto our purposes, here is a sketch of the position the endorsement of which connects me to a different mountain than Taylor's Colline de la Croix.

In the story of the genesis of men and women, the thinkers behind the Bible set out the view that the human sector is alien to (extra-human) nature. Since paganism was at the time the only ism in town, what is advanced *is* – and is presented as such – epoch-making, though most who address its revolutionary character miss its philosophical character.[4]

The biblical conception of men and women resembles the conception that informs the charter documents of the American Republic. On what took place at the inception, and on how and why what took place was significant to the American Revolution but not to the later one in Russia, the documents leave us guessing.

The *aperçu* of the Bible's thinkers is that human beings are not entirely natural. The depiction of God enlivening the first man conveys the thought that men and women have in them something of the extra-natural.[5] My subtitular phrase refers to the breath of life with which God inspires what he "formed … from the dust of the ground" (Genesis 2:7). "Turbocharged humanism" doesn't label a model of humanism that *contrasts with* a naturally aspirated model. It's pleonastic.

Taylor's claim is that if you scratch a self-styled exclusive humanist, a residually religious person will be revealed. In my view, there are no honest-to-goodness exclusive humanists, only self-styled ones. "Exclusive humanism" is an oxymoron, like "religious atheism."[6]

Humanism is *the* issue between (Western) non-believers and believers. That (as I read the Bible) is how the thinkers behind the Bible view it. Millennia away from modern atheism, they express themselves, however, as the times dictate. Paganism and atheism connect internally in one direction. Modern atheists hold that reality is exhausted by its natural part. So the Bible is against atheism because atheism consorts with naturalism. The straight existential question regarding God is a side issue.

I will develop the thesis via a critical discussion of Taylor's book. Central to the discussion is a striking episode in the Bible to which Taylor refers, a dramatization of the rejection of the other gods.[7]

Effects and Causes

A Secular Age reads as abstract sociological analysis eked out on one side by real-world history and by intellectual history on the other. Tackling religiosity in sociological terms is sensible. Religiosity doesn't come down to one's profession of belief in the existence of a deity. Social and institutional forms and modes of expression are also ingredients. But Taylor talks about religion too. "A reading of 'religion' in terms of the distinction transcendent/immanent is going to serve our purposes here" (15).

To transpose this talk, professional philosopher's talk, onto the level of institutional arrangements, characteristic symbols, social practices, and the like would require a Rylean *The Concept of God*.

Ontology is where the action is. Although the action can be illuminated from the social and the institutional angles, such lighting leaves the face of the thing in shadows. Why does Taylor proceed back-to-front? It's because in the last analysis religion is not his focus.

Commenting on the claim quoted above, Taylor states that "defining religion in terms of the distinction transcendent/immanent is a move tailormade for our culture" (16). "For *our* culture" means "for Western culture." The transcendent factor – an extra-natural entity, a state of being apart from space and time – is foreign to a belief-system like Buddhism. Approaching the matter from the standpoint of religiosity, a standpoint not specifically Western or Eastern, Taylor therefore at least soft-pedals the ontological matter.

The approach via religiosity has the potential to beg the question against philosophy *qua* "science" of fundamentals. As the following scenario illustrates, religiosity doesn't require religion.

Driving on the left side of the road and driving on the right side are functionally indistinguishable. Crossing over wouldn't change the degree of difficulty of getting from here to there. But Buddhists might say that in worshipping God their Christian counterparts are driving over an existential precipice. In effect, the Buddhists are here charging the Catholics with religiosity without religion. They go through the motions. They feel the emotions. Yet they are out of touch with the underlying notions.

At first sight, Taylor's attitude towards Buddhism seems ecumenical. But if ecumenism underpins his soft-pedalling of the ontology, that's a problem. Tolerating the follies of others is often the price of social harmony. Pretending that fools are sages is itself folly. With a few shrugs of the shoulders, latitudinarianism can slouch into appeasement.

Reading *A Secular Age*, one little gets the sense that Taylor is bending over backward. These Cassandrine sayings, that is, seem alarmist. What looks like an easy-going attitude is more an effect than the cause of the emphasis on religiosity (and hence the de-emphasis on religion). As much as I differ from Taylor regarding religion, I agree that the tent of religiosity is wide enough for saffron robes *and* cassocks. Buddhism in its culture and Catholicism in its are functionally similar. The same functional thing is visible in a subculture like soccer, with its saints and its shrines, its dress codes and rest-day rituals.

Religiosity does not seem, then, to have an essence. The same may not be inferred about religion. Should it be objected that that which is found on the level of custom and practice only deserves to be called "religiosity" if it is rooted in religion ("soccer is a 'religion,' not a religion"), that reinforces my point. Where otherwise than in passing does Taylor discuss religion?

We are still no wiser as to why Taylor places religiosity first. A line that I'll now quote from the book gives us a leg up.

"[Distinctions like the immanent/transcendent distinction] have been reconstructed or redefined in the very process of modernity" (ibid.). Taylor is talking here not of a contrast like that between Christianity and Buddhism, but of one within the frame of a single faith's historical career. The clear implication is that a common ontological denominator is unlikely to be found when one looks at the manifestations of (say) identifiably Christian religiosity through time. This, if so, is a stronger point than the point that Buddhism differs from Christianity.

As in the previous case, what Taylor says here is, I think, more effect than cause. The measure of independence it does have is only on the side of method. Since the methodological basis is flimsy, there is more to the story. That's the good news for Taylor. The bad news is that the other part is problematic too.

The Continental Style

Taylor's discussion is very much in the Continental mode. His treatment mixes phenomenology and historicism.

Phenomenology itself is not by nature anti-essentialist. The objective of Edmund Husserl, its modern seminal thinker, is to isolate the invariant structures of experience. Nonetheless, phenomenology does by its nature focus on things from the side of consciousness, rather than from the side of the things that are *taken up* through consciousness.

The addition of the historical dimension complicates the defence of essences. The quintessentialist, Plato, does not deny that the timeless Forms have temporal (contextual) reflections. The Forms are an integral part of the metaphysical analysis of appearance. But so much is the flux at odds with their immutability that Plato works overtime to prevent the Forms themselves from being implicated in temporality.[8]

For historicists, time isn't only the scene of truth. Although this does not preclude their endorsing essentialist positions, their accounts tend towards anti-essentialism. Nietzsche's genealogical approach has been influential in this regard. The corrosive critique of Western truth and rationality that it generated led, by a tangle of byways, to post-structuralism and deconstruction.

Here is an illustration of the Nietzschean approach in an instance where its aptness can't be denied. The illustration brings into relief the difficulties that confront one who, like Taylor, offers an essentialist position from the Continental perspective.

Baseball is played according to the rules. It's foolish to represent the rulebook as more than a stabilization of one phase of a living organism. The designated hitter rule cannot be lamented for adulterating the game. Still, the sacrifice of versatility could reasonably be deplored. "What next? Field players who do not know what it's like to strike the rock with a staff?" When genetic treatment is appropriate, sociological sensitivity is appropriate too. In some ages, specialization might be rated above versatility; in others, the jack-of-all-trades might be king.

"Baseball is a religion." That claim is sometimes heard. It would be better to say, then, that a halo of religiosity surrounds more rabid instances of baseball fandom.

A single at-bat does not make a summer. Our question is whether *religion* has an essence. Taylor's sociological approach inclines him against thinking ontologically. I haven't been trying in this section to establish that the ontological matter is basic to our issue, only to give a sense of the friendliness of the Continental way of doing philosophy to the sociological approach. Because Taylor operates in the phenomenological style, he is unlikely to see the prominence of sociological analysis as occulting an ontological level.[9]

Taylor (who is critical of post-structuralism and deconstruction) should be more essentialist in the non-historicist way with regard to religion. His error is about *where* the action is, not about *what* it is. Is the preceding diagnosis accurate? That can be debated. There is also the point, which I have so far merely stated, that religion has an essence.

There are signs that the sociological approach belies Taylor's underlying view. One is his critical attitude towards Judaism, another, his stress on the human element.

Given Taylor's warmth towards Buddhism, one expects openness to Judaism, the more so given the Montrealer's proximity to Jews. The expectation is disappointed. To exemplify the difference between the Jew and the Christian, Taylor quotes the story of the Samaritan. The Gospel is critical of the Jews for responding only to the need of their co-religionists. On what grounds is this objectionable? *You* may not like it, but if it's another practice, with an us-and-them attitude at its base, how can the criticism stick? The criticism, like the defence, requires more for its validity than the facts of practice or the needs of social lubricant. Anyway, some might regard a modicum of friction as enlivening. *Taylor is imputing to the Jews some kind of mistake.*[10] This is a betrayal of what he says about the reconstruction/redefinition. *The basis of his criticism is surely ontological.* The Jews of the time can be charged with mistreating people because, Taylor is saying, of what people are and what this entails in the matter of personal relations. This may be so. But on the level of practice, there is in the conduct of the Jews nothing to criticize.[11] That women are people does not mean they should suit up in Yankee pinstripes. So whatever the criticism is, it goes beyond the matter of religiosity.[12]

Taylor contrasts the crucifixion of Jesus and the execution of Socrates. "Unless living the full span were a good, Christ's giving himself to death couldn't have the meaning that it does. In this it is utterly different from Socrates's death, which the latter portrays as leaving this condition for a better one" (*A Secular Age*, 17). Plato's transcendent complementation demotes human life. Real value is elsewhere.[13]

Since alternatives exist (Cohen's Marxism stresses classes), Taylor's got some justifying to do. It's not enough that he accepts human life to be of basic value. Why is Platonism, which differs from Taylor's Catholicism on this, mistaken? The Bible addresses the matter in telling of God breathing life into the first man and in describing the transgression in Eden. Taylor is silent about God's nature. He goes no further than to describe God's functioning.[14] The problem, as I see it, is that he does not understand the god of Abraham. He is interested in the wrong thing.

Fullness

Taylor focuses on religiosity, which he understands in functional terms. This makes the sociological analysis appropriate. But Taylor says more. The key idea here is the idea of *fullness*. This is how Taylor gets God into his picture.

For Taylor, the modern secular ensemble is the confluence of three negative streams, each of which developed through a slow but steady erosion, from about 1500 onwards, of an "enchanted" view of the world: the *removal* of God from public spaces; the *emptying* out of places of worship; the option of frank *disavowal* of belief. Here's Taylor's telegram. "First, science gave us 'naturalistic' explanation of the world. And then people began to look for alternatives to God" (26). This "'subtraction' story" (ibid.) Taylor rejects.

Immediately relevant to our issue is Taylor's singling out the third element as the real marker of the modern ensemble as secular. But what is it to disavow belief? It's to say that God (something transcendent) does not exist. By implication, it's to say that immanence is all. "Disavow" is hazardous here to the truth. *The disavowing* isn't what counts. That can consist in person's absenting themselves from a place of worship. *What's disavowed* is what counts. This has to do, primarily, with religion. It's claimed that there is no religious subject-matter as there is no phlogiston. I make this remark because it supports my view that Taylor treats God functionally – a cardinal sin against the Bible.

We come here to fullness. I will show that Taylor's account of this crucial notion begs the question against the Bible.

Religious attitudes, according to Taylor, are rooted in the sense that many men and women have had, and continue to have, that human reality, taken as self-contained as to value and meaning, is a pale thing, shallow, inane. "Is that all there is?" as Peggy Lee sings. Institutionalized religion with its forms and usages is the frame within which filler has traditionally been supplied. The varieties of spirituality that have mushroomed of late as the old forms have withered also testify, as Taylor points out, to dissatisfaction with the quotidian.

Fullness, a load-bearing pillar of Taylor's discussion, is not a clear notion. Would Taylor also look down on a person at whose pleasures the élite sneer? What malicious spirit powers the dismissal as trivial the pursuits to which the person is given? Mightn't private envy feed the contempt? Regretful of self-exclusion from the activities, they belittle those who partake. To speak of "real satisfaction" here is to beg the question. This is not *ipso facto* to endorse wholly material measures of success. But let's be fair. Looking back, many who have made good materially derive satisfaction from what the resources enable. Typical bucket-list items are activities so far forgone in a workaday life: a trip to the East, hang-gliding in the Andes, dining at El Cellar de Can Roca. Few list service in an orphanage, reading the whole of Proust, donating blood.

The murkiness of the notion of fullness notwithstanding, observe how it verbally associates with Taylor's "reading of 'religion' in terms of the distinction transcendent/immanent." Talk of fullness suggests that one must *exit* the sphere of the immanent, move *outside* it. One must *fill out* what is missing.

We don't only speak of *filling out*; we also speak, as idiomatically, of *filling in*. The superficiality that Taylor decries could be a failure not of breadth (I am out of touch with God), but of depth (I am out of touch with myself). Taylor's mention of the immanent/transcendent contrast should not be allowed to do the deciding between the two, especially as he supplies only a functional account of God, an account of a rather Feuerbachian sort.

Taylor's core point about the modern secular ensemble is this: the structure of religiosity is *from* a feeling of lack *to* what fills it. Taylor's discussion makes extensive use of this structure. The phases of European thought (Descartes and rationality, Goethe and Romanticism, Kant and moral self-legislation) are represented as ways of refilling the vacancy created by the world's disenchantment. The structure is thus maintained. "The structure of *religiosity*." Could it not be the structure of *religion*? Could it not be the ontology that is retained? Taylor fuses the structures, assigning priority to religiosity. The God-function isn't ontologized. The ontology is functionalized.

"Unless living the full span were a good, Christ's giving himself to death couldn't have the meaning that it does. In this it is utterly different from Socrates' death, which the latter portrays as leaving this condition for a better one." Observe Taylor's "full." Fullness is ascribed to a human life. This is more like my sense (and, I hold, the biblical sense) than it is like the person's whose words were quoted.

A failure to see a difference for what it is powers the increasingly Scholastic attempts of naturalists and reductionists to burrow to a common denominator. They are superficially profound out of profound superficiality. Taylor, profoundly superficial out of superficial profundity, doesn't correct them. His sociologically inflected discussion substitutes the cart for the horse.

Taylor begins his genesis story of secularism with Latin Christendom. He traces the shift from the hierarchical structuring that the Church clamped on society to the flattened secularity of modernity, arguing that the shadow of the structure – the "residue" of religiosity – remains.[15]

European culture's inheritance from the Bible is more solid than this spume upon a ghostly paradigm. The inheritance, the Western conception of what men and women are (*this* is the horse), has, moreover, no hierarchicality about it. God's position at the apex of a theological pyramid is irrelevant to it, as, therefore, are the associated social structures (*these* are the cart).

In his valedictory oration (Deuteronomy 30:12) Moses tells the Israelites that what he is offering "is not in [the] heavens, that you should say, 'Who will go

up … for us, and get it for us so that we may hear it and observe it?'" Yet Moses
ascends a mountain, doesn't he? Let's leave Mount Royal for another high place,
there to consider the apparent inconsistency.

"A hairy man with a leather belt"

Elijah, the biblical character associated with Mount Carmel, carried out his
mission during the reign of Ahab, who "did evil in the sight of the Lord"
(1 Kings 16:30). Pitting the prophet of God against "the four hundred fifty
prophets of Baal and the four hundred prophets of Asherah" (18:18), the contest
on the Carmel is a distillate of the biblical revolution. The story is less allusive
than Abraham's story, also the story of a person at a crossroads. To extract the
message, I will proceed by drawing out a similarity between Elijah and a well-
known figure of Christian ceremonial.

Elijah figures in the festival commemorating the exodus from Egypt. Towards
the end of the celebration the front door of each house is opened and the celebrants, having placed for him at the centre of the Seder table a brimming cup
of wine, sing a welcome to the prophet, expressing hope for the messiah's arrival
"speedily, in our time." In the (supposed) historical event on which Passover is
based, Elijah has no part. It's the same with Santa Claus and Christmas. The
custom in the Christian case is also to set out refreshment for an unseen guest,
who passes over no house in which the festival is marked. Nor is this all. Elijah
is described as "a hairy man with a leather belt around his waist" (2 Kings 1:8).
Add a few pounds and a jolly mien, and such a one could do a December stint
in the mall. Indeed, aren't both Elijah and Santa Claus associated with animal-
drawn carriages that fly – a sleigh and reindeer, a chariot of fire harnessed to
fiery steeds?[16]

Santa Claus brings gifts – an excellent way to impress the young. On a more
abstract plane, what Santa Claus brings corresponds to God's gift to men and
women. Elijah also brings a gift. What gift? To extract the answer we must
appreciate that Elijah, with one important difference, stands to the central figure of the Torah, Moses, as Santa Claus stands to the magi and to God. The
business of Santa Claus can be seen as infantilizing the Christmas message;
redemption does not come gift-wrapped. In Elijah's case, the connection is
internal to core Hebrew scripture.

Fire and Rain on the Mountain

Declaring himself the only prophet of the Lord left, Elijah challenges the Israelites. "How long will you go limping with two different opinions?" (1 Kings 18:21).
The prophets of Baal, four hundred fifty in number, agree to a winner-take-all
contest.

Elijah sets the rules.

> Let two bulls be given to us; let them choose one bull for themselves, cut it in pieces, and lay it on the wood, but put no fire to it; I will prepare the other bull and lay it on the wood, but put no fire to it. Then you call on the name of your god and I will call on the name of the Lord; the god who answers by fire is indeed God. (23–24)

The votaries of Baal stagger about their altar; they bellow the name of their god; they cut themselves with swords and lances. To what effect? "[N]o voice, no answer, and no response" (29).

Elijah trash talks with the best: "either [your god] is meditating, or he has wandered away, or he is on a journey" (27). The only explanation of Elijah's mockery is conviction that *nothing* of the sort will work. Not that the Baalites are gibbering when they speak of their gods. Rather, they know not of what they speak.

Given the failure on the Carmel, what, some may wonder, took so long? As long as base-Baal was the only game in town, control of the media and powers of suggestion were able to fill the stands. Now the worshippers are challenged. Rather like the child who draws attention to the emperor's nakedness, Elijah is underscoring a suspicion that many of them might harbour.

Elijah is portrayed as confident. Whence the assurance? Does self-confidence light fires?

Elijah does not say "Let There Be Fire" and piously wait.[17] He shifts stones about like a shell game tout: "come closer to me" (30). Then he has the assembled fill the trench, thrice, with "four jars of water" (33–4). The hint, carried in the line "the fire of the Lord ... even licked up the water that was in the trench" (38), is that the jars contain a combustible. When heated, water boils and steams. Oil? Tongues of fire lick it up.

Jezebel isn't amused. Later in the action, on the run from the Queen's hit-men, Elijah questions God's protection. "He was afraid; he got up and fled for his life" (1 Kings 19:3). In juxtaposing the bravado on the mountain and the flight to the wilderness, the text winks that Elijah's confidence on the Carmel is self-confidence.

How hard Taylor tries to remain ecumenical in commenting on Elijah's performance (73–4), a tendentious stance at odds with the biblical point.

> One of the potentialities of Christian faith was a reversal of the field of fear. The power of God will be victorious over all evil magic. So much is common to all variants of the faith. But this victory can be understood as that of white magic over dark magic. Or it can be understood as that of God's naked power over all magic. To draw on this power, you have to leap out of the field of magic altogether and throw yourself on the power of God alone.[18]

This "disenchanting" move is implicit in the tradition of Judaism, and later Christianity. Fundamental to both is a break with a world in which what they judge to be bad magic, worship of pagan gods and forces, is rampant. But this breach can take one of two forms; in a sense, it hovers between them. We can see this when Elijah humbles the prophets of Baal on Mount Carmel. In challenging them to see which God will bring down fire on the offerings, and showing that they can't deliver, while he can, he is in a sense deploying a victorious counter-magic to theirs. But the point of the story, which Elijah drives home, is that their magic is empty; it is utterly ineffective; their Gods have no power.

I mentioned the connection between Elijah and Moses. Elijah is in fact a version of Moses. Two parallels between their stories are pertinent.

Moses's contest in Pharaoh's court parallels Elijah's confrontation. Anything that Pharaoh's magicians can do Moses shows that he can do better. Taylor's words therefore apply more to him: "he is ... deploying a victorious counter-magic." The second parallel concerns Elijah's flight after *his* victory. Back in Egypt, Pharaoh's forces pursue the Israelites. In both cases, those on the run end up in the wilderness after a multitude of their antagonists meet violent ends.[19] In the wastes of Sinai, Moses experiences his main theophany. Fleeing from Jezebel's posse, Elijah also finds himself at Sinai. To Moses God had said (Exodus 33:21–2): "See, there is a place by me where you shall stand ... while my glory passes by." To Elijah (1 Kings 19:11): "Go out and stand on the mountain before the Lord, for the Lord is about to pass by." God appears to Moses, though only partly: "you cannot see my face, for no one shall see me and live" (20). And Elijah?

> Now there was a great wind, so strong that it was splitting mountains and breaking rocks in pieces before the Lord, but the Lord was not in the wind; and after the wind an earthquake, but the Lord was not in the earthquake; and after the earthquake a fire, but the Lord was not in the fire; and after the fire a sound of sheer silence (11–12).

The text's summary of the efforts to elicit Baal's reaction was quoted: "there was no voice, no answer, and no response" (18:29). Two silences; one the silence of nothingness; the other, the voice of non-natural being.

God (Deuteronomy 33:23) had appointed Joshua to replace Moses. Immediately after the quoted experience Elijah, in a departure from precedent, anoints his own successor, Elisha. Hereafter, it is down to us.

Père No-El

A popular construal of "sheer silence" has it that God speaks from within, through conscience. Why should God not speak externally?

As in the foundational cases of Abraham (in the personal sphere) and of Moses (in the national one), on the Carmel we have a shift from a pagan system. The prophets of the Baal are supplicating to a god with a fiery mode of expression. Since the pagan deities speak through nature, this is as expected. The difference therefore accentuates the fact that God, the Bible's deity, is outside nature. But there is more to it.

Elijah's anti-pagan message is less triumphal than Moses's. Fear of fire and rain (as opposed to caution) is inappropriate. In this respect, Taylor's "reversal of the field of fear" is correct. That the biblical view is salvific can't however be inferred.[20] The view exposes what, by the lights of the thinkers/tellers, the human condition *is*. Then it's our turn. On the biblical side, we have an anti-theophany. *God does not appear.*

A single mention apart, Moses is absent from the Passover Haggadah. Anticipating the obvious question, the compilers insert a Torah passage. "'The Lord took us out of Egypt,' not through ... a messenger. The Holy One ... did it in His glory by Himself!" We are to think of what happened as we think of the first man: it's God's doing. Elijah's story shifts exultation downwards. A ragtag newly liberated from bondage is more in need of sugar coating than a group sovereign in its region. Accordingly, it's as it should be that Elijah's gift suits *us* better. Moses is an absent presence at the festival of liberation. Elijah is a present absence. As God does not appear to him on Sinai, Elijah does not appear to us, the untouched liquid in his cup to extinguish our childlike faith.[21] I would conjecture that Elijah's non-appearance is designed to remind us that *God does not appear to him.*[22] As Elijah was on the Carmel, so we are wherever we may be: on our own.[23] "[The word] is not in [the] heaven[s]."

If the word is immanent, why (it might be asked) did Moses ascend? In fact, the representation of the message as descending goes beyond saying that it's a higher message. Like Descartes's dualism, the Bible's anti-paganism belongs to philosophical anthropology: men and women are not entirely parts of nature. In this regard "from on high" means "from outside nature." The Bible occasionally reverses the orientation: "Out of the depths I cry to you, O Lord" (Psalm 130:1). Same difference.

The story of the rain in 1 Kings 18 bears this out. In sending Elijah to Ahab, God had promised to send the rain as a sign:

> Elijah went to the top of Carmel; there he bowed himself down upon the earth and put his face between his knees. He said to his servant, "Go up now, and look toward the sea." He went up and looked, and said, "There is nothing." Then he said, "Go up again seven times." At the seventh time he said, "Look, a little cloud no bigger than a person's hand is rising out of the sea" ... In a little while the heaven[s] grew black with clouds and wind; there was heavy rain (42–45).[24]

I daresay meteorologists wouldn't be the butt of jokes if a predictive success rate of one in seven were satisfactory.

In the story in 1 Kings, Elijah is a Père No-El. In two senses. One: No El. Nature is not an object of worship and reverence. Two: No Père, no Father, in the sense of Christianity. There is the natural world; and there are men and women. That's the whole of it.

Santa Claus and Anti-Claus. Santa Claus's refreshment is taken. Elijah's is untouched. Did Elijah not come? He came. To teach that there is nothing transcendent of us that makes us the transcendent beings that we are.

Taylor, like Elijah, offers two options: God's white magic against the black magic; or, God's naked power. The moral of Elijah's story is that there is no power save the power of the truth, the truth (as the Bible sees it) that it's up to us. This, nearly enough, is the message of Moses's valediction. But in the presence of Pharaoh's magicians Moses does perform white magic. This, again, is why Taylor's gloss applies more there. It's also why he stands in need of correction. In using the idea of fullness both in the pagan frame and in the theistic one, Taylor loses the ontology.

The matter, from the Bible's viewpoint, is much less fraught on the critical side too. Taylor says "black magic." Where's the magic, black or white, in the doings of the prophets of Baal? They are trying to elicit fire. We have become excellent at that. Our efforts with precipitation are by contrast more miss than hit. Which is what the Bible goes out of its way to tell us in telling us the story of Elijah and the rain.

Is the biblical position anti-religious? It is anti-pagan. Theologically, the pagans miss God. Ontologically, they miss the particular. Missing that, they lose themselves.

Being anti-pagan, the biblical view is anti-naturalist. It is also, in its assertion that men and women are alone, broadly humanist. "How does this differ from exclusive humanism?" The role that God plays, the role of the particular, sets the two positions apart. God ratifies the "smallness" of men and women.[25]

The Cardinal Sin

There are cardinal numbers ("one, two, three") and there are ordinal numbers ("first, second, third"). The latter line up on the functional side. The Bible's basic philosophical claim is a cardinal one: each man and each woman is one, as God is one. The thrust of monotheism is that God, the extra-natural one, transmits his particularity to men and women. The thinkers behind the Bible are taking a non-reductionist stand: the being of men and women eludes the terms that pagans have available. When God appeared to him in Ur of the Chaldeans, that is what Abraham came to appreciate. Dramatized in geographical terms, Abraham's departure in answer to God's call is (=) his recognition of his native culture's inability to accommodate men and women. That's what Elijah is teaching. Our actions must be sensitive to the core value: individual human life. The approved patterns of behaviour must be adjusted to it. Thus the Ten Commandments.[26]

Taylor quotes a scene from *The Possessed*. The exchange between Shatov, the novel's tragic figure, and the midwife Arina Prohorovna could be seen as an exchange between God and Zeus at the appearance of the first man.[27]

> "The mysterious coming of a new creature, a great and inexplicable mystery; and what a pity it is, Arina Prohorovna, that you don't understand it."
>
> ...
>
> "There were two and now there's a third human being, a new spirit, finished and complete, unlike the handiwork of man; a new thought and a new love ... it's positively frightening ... And there's nothing grander in the world."
>
> "Ech, what nonsense he talks! It's simply a further development of the organism, and there's nothing else in it, no mystery," said Arina Prohorovna with genuine and good-humoured laughter. "If you talk like that, every fly is a mystery."

The Bible-writers would have delighted in Shatov's formulation. It's not first, second, and third. It's one, one, and one. Exactly what (in translation) the first man said: "this one shall be called Woman, for out of Man this one was taken."

Taylor sees the truth from the standpoint of structures and forces outside the control of human agency. *A Secular Age* is, like *War and Peace*, epic. Better suited to Taylor's view than Dostoyevsky's Ivan Shatov is, on the negative side, Tolstoy's Ivan Ilyich, a man whose despair is due to a feeling of the absence of transcending fullness from his life; or, this time positively, Pierre Bezukhov of *War and Peace*, who yearns so hard for spiritual fulfilment.

Failure of fullness isn't the problem; alienation from the holiness of the particular is.

An Unconnected Cog

Plato is a rational pagan. The Greek idea of cosmos, an orderly whole, is basic to his understanding of the world. Science's delegitimization of the idea is, Taylor says, problematic for religious men and women. It goes along with God's removal from the picture. Problematic the delegitimization may be. For Plato, it certainly would be. The Bible's story is closer however to the story of the Big Bang.[28] God's basic role is the Genesis 2 creation of men and women. God did not teach Abraham cosmology. The misreading also leads Taylor to tell a complex story that involves deism: he does not contend that God was banished when science came along; rather, he likens God to a clockmaker who, once the timepiece is tick-tocking, no longer interacts with the flywheels and the sprockets. I do not contest the story's accuracy. But Taylor is not writing as a historian. The intellectual history in *A Secular Age* is part-and-parcel of Taylor's attempt, as a religious person, to defend the claim that the modern secular ensemble is not exclusively humanist.

A Plea for Ontology:
Thomas Nagel's *Mind and Cosmos*

Doubting Thomas

Within the ivied walls, time stands relatively still. Asked to apply "warp speed" there, a low-grade wit might pick out the rate at which scholarly books warp as they gather dust on the library shelves. In contrast, the speed of the scholarly world's reaction to Thomas Nagel's *Mind and Cosmos* puts one on the bridge of the starship *Enterprise*. The range of responses to the book's publication matches their rapidity. More exuberant admirers of Nagel trumpet the second coming of Galileo. The words of a top cognitive scientist typify the mood at the other extreme: "the shoddy reasoning of a once great thinker."[1] The polarization yields easily to explanation. Nagel is assaulting the received position about the relations between the titular notions. The book's subtitle is explicitness itself. "Why the Materialist, neo-Darwinian Conception of Nature Is Almost Certainly False." Conditioned to lie low,[2] opponents of orthodoxy are emboldened. Unable to lump Nagel in with the throwbacks who hang Rockwell at home and whose worldview in foreign affairs centres on Roswell, occupants of the materialist-Darwinian citadel train *their* artillery at doubting Thomas.

"I think, therefore I am." "To be is to be perceived." "To be is to be the value of a variable." These are the calling cards of, respectively, René Descartes, Bishop Berkeley, and W.V. Quine. Several decades ago, Nagel posed a question that has become *his* pasteboard: "What is it like to be a bat?" Chiropterologists detail its physiology. Its habits they describe. Why not knock on *their* door? Nagel's point is that students of science can't enlighten us as to what it's like from the inside to hurtle through lightless caverns navigating by (to us) supersonic squeaks.

The heart of Nagel's book is the contrast between outside and inside. Here's what the philosophical stethoscope registers: "Inside not nothing. Outside resources unequal. Inside not nothing. Outside resources unequal." In focusing on the historical or genetic issue that biochemists address in explaining the emergence of life and with which evolutionary theorists deal in accounting for the presence among living creatures of reflective reasoners, Nagel is giving the shape of theory to his thoughts about the irreducibility of the subjective.

Over the years, Nagel has worried in print about the fit of life and mind in the world of matter in motion. No one even passingly acquainted with his reflections on the inside and the outside could mistake Nagel for an insider.[3] That being so, Pinker's apoplexy is theatrical. In a world in which tomorrow's wisdom turns out with predictable frequency to be today's lunacy, it's worrisome that the materialist-cum-Darwinian is so incurious about the shape of an effort to say how life and mind might otherwise have emerged. True, Nagel's amalgam of a principle of life irreducible to biochemistry and a teleological account of historical development[4] leans heavily on the destructive aspect of his case. As such the amalgam is more unstable than the reductive positions. Nagel is under no illusions. But what's taken Pinker & Co. so long? Why wasn't the squib about syllogistic sloppiness and faded glory fired off a decade earlier against, say, Colin McGinn?[5] What about the questioners of the compatibilist analysis of freedom of the will? Kant, a fully armed non-materialist anti-reductionist freedomite, and a philosophical voice one ignores at one's peril, calls compatibilism "a wretched subterfuge."[6]

"The obscurantists of any generation," quoth A.N. Whitehead, "are in the main constituted by the greater part of the practitioners of the dominant methodology." Whitehead's generalization applies in the present case. The main currency of the naturalizers is the promissory note. In his prosecutorial guise, Nagel puts the signatories in the dock. But Nagel too is making a leap of faith. "About the specifics of how it's done I haven't a clue. It's got however to be doable my way."[7]

So extreme is the polarization that productive engagement seems impossible. In this discussion I'll carve out a midway position. "If wishes were horses?" I have a solid ground for proceeding thus. Both sides have failed to notice a runner in the case of Nagel.

Three Questions

The naturalizers speak in chemical terms of the emergence of life. The anti-naturalizers liken this to sleight of mind. The anti-naturalizers speak of the principle of life that isn't part of the order of things conceived as matter-in-motion. *This* sticks in the naturalizers' throats. Beneath these reciprocal bafflements, two things are *not* in dispute. Life exists. Higher cognitive processes exist. Mystery may surround how these things came to exist. That they exist is however no mystery. If the rabbit produced in the course of the magician's performance were a mysterious rabbit, a hologram, the happenings on stage would not mystify in the intended way.

Nagel asks *the L-question*: "What is it like to be a bat?" As my production of the rabbit shows, a different question asks to be asked. "What is it to be a bat?" This isn't a request for identification: "Which among things are bats?" So it doesn't pose *the ID-question*: "What are the criteria for identifying such things?" It is, rather: "A, B, and C among things are bats. What is it to be one?" Doesn't answering this, *the B-question*, have a bearing on the issue that the L-question raises? The closest Nagel gets is some variant of the ID-question.

The L-question is Nagel's trademark. Nagel assumes, as do his opponents, that we know what askers of the question are asking it about. But it's the answer to the ID-question that we know. "Being a bat is like being *that*." This doesn't even hint of an answer to the B-question. If you told me what it's like to be *that*, sc. a bat, you'd still owe me an account of what it is to be *that*, sc. a bat.

Chiropterologists, questioned about the flighted mammal, are helpful. They do not however answer the B-question. The B-question, one of ontology, is as such less scientific and more general. My approach is in this regard as in Aristotle's *Metaphysics*.

> There are several senses in which a thing may be said to be …; … in one sense it means what a thing is or a "this," and in another sense it means that a thing is of a certain quality or quantity or has some such predicate asserted of it. While "being" has all these senses, obviously that which is primarily is the "what," which indicates the substance of the thing. (1028ª10–15)

In what sense do we say things, bats for example, to be? Is the thing we're talking about said to be as a quality is said to be, or as a quantity, or what? "What," Aristotle would phrase it, "is the substance of such a thing?" Focus on the B-question can supply material relevant to the dispute between the naturalizers and Nagel. The answer to the B-question *constrains* those who ask the question that Nagel and the naturalizers are asking and about which they disagree.

Descriptive Ontology

Nagel's positive position is rife with speculation. Yet from a historical perspective he does have a point. Dualism, an entailment from the father of modern philosophy, is anchored in Descartes's appreciation that mental phenomena do not yield easily to the rationalizing resources of early modern science: measurement, quantification. "The great advances in the physical and biological sciences were made possible by excluding the mind from the physical world" Nagel, 2012, 8). Did Descartes believe that nascent science needed breathing space to gather strength, or was his view that the mind resisted incorporation? The question is still a live one. Nagel says that Descartes's initial position was designed to assist the new enterprise by cordoning off a vulnerable spot. Isn't the implication that Descartes likened the resistant part to the prodigal son? Nagel's formulation wavers, possibly because of this: "[substance] dualism ... abandon[s] the hope for an integrated explanation [of mind and cosmos]" (ibid., 49).

Characterizing the subject-matter of Descartes's thinking doesn't oblige one to choose. The data that Descartes addresses are available to men and women in the street, and available to the scholars because it's through the street door that they enter the study. Descartes recognizes mental phenomena. He recognizes material phenomena. Neither recognition is the output of scholarly processing. No one in the street believes that they must choose between materializing mind or mentalizing matter. If Descartes is minded to put matter over mind or if it is material to him to put mind over matter that will be for independent reasons. An antecedent ranking would open him to the charge of dogmatism.[8] In the new intellectual world that "Let there be certainty" brought into being, some, notably Berkeley, elevated the mental side over the material. That too was an option within the Cartesian frame.

Nagel comes forward to advocate for "the untutored reaction of incredulity to the reductionist, neo-Darwinian account" (2012, 6). The reaction that Nagel is in fact defending is, as I will now explain, not of the sort that any Dick, Harry, or even, for that matter, Tom, would offer.

What has the point about the neutrality of the data to do with our dispute? All the parties assume that the identity of what they are talking about is clear. In fact, they only know which things make up the subject-matter of dispute. The assumption is implicit in a criticism that Nagel levels against Strawson's treatment in *Individuals* of the relation between the mental and the material.

"[W]hile internal understanding is certainly valuable, and an essential precondition of a more transcendent project, I don't see how we can stop there and not seek an external conception of ourselves as well" (2012, 30). By "internal understanding" Nagel means "understanding of presuppositions and of the underlying structure of how we think about things."[9]

Nagel is right to say that Strawson, whose efforts are geared to this last, leaves open how to account for the existence of persons in the physical world. This, to Nagel, indicates that Strawson the descriptive metaphysician downs tools before the whistle. The problem, however, is that what Strawson puts forward is *irrelevant* to the dispute. It's not descriptive metaphysics itself that is irrelevant. It's *Strawson's* descriptive metaphysics.

In his account of persons, Strawson tells us that persons sustain both M-predicates ("weighs 60 kilograms") and P-predicates ("is delighted"), adding that the concept of a person does not *à la* Descartes fuse a mental part and a material part. Observe that to say that a person is the bearer of both material properties and of properties that engage consciousness is not to say what it is to be a person. "A sustainer of both" is no answer to "What kind of thing is it that sustains both?"

The B-question seems to be natural for Strawson to ask. It falls within the ambit of the search for presuppositions and structure. But he doesn't ask it. *Why* doesn't he?

The author of *Individuals* is pressing to establish that effective grounds for identifying an X are a condition for Xs' being objects of thought and discourse. No entity without identifiability. "Individual" in Strawson's title *means* "item with effective identification conditions." Individuals come in two classes: the general ones (properties such as redness and honesty); and the non-general ones (concrete things such as trees and tables). Strawson is at pains to establish that the non-general ones are effectively identifiable only because they are located in space and time or are linked to other effectively identifiable non-general spatio-temporals. *That* is the book's driver.

A property can be a Strawsonian individual. So can a physical object. *Strawson's major term of art is not, then, a category label.* His concern is the conditions for qualifying as an object of experience and of discourse, not *the what-it-is-to-be* of, say, a table, or *the substance* of, say, a football match.

Who can be surprised that Nagel should move past Strawson to his, Nagel's, main (description-transcending) issue? Strawson's question is far to the ID-side.[10] Something is missing – *missing on the descriptive level*. The missing thing bears on the dispute about naturalization. That Strawson omits it doesn't mean that it isn't present on his level of operation, a level on which both parties to the dispute can be in agreement. As I see it, this level *has* distinctive ontological content, content that Strawson's Kantian interests cause him to overlook.[11] Part of an internal account, the content substantively constrains "[the] more transcendent project." For this content, we can look to a theistic source, the Bible.

Nagel understands the affinity that his denial of reduction has for his repudiation both of Darwin and of Western religiosity. As it is usually taken, the view that God is responsible for life and for the existence of human beings is a denial of the naturalizers' position. But, taken in this way, the view raises more problems than it solves. Isn't God also responsible for insensate matter?

"As it is usually taken." The implication is that the usual taking of the Bible is a mis-taking. A large part of what leads Nagel not to look at the Bible is, I'm sure, the general view of it as on a par with Disney. As the case may be, I'll now show that the Bible answers the B-question. It is, therefore, a better essay in descriptive metaphysics than is *Individuals*.

Description before Worship

The Bible's opposition to paganism is not the party of heaven's attempt to wrest control of the minds and hearts of people from the powers on, say, Olympus. Paganism should be forsworn because of its mistaken view of reality. Who are the pagan deities that God enjoins Abraham to abandon? The Bible is teaching the error of a restrictedly nature-based conception of things: the pagan gods are only part of the story of men and women – indeed, the less important part. In the name of self-understanding, men and women will have to speak a language that is Greek to them.

I'll assume that talk of God's calling Abraham, and talk of Abraham's accepting the call, convert with talk of Abraham's having a "Eureka!"-moment. The assumption, which pre-empts the straight existential issue about the Bible's deity (principles are not entities), brings out the affinity between Abraham and Nagel. Both affirm an extra-physical principle that is, as Kant would have put it, original.

Nagel associates theism with the Bible and with its account of the genesis of life and mind. Abraham should not however be seen as pursuing, from the outset, a religious agenda. Be the Bible's ultimate commitments as may be, they rest on an analysis of the constituents of the world, non-living and living, sentient and possessed of higher consciousness. The analytic results may have implications of a religious sort. Acceptance of such implications as there are is however a (rational) consequence of the *analysans*, not a precondition of understanding it. The same goes for science.

When Abraham rises in Beer-sheba and "call[s] ... the name of the Lord," he is advancing the new view of things. Two and a half thousand years before Augustine, he is calling out *contra paganos*. He is advancing *his Mind and Cosmos*. In broadcasting the name of the Lord, he is *asserting* the new principle.

What is the text of the inaugural lecture in Bibleism? What Abraham said begins with the most famous line of the Bible: "In the beginning." That's no coincidence. For what he said *is* the beginning of the Book of Genesis.[12] Abraham gives an account of the world, of its genesis, an account in which the non-pagan principle is central. The assertion in verse 34 of chapter 21 about extended residence in Philistia tells us that despite Abraham's Pauline gesture, the place, conceptually speaking, remained alien. Among the pagans within earshot he made no inroads. It is therefore as it should be that chapter 22 presents the Akedah, the test of Abraham. Having met with no success, will he think better of the enterprise, like the scholars whose books are warping in the library?

The position that Abraham supports is, on the descriptive side, Strawsonian: people are irreducible. Strawson, in the formal mode, says that the concept of a person is "primitive." The Bible says more. It answers the B-question.

First Nature: Genesis 1

In the creation story of Genesis 1, the Bible's treatment of physical reality is genetic. The text describes the birth and early development. Order slowly emerges from a beginning state of maximum disorder. The Bible sees the physical world as a system: you cannot have wet regions coming to be out of a moist condition without dry(er) regions coming to be, an upper part without a low(er) one, light without dark.

Genesis 1 supplies a categorization into system and elements of system. The elements, *essentially* of the system, are as natural as the system. The developmental story is of a chaotic initial state being differentiated into distinct regions, and then of the regions coming to be inhabited by the things that inhabit them. It's not a coincidence that the account has an affinity with pagan cosmogonies. The writers are *quoting* the Babylonian writings.

The Bible's account differs in two salient ways from the pagan ones. The Bible's account is free of myth. Technological, not mythological, it borrows its models from common-or-garden interaction with the world. Here's an example.

Attired as we often are in rubber boots, furled umbrellas at the ready, the existence of upper waters is well-known to us. Why don't the raindrops keep falling on our heads? God is said (1:7) to insert between the upper waters and the lower ones a divider with spillways. We ourselves do this sort of thing when we install a sprinkler system.[13]

In the Bible's cosmogony, the character called "God" is behind what happens. There is none such in pagan accounts.

Though salient, this second difference isn't however as strong as it's usually taken to be. God is placed behind everything because God is the Bible's new principle, not because God does the job. To appreciate this, return to the Bible's treatment of the emergence of living things.

The paradigm of the process of emergence is given in these verses. "And God said, 'Let the earth bring forth vegetation: plants yielding seed, and fruit trees of every kind that bear fruit with the seed in it'" (9). "And God said, 'Let the waters bring forth swarms of living creatures'" (20). "And God said, 'Let the earth bring forth living creatures of every kind: cattle and creeping things and wild animals of the earth of every kind'" (24). God does not create the plants, or the marine creatures, or the wild animals. The principles that govern the locations generate the occupants. Obviously, the specifics of the various processes the writers do not know. Their fullest sense of them is in the case of the fish. The idea is that the churning of the waters brings forth the yet more organized parts.

The thinkers behind the Bible are honest about all this. The plants, they say, come to be on the solid earth, the fish, in the substantial water. As aware as we are of how insubstantial a bird in the hand feels, the thinkers do not see how such things could congeal out of thin air. They therefore tiptoe.

In design, the biblical story of life's emergence is, then, a natural story. The principles governing the physical world underpin the differentiation into regions and the further organization of the contents of each region into the living things found in it. Life is (just) a much higher (and later) degree of organization. The naturalizers would say "Amen."[14]

And so, the Bible's non-pagan principle, the principle represented by God, does not play a substantive role in Genesis 1. The first part of what Abraham declaimed to the world in Beer-sheba isn't distinctively biblical.

Even accepters of what I've said about the account of the physical world will gainsay the preceding sentences. Verse 26 has God saying: "Let us make humankind in our image, according to our likeness; and let them have dominion over the fish of the seas, and over the cattle, and over all the wild animals of the earth, and over every creeping thing that creeps upon the earth." Isn't the claim that God, the new principle, *is in the world at this stage*?

It isn't. Only in the second chapter of Genesis does the reason emerge for which such a principle is required. I'll get to that shortly. Here, I'll say enough to make clear the meaning of verse 26's "in [his] image, according to [his] likeness."

The emergence of men and women on the scene is understood along the lines of the emergence of the rest of the creation (up to then). The various species of living things, including ours, come into existence in accordance with the principles that govern the natural world. The image and likeness claim is the Bible's way of clarifying a difference, descriptively present already. God, because of his nature, has no physical niche. In the claim that men and women are fashioned like God is the point that men and women are like God *in that respect*. To have dominion means not to be domain-bound.

Who doesn't recognize that the behaviour of one species has this greater plasticity? But the plasticity isn't regarded in the Bible either as more than a striking difference or as inconsistent with paganism. Confirmation is supplied by the fact that God, at the end of the Genesis 1 creation story, declares the whole, inclusive of the human part, very good.

Second Nature: Genesis 2

Both Genesis 1 and Genesis 2 answer the B-question. Both mention God in answering it. The two answers are mutually irreducible. According to Genesis 1, the physical world is a system; its constituents are parts, essentially so. Humankind differs in not being niche-bound.

Given that humanity is in existence at the end of Genesis 1, what need of Genesis 2? The second story, *the posterior analytics* of mind and cosmos, says something absent from Genesis 1, *the prior analytics*. Each man and each woman is, it says, an ontologically separate being, a particular. True, each is a non-general individual, in Strawson's sense. But, unlike Strawson, the Bible is answering the

B-question. To be a man, to be a woman, is to be a particular. There is no such notion in Strawson; none in Nagel or in Nagel's adversaries either.

Lest concision occult the point, I'll state again that what is true of the emergence of humanity in Genesis 1 doesn't transpose to the coming into being of the man and of the woman. In Genesis 1, humankind emerges naturally. In Genesis 2, God does the creating. Since humanity exists prior to this creative doing,[15] subtlety is required when one approaches the Genesis 2 account.

Recall Michelangelo's depiction of what Genesis 2:7 describes in words. We concluded that the portion of the physical world that has the physical form of a man is alive *before* contact with God's digit. The Bible says (in the English version): "and the man became a living thing."

A living thing becomes a living thing. That's worse than uninformative. Informative is the claim that God imparts a bit of himself to that portion of the world. He makes that thing to be as he is, namely a separate thing. *The man becomes a particular.* Particularity is what the members of a biological species like *Canis lupus* lack.

I will content myself here with illustrating the point in the mode of the descriptive ontologist. A part of your automobile, a tire for example, is an individual. But it's immaterial to you, the owner, which (comparable) tire is mounted on the rim. This is not true for particulars. That's why we feel uneasy when it's written that Job was made whole through the supply of a substitute spouse and replacement children.[16] The first man says of the first woman that she is "bone of my bones and flesh of my flesh." The words bring out the particularity. "I am one. This is another one."[17] The normative story in the Bible is the story of the whole chain of particular men and women, whose links we, each woman Jill and man Jack of us, are. Indeed, God's self-identification in the Bible, "I AM" is an assertion of (ontological) particularity. Which, again, confirms that Genesis 1 is not distinctively biblical.

This, then, is the Bible's position on naturalization. "To be a person is to be a particular." This answer to the B-question, an ontologist's answer, is unavailable to pagans.[18] And, we've seen, Strawson can't have it either. Absent from *Individuals* is precisely what is distinctive of persons. In rejecting the Bible's theistic line, Nagel deprives himself of a better version of what he praises Strawson for furnishing.

The answer to the B-question is available independently of the L-question. Still, it's hard to believe that As and Bs differ only in that As are particulars. I can see no decisive ground however for maintaining that the L-question applies to particulars and to nothing else. What would Nagel say? True, he regards the L-question as applying to things that fall into both categories. But the ontological categorization isn't part of his thinking. Implied is that the L-question itself is peripheral to the debate. What has emerged as central from the vantage point of present concerns is the notion of extra-system unity that particulars have.

Possibly relevant here is something like Kant's unity of apperception. Perhaps this unity is part of Descartes's "cogito." Isn't the conclusion of the "cogito" the same as God's self-identification? "Thus you shall say to [the Israelites]," God instructs Moses, "I AM has sent me to you."

Strawson's descriptive metaphysics is "an essential precondition of a more transcendent project." This makes little sense coming from Nagel, I commented, save as a polite salute. I have now, as promised, given it more sense. The ontology is missing from Strawson. The fact that each person is a particular constrains "[the] more transcendent" project. Unfortunately, the idea is not available even to Nagel. He does not think (as Descartes, if he is a substance dualist, thinks) that naturalization is a non-starter.

The naturalizers cannot explain particularity. Particularity goes beyond individuality, which is as near as pagan resources can get. Paganism is ontologically incomplete. It excludes distinctively human reality. What better way to say this than by saying that pagans don't recognize God?

15
Phenomenology and Analysis: A Bridge over the Waters

Between the Covers

Nineteen sixty-two saw the publication of an English translation of Maurice Merleau-Ponty's *Phénoménologie de la perception* (Gallimard, 1945). For a book to be bound between the red covers of the International Library of Philosophy and Scientific Method was a coup in the English-speaking philosophical world. How great the honour of rubbing up against Wittgenstein's *Tractatus Logico-Philosophicus*, the study of which remains a rite of passage into the twentieth century's distinctive philosophical thought.

Through my graduate school years at Oxford, from the mid-1960s to the early 1970s, *Phenomenology of Perception* was in vogue. We even had a jokey name for the author: "Morris Bridgewater." Did the book's publication mark a watershed for phenomenology in the citadel of English philosophy? A contemporary Oxford connection, one in which Merleau-Ponty figures obliquely, provides an amusing entry to the issue.

Along with several of my Balliol chums, back then I eagerly awaited the latest instalment of Anthony Powell's sequence of novels *A Dance to the Music of Time*. In the penultimate, eleventh, volume, *Temporary Kings*, which appeared in 1973, Pamela Flitton, the female protagonist who takes a back seat to no one in the casual cruelty that narcissism trails in its wake, bruits it about that the French writer Léon-Joseph Ferrand-Sénéschal "croaked" while the two were in bed – a foreshadowing, this, of her post-mortem coupling with the American scholar Russell Gwinnett (*she* is the stiff in this encounter). Powell's Ferrand-Sénéschal is loosely based on Merleau-Ponty, who in fact had had an affair with Sonia Orwell. Because Ferrand-Sénéschal is a French intellectual, but even more because Merleau-Ponty's colleague the batrachianesque Sartre cannot fail to come to mind, "croak" is positively Aristophanean.

Ferrand-Sénéschal expires in the bed of the frigid Englishwoman: literally a fatal female. That appears to have been the fate of French phenomenology in the philosophical hotbed of Albion. How, one wonders, did the real-world Ferrand-Sénéschal's sheets came to be inserted between the same red covers as Wittgenstein's? Perhaps because of the fate of the members of the Vienna Circle, with whom in the mid-1930s he had had philosophically fruitful contacts, intellectual goings-on across the Channel worked like a muleta on A.J. Ayer, at the time the general editor of the International Library.[1] Could it be that, having lent to the enterprise the celebrity he had acquired through *Language, Truth, and Logic*, Ayer took the bows and delegated?

Another Oxford priest can be enlisted to add a few brushstrokes to the intellectual *esquisse*, in the process moving in the direction of a reason for Oxford's dalliance with Merleau-Ponty.

Jerry Cohen arrived in England early in the 1960s. In his romp through Marxism – *If You're an Egalitarian, How Come You're So Rich?* – he makes reference to the conflict between American and English philosophy over the analytic/synthetic distinction, a conflict that Quine's "Two Dogmas of Empiricism" ignited. Cohen reports that when he was wavering between Harvard and Oxford, a mentor advised him to go south. "Quine," the Horace Greeley of the piece opined, "can put Ayer in his pocket." Not heeding the counsel, Cohen plumped for not so jolly postwar Olde England over New England, and eventually did his sculling among the necessitarians on the Cherwell rather than in the contingent along the Charles. Could it be that the warmth towards phenomenology, however tepid, has to do with the dispute about the analytic and the synthetic? As I see it, it's not incidental to the matter that in collaboration with H.P. Grice, P.F. Strawson, my crypto-phenomenologist, authored "In Defense of a Dogma."

For one who was so reflective about how he was intellectually formed, Cohen's overall stance here is uncharacteristically self-opaque. Oddly, he doesn't bring his scholarly work to bear when he comments on the analytic/synthetic distinction, this despite that Marxism has a root in Hegel's phenomenology. Cohen's extended critical engagement with Harvard's John Rawls ups the oddity. For Rawls's openness to inputs from the sciences – psychology, economics – puts him in Quine's orbit, not in Ayer's. From a more theoretical perspective, the mentioned engagement seems less strange, however. The way that Cohen's considered position sinks the person in the wider whole says "Cambridge."

What's the link between a phenomenologist like Husserl and an analytic philosopher like Strawson? The phenomenologist explores the unavoidable influence on what is experienced of the defining feature of consciousness: its meaning or intentionality ("aboutness"). The analyst seeks out propositions whose truth, assured by the meaning ("intensions") of their constituent elements, is (also) prior to the empirical specifics.[2]

I'll do a MacArthur on Merleau-Ponty. My topic, as the preceding lines indicate, is a more general one: the connection between Continental and

England-based philosophy. To locate the point of parting of Abraham and Lot, I'll go two centuries back beyond Hegel to what many see as the birth of the modern activity in a stove-heated room ("poêle") in Bavaria. I'm referring to the real-world correlate of what Descartes intellectualizes in *Meditations on First Philosophy*, a work of intense interest both to philosophers of the analytic tradition and to phenomenologists. On the foundation of an interpretation of a key part of Descartes's argument, I erect an imaginative reconstruction that clarifies the connection.

In the *Poêle*

I focus on two parts of Descartes's presentation in his chief work: the critique of the senses, and the role of God.

An obstacle to claiming Descartes for phenomenology is that the set-up in the *Meditations* looks to involve a rejection of the practical life-world that is phenomenology's fulcrum. Consider these sentences, from the first paragraph. "I have expressly rid my mind of all worries and arranged for myself a clear stretch of time. I am here quite alone, and at last will devote myself sincerely and without reservation to the general demolition to my opinions." Isn't this a neutralization of what Heidegger calls "Sorge," the attitude of care or concern? Isn't Descartes's project of careful reflection care-less? Indeed, central to the interpretation of Descartes given by one of the most astute of the preceding generation of Oxford-trained philosophers (Williams 1978) is the idea of "pure enquiry," enquiry aimed at the truth and nothing but the truth.

The perception of the Meditator as leaving the bustle behind might be in the eyes of the perceiver. Couldn't the idea be that beyond the belief in them, the character of the propositions believed is a function of the pressures of the quotidian? Worried men and women sing worried songs. Instead of being a ticket to a rarefied plane of pure ratiocination, the meditative stance (whatever it is) might make possible a *proper* attitude towards the world.[3]

After saying what the quoted lines report, the Meditator sets to critiquing his stock of beliefs: "whatever up till now I have accepted as most true." The text is invariably seen to have the following logical structure. The required leisure secured, the Meditator "seriously and without reservation" pursues the project. The "clear stretch of time" is the opportunity to get on with the job.

This makes sense. But there's a downside. In our current reading of it, the remark about the Meditator's condition corresponds to what authors nowadays hive off to front matter: "I couldn't have done these researches but for the leave of absence." That Descartes makes the remark in the body of the work that he so painstakingly composed supports the suggestion that "careworn" and "worry free" aren't psychological labels.

Attention to a problem that affects interpreters who tread the more trod-
den path furnishes backing for the reading on which the two parts connect.
To elicit the problem, I start off by examining the part of Descartes's treatment
of everyday belief that bears most directly on phenomenology, the argument
against the senses.

Garage and Hangar

To undermine sense-involving experience, to do it *as a philosopher*, one must
first identify a logically necessary feature. Then one must show that sense-
involving experience, because so featured, is open to a scruple of the sort that
Descartes expresses by asserting that the beliefs acquired along the sense-
involving route disappoint the requirements of a rational person.

On most interpretations, Descartes's criticism of the senses is said to be
incomplete until absolute doubt is reached. At that point the Meditator discovers the indubitable *cogito* and the constructive movement begins. How do the
extreme doubt-makers – malign God and malicious demon – work?

You conceive the plan of flying from London to New York. On reflection, you
conclude that no sane person would attempt the crossing. For, mistaking the
Bentley for a Boeing, the person might end up in the Celtic Sea off Land's End.

True, if you are prone to confusing garage and hangar, then, assuming you
can keep track of the efficacy rankings of the modes of transport, your best
course is to stick to the hearth. But where in this is an objection to an airplane
as transoceanic transport? Grant that a person can confuse A-type things with
things of type B. Who would specify as a defining condition for being an A the
possibility of being taken for a B?

A second scenario. Your plan is to travel to New York on the Concorde.
Research uncovers that mechanical problems affect a high percentage of these
aircraft. "Cogito ergo sum, perhaps," you conclude, "but in concordiae nulla
salus." Since the Concorde is the only way stateside that you are considering, up
to London you go to see the Queen.

This example, matching in structure the opening phase of Descartes's argument against the senses, has three interpretively pertinent features. One: The
problem is a problem with the Concorde. Two: The criticism moves from the
general (the model) to the particular. Suppose the design of the flaps is the
problem. The flaw is not, if so, peculiar to the particular flying machine that you
would board. Both features correspond to features we look for in the argument
against the senses. Three: The example disappoints our analytic desires at the
right point too. Even if the Concorde has a design flaw, that does not mean JFK
cannot be reached on it. God saved the Queen on more than one occasion. If
Descartes's "general demolition" is to be sustained, a reading must be supplied
on which the senses *never* get us to JFK.

Interpreters see what Descartes says about the senses prior to the introduction of the radical doubt-makers as exemplifying the third Concorde feature: Descartes's is only a "some" point. Since more extreme doubt-makers are then wheeled in (dreaming, for example), the interpreters down their tools. Unfortunately, once Descartes reaches the bedchamber, he is dealing no longer with a problem affecting the operation of the senses. The argument is that waking experience can be confused with dreaming. Accordingly, the opening part, which has the right form, remains on the tarmac.

What about the preceding argument? Perhaps Dover and Calais inform the phrase "chalk and cheese." But who among us has not reached for a wax fruit on the coffee table? Yet how does the inedibility of the decorative pear detract from the pleasures of the real one? Anything can be confused with anything.[4] On the truth of that we have Descartes's clinical note. "Madmen … firmly maintain that they are kings when they are paupers[. They] say that they are dressed in purple when they are naked, or that their heads are made of earthenware, or that they are pumpkins." Nor, as the text itself indicates, is it the case that in our everyday activity we are (as the unclothed lunatic and the drowsy recumbent might be said to be) careless. "Yet although the senses occasionally deceive us … there are many other [sense-acquired] beliefs about which doubt is quite impossible." The person who says this is obviously exercising judgment.

"Relying on the senses is a flawed way of forming beliefs since you might be dreaming" is a poor (not to say a batty) piece of reasoning. So if an argument can be found in the text that strikes at the senses because of *what they (or their deliverances) are* rather than because of *what they (or their deliverances) might be confused with*, it would *ceteris paribus* get the nod.[5]

Seek and you shall find. In addition to making the problem with the senses a problem *with the senses*, and to supplying the requisite generality, the way of reading that extracts the argument has several other welcome effects.

I conclude the preliminaries with a point about the extreme doubt-makers. From a structural perspective, these fill our bill. While exemplifying the attractive features of the Concorde example, they are free of the unattractive feature. Dreaming is (supposed to be) a problem for the rational believer because that kind of experience is no basis for acquiring (true) beliefs about the world. The same goes for madness. Descartes uses dreaming, madness, and so on *because* they exemplify the mentioned features. They *model* what he thinks to be true of common-or-garden sense-experience.

Dreaming and insanity and the evil genius do what we want done. But at the wrong place. Descartes knows this. He uses the ideas to model what he holds the situation with sense-experience to be, not to prove the situation to be that.

The Argument

Beginning the critique of the senses, the Meditator says that the senses *occasionally* deceive. If some cases of sense-experience are not deceptive, being a case of deception isn't a necessary condition for being a case of sense-experience.

Ideally, we want an argument formally identical to the Concorde example but whose quantifier is "all." Looking beyond the early point about (occasional) sense deception, most interpreters focus on Descartes's claim (as they see it) that the subject can *never* be sure that they are experiencing via the senses.

In my understanding, the "some"-claim (as we are calling it), part of which I quoted above, from early in Descartes's presentation only *looks like* one. When the Meditator states this – "Yet although the senses occasionally deceive us with respect to objects which are very small or in the distance, there are many other beliefs about which doubt is quite impossible, even though they [too] are derived from the senses" – he is requesting amplification, not putting forward an objection. "Yet isn't it true that we do sometimes get the straight goods via the senses?" As a response, "You might for all you know be dreaming" isn't any good. While Descartes *qua* rationalist[6] categorically rejects the adequacy to reality of sense-based representation, underlying the difficulty of distinguishing dreaming from waking is this conditional: "Cases of deception apart, if one is using one's senses, one is thereby supplied with an accurate representation."

Those who are puzzling over the text need to bear in mind the form of the *Meditations* – an internal monologue. It's not immediately obvious whether what is being said advances the argument or only makes a criticism that requires the arguer to back and fill. An interpreter must always be wary of the move from "The text has 'p' in an asserted form" to "According to Descartes, p."

The position usually taken is that the quoted lines fall into the second category. "Why, otherwise, would Descartes have proceeded to ratchet up the doubt?"

This is less than decisive. In the internal monologue, one and the same person takes both sides. Happily, *The Search after Truth*, an earlier Cartesian text,[7] presents three parties interacting over the matter: Polyander, Epistemon, and Eudoxus. Polyander is, by name, the Everyman of the piece, expressing the views of an intelligent non-philosopher. Epistemon, Mr Know-It-All, takes the stance of a Scholastic thinker of the time. Eudoxus, the Good Believer, is the Socrates of the piece.

In *The Search*, it's Polyander who makes the claim quoted three paragraphs back. "I am well aware that the senses are sometimes deceptive if they are in a poor condition, as when all food seems bitter to a sick person; or if their objects are too far away." The implication here is as before: other cases exist in which the senses deliver the straight goods. That is also the position of common sense. Eudoxus responds that he must go further to persuade Polyander ("to make you fear") that the senses deceive even when the circumstances are of the "many other" sort. "For the purposes of converting the Polyanders, the argument," he is saying, "has to be expanded." The implication is that without expansion the desired effect on the audience won't be achieved, even though the argument is in itself good enough.

This too can be debated. But find me find an interpreter of the *Meditations* who wouldn't put Polyander's lines about the senses into Eudoxus's mouth? The portioning out of the assertions and questions in *The Search* is therefore a call to reconsideration. The presumptive implication is plain: it's the man in the street who mentions occasional sense-deception to block the "general demolition."

The presumption awaits a suitable argument. The argument is this: sense-experience has a specific structure. The formulation in *The Search* is a clearer window here than is the formulation in the *Meditations*. Polyander lumps the medical condition of the sense-perceiver (sick) with the locational condition of the object (distant). Sickness is an abnormality. Generalized (at some distance or other), the latter condition is unavoidable. *The Search*'s formulation is also more informative. It speaks of what all would agree is an infirmity, suggesting that the same problem affecting the radical doubt-makers affects the senses directly. Since we agree that the radical doubt-makers sustain the "all" point that Descartes needs, it's implied that the first part of the argument does too.

The point? *All* cases of sense-perception are infirm. Even when the senses are functioning optimally, we cannot "recognize the truth" by their means. The conditional of which I spoke above is thus rejected.

This reading cracks a few hard nuts. Consider the claim, early in the *Meditations*, that for the sake of "the general demolition of my opinions" It isn't necessary to examine them all. If you must do X to accomplish Y, isn't failure inevitable if accomplishing X is "something I could perhaps never manage"? On the preceding reading, it is only necessary, as the Meditator states, to examine the principles on which my beliefs rest. If the process of belief-formation by means of the senses is faulty, then all the products are suspect. There are historical gains too. It's no infirmity of sense that it "tells" us that objects on earth tend to a state of rest or that the sun, also, rises. Nonetheless, both are, for Descartes, epitomes of the pre-modern worldview. Better sense is thus made of what is labelled "Descartes's rationalism."[8]

Deception and Certainty

The argument against the senses, as it has now been interpreted, exemplifies the first two features of the Concorde example. Also, the problem with the example, its third feature, is overcome.

The Meditator is seeking a quality labelled "certainty." The usual view, which accords with the analysis that I rejected, is that if a story can be told about the acquisition of a belief, and that story differs from the story that would be told of how the belief is (as we think) actually acquired, the belief is uncertain. I come to hold that the sun is shining on the basis of what I see. Since I might have come to hold the same while dreaming or by cortical stimulation, the belief fails to qualify as certain.

On the preceding account, having certainty means being in possession of all the direct evidence.[9] As a mode of belief-formation, sense-perception falls short not because for all the believer knows they might be lying abed. Rather, *qua sense-perceiver*, they have only part of the direct evidence.

Sense-perceptual access to the world is in principle deceptive. The word "deception" is instructive. Its etymology is "grasp from the outside." Which is what Descartes, on this analysis, is saying about such access.

This approach has the additional merit of explaining why the doubt stops at the *cogito*. The outside-ness that structures sense-perceptual contact is absent in the case of one's own mental conditions. To characterize beliefs about such a condition as incorrigible is to say that no direct evidence is lacking to the person whose condition it is, from which it follows that no other person is in a position to offer correction. Also, God's role is deepened. It's not only that God, being by nature maximally knowledgeable, is therefore, *qua* sky-high benevolent, a reliable deliverer from false belief. God, in Augustine's marvellous formulation a circle whose centre is everywhere and whose circumference is nowhere, makes sense of the truth. Such is God's kind of grasp that he, cognitively, is not in our disadvantaged condition. Luke 12:17: "the very hairs on your head are all numbered."

Since human subjects, as sense-perceivers, possess only a fraction of the evidence, they are never in a position justifiably to assert the relevant proposition. The missing data might tell another story. As we know, many an X established "beyond a reasonable doubt" never in fact occurred. Cases of the kind where the Polyander of the piece does agree (when the object is distant, when it is tiny) are no different structurally from cases of the "optimal" kind. Deception is a normal cognitive condition. As subjects whose actions are adjusted to their beliefs, it is how we are in the world. The hyperbolic doubt-makers are superfluous to the logic of the argument.[10]

It will obviate misunderstanding if we *derrida* the word "deception." "De-ception" betokens permanent deferral of completeness of grasp. Descartes's critique of the senses is an attribution and a critique of that condition. Certainty, then, is another cognitive condition, one that makes good the constitutional defect of the permanently deferred one.

When Descartes speaks of being careworn, he is speaking as a philosopher, not as Dr Phil. The case has now been concluded that he *is* speaking of our normal cognitive condition. The interrogation of sense-experience follows directly upon the description of the Meditator's installation in the *poêle*. To not have leisure is to act hastily. To act hastily is to make judgments that should be deferred. Descartes is speaking not of a local condition that taking it slow might cure. The condition is a general one, a condition of (so Descartes sees it) evidentiary deficit. More than a vacation from getting and spending is needed to make good the evidentiary shortfall. "For we know only in part ...; but when the complete comes, the partial will come to an end" (1 Corinthians 13:9–10).

In critiquing the senses, Descartes is critiquing a way of being in the world, the hasty way, the premature way, the way of the sense-perceiver. It is appropriate, then, though possibly question-begging, that the oven-imagery is obstetric.

God, and the Divide

Is the God-like position a measure of truth for Descartes, or is it Descartes's upwards projection of proper cognitive immersion in the world? The first of these moves in the direction of English philosophy. The second is phenomenological. On the first, the non-de-ceptive mode of cognition is what gives, slightly misleadingly, the truth-conditions. On the second, it is a mode free of the worries of the finite subject. Let me state the difference in a more "logical" way.

Polyander fills out what is stated in the *Meditations* about the problem that affects sense-experience. In the *Meditations*, we have only "the objects are small, or distant." Polyander elaborates: "as when we look at the stars, which never appear so large to us as they really are." Judgments are made relative to one's (local) position. Generalizing, it might be said that our descriptions of things retain a measure of relationality, of perspectivality. It's always "as seen from some point of vantage." One of the *relata* is (or involves) consciousness. Accordingly, the God-like kind of cognition overcomes the relationality. The difference is that the human claims are (implicitly) relational. How is this a flaw in them? Being what we are, *it* is what *they* are. The God-based claims are non-relational: they represent things adequately. The position would be, then, that from the standpoint of truth, relational claims are anchored in non-relational ones and that divine cognition drills down to the latter.[11]

I said early on that careless claims are claims of a certain kind. The proposition that some claims are of the hasty type repeats the point. A care-less claim is one made with less care than is possible – less, in Descartes's terms, that God can exercise. We can call them intrinsically relational claims or constitutionally perspectival ones. They bear in their content the marks of the limitation. Care-less claims are the claims of de-ceived subjects.

Here's a representation of the subject (S) and the object (O) relating to each other that captures the criticism of the senses.

The defect of sense-experience is that the sense-perceiver S, *qua* outside the object O, has only partial (direct) information about it. Consider a second subject T situated elsewhere relative to O. T's (direct) information about O will differ from S's. This is so even if the experiential conditions of both are optimal. Sense-experience is, then, *essentially*, or *by its nature*, de-ceptive. Certainty is available either when S and O coincide (the case of mental aware-ness) or when S occupies all (external) positions relative to O (God's case). The first of these is not sense-experience, and the second exceeds the reach of subjects of our sort.

Is certainty understood from the standpoint of O, or of S? If O, "No" to phe-nomenology. If S, "Yes."

Descartes invented analytic geometry. When we superpose the coordinate scheme onto Augustine's theo-geometrical image, these questions arise. Does God have an omni-perspective or is he object-coincident? Is the origin of the coordinate scheme everywhere, or is there no origin? The English tradition, opting for the latter, sucks subjectivity from the scene: God is the measure of truth. The Continental tradition spreads consciousness over the whole: God is the non-de-ceived (the global rather than local) consciousness. It's easy to see how the critique of God understood along the latter line would lead (once a temporal coordinate is added) from a Hegelian-type position to postmodern views of the sort that predominate on the Continent, including the philosophi-cal co-option of Freud, and how the construal of God as a metaphorical mea-sure of truth could lead in the direction of programs of the sort one finds in the English-speaking philosophical world.

Does God have a point of view on things? This is not a question I can answer, and not because I, like Pope, presume not God to scan. The present project is more down-to-earth: to identify the point in Descartes's philosophy where the two sides of the Channel become two philosophical solitudes.

I will now show that the phenomenological approach that would say that God's relation to the world is (=) the original intention is, in a transposed form, present in English philosophy, and present at the time when Merleau-Ponty's book appeared in English.

P-predicates and P-pronouns

Strawson plays the role in this discussion of crypto-phenomenologist; perhaps even of phenomenologist *malgré lui*. To lay bare the tendency, I will connect two pieces of his philosophy that Strawson advances separately. One: The idea of P-predicates. Two: The thesis that singular terms cannot be eliminated in favour of quantifiers and variables.

In *Individuals*, Strawson offers a philosophical anthropology. From a categorial perspective, persons are non-general individuals, as are trees and fish and planets. Persons have clear identification and reidentification conditions (this is essential for status as an individual), and they have spatio-temporal characteristics (this is what makes them non-general). What differentiates persons from (other) material objects is the fact that a range of consciousness-involving predicates ("P-predicates") applies to them alone.

Strawson wants to capture the distinctiveness of persons without paying the price that Descartes remits: the acknowledgment of a wholly different realm of being. Strawson gets what he wants by arguing that the characteristics (states of consciousness, etc.) that set men and women apart could not intelligibly be ascribed were they not linked to spatio-temporal objects. Among non-general individuals, only spatio-temporal ones *have* well-defined conditions of identification and reidentification.[12]

Think of this what we will, phenomenology has, unknowingly, already been sinned against. Heidegger, in claiming to be doing ontology, is denying that he does (just) metaphysics. The status of men and women is ontological in an irreducible sense. Men and women have a different mode of being. Heidegger's answer to the question of philosophical anthropology – "What is Man?" – is not that men and women are physical things of a distinctive sort. Trees and fish and planets too are each of them of a distinctive sort, like to one another and unlike other things.

Strawson doesn't recognize ontology as a separate compartment of metaphysics. This blocks him from acknowledging phenomenology. The applicability of P-predicates to men and women marks them as different from the individuals to which the P-predicates can't apply. But it doesn't mark them as being in the world *in a different way*. All non-general individuals are in the world as space occupants and temporal continuants. In structure, Strawson's (philosophical) position in anthropology is Aristotelian. Though they differ more from other animals than the latter differ pairwise, in *Individuals*'s last analysis men and women are still animals – animals with benefits.

Subordinating ontology to metaphysics – treating all differences between types of things as differences capturable in terms of predicates – puts Strawson at odds with phenomenology. But his stand on singular terms goes in the opposite direction.[13] In maintaining that the basic needs of discourse require demonstratives such as "this," "that," "here," "there," "I," "you," Strawson is maintaining that the origin point of the coordinate scheme requires a consciousness-type principle. Quine accepts only the impersonal pronoun "it." For Quine, no coordinate system has privileged origins.

P-predicates are therefore but half the story. The point goes along with a point about P-pronouns. The latter Strawson makes in the frame of a treatment of the conditions for discourse much more specific than *Individuals*'s treatment of the conditions for identification. Needless to say, language is peculiar to men and women. To God too, in the biblical account, it is peculiar. In the beginning God *said*.

That is the point. It matches what Strawson says in his opposition to Quine. The beginning is the coordinate scheme's origin, with the speaker/subject anchoring the process of entry into the world. This is phenomenology.

Strawson does not connect the two when it comes to persons. Descartes, if he is read in one way, does. God is the origin that is spread all about. God is the large "I." We, finite subjects (persons), are small versions.

Strawson's treatment of action is revealing here.[14] It reveals a philosopher tongue-tied by the subordination of ontology to metaphysics.

The treatment of action takes place in the field of thought of *Individuals*. Strawson's point is that attitudes such as resentment make no sense unless men and women are responsible for what they do. To put it that way is to say that a specific range of predicates applies to persons, predicates that justify attitudes like resentment and blame: "did," "performed," "perpetrated."

Proceeding through Strawson's presentation, a reader who isn't philosophically co-opted will feel an urge to give him a shake. Strawson wants to say that men and women are actors in the full sense. By contrast, non-human things are (merely) parts of systems.[15] Does one blame a storm for flooding the basement? The upset when the cat rips the upholstery is at oneself for having left the door ajar. The direct way of expressing the contrast is in phenomenological terms. "Each man and each woman is in the world as an actor, a performer, a doer. Felines and floods aren't." Drawing the distinction metaphysically, Strawson is restricted to the claim that the ascription of responsibility in the human case would make no sense unless men and women differed from other creatures and things. Why did he not appreciate that the point that personal pronouns are needed is an ontological point, their function being ineluctably non-general?

"Oxford," said the chronicler Anthony Wood of the city of his nativity, "is no good air." Could the philosophical mists along the Cherwell be obscuring the view of the life-world on the side of Magdalen Bridge across from the dreaming spires?

Epilogue:
The Acts of the Philosophers

It's real and it's true that God took our people out of Egyptian slavery three thousand three hundred plus years ago. This happened, and it happened with incredible supernatural miracles. It's true that our people stood on the desert floor at Mount Sinai three thousand years ago and the creator of the universe revealed himself to our ancestors.

– Rabbi Michael Skobac[1]

Not History

"The Bible is a work of philosophy." Even readers convinced by the argument that the Bible penetrates to the level of philosophy will I expect see this prefatory assertion as hyperbole. To bring the curtain down, I address a main source of resistance: the story-likeness and, as it seems, the historical content of the Bible.

What role – what kind of role – do the major biblical characters play? Much of the specifically historical activity,[2] as it seems, concerns invariants of being, not occurrences or happenings, real or imagined, in the world or beyond it. Much of it, that is to say, is philosophically significant. Howsoever natural it may be to view the events under the rubric of history,[3] whether of the common-or-garden strain or of the providential/miraculous variety, they are better understood in terms of the Bible's distinctive philosophical principle, and the dialectical context, monotheism versus paganism, into which the Bible is injected.

If its narrative texture and its dramatic content were the composers' way of imparting the philosophy, the Bible would differ not at all from many other products of the philosophical assembly line whose mode of presentation goes beyond analysis and argumentation. Distinctively among such products, the Bible is a *philosophical* story. The thinkers responsible for the chapters and the verses are offering, so to speak, *philosophical acts*. The acts are not (or are only

incidentally) historical. They are connected internally to the Bible's philosophical principle. It's due to the influence of Greek philosophy that the mode of
presentation's tight synchronization with the philosophical truth as the thinkers
behind the Bible understand it escapes readers.[4]

A Kantian parallel clarifies why the acts are more than vivid accompani-
ments to the lecture. Kant maintains that the truth of "The bisectors of the
interior angles of a triangle meet at a point" is a function of more than the
connections between the concepts used to formulate them. Too, it is a function of intuitions – first-level instances of the concepts. The corresponding biblical claim is that distinctively human truth depends on particulars.
The discussion of Strawson is pertinent here. We have more than special or
distinctive predicates, P-predicates. We have special or distinctive things,
P-things.

The Kantian parallel goes beyond structure. The intuitions are spatial and/or
temporal. Space and time themselves, not only the ideas (concepts) of space and
time, are implicated in the truths.[5] This matches the Bible's point of metaphilo-
sophical deviation from the Greek bequest. Biblical thought assigns a status to
something concrete, a status unavailable on the Greek side, where generality-
hungry metaphysics squeezes out particularistic ontology. The Greek side relin-
quishes the lowest level on the ladder of cognition, the level of (non-conceptual)
instances,[6] to men and women in the street.

Kant's claim about intuitions (to finish up the comparison) distinguishes him
from the rationalists, who are pure conceptualists. The Bible's claim about particulars distinguishes *it* from paganism, of which, *mutatis mutandis*, a similar
thing can be said.

As a major player in the biblical drama, it's as it should be that God's acts
too are philosophical. Since it is through God that the principle of particularity is conveyed, one is apt to think that these acts will be paradigms. The
thought, though not without truth, must be qualified. The things said of God
in the Bible that don't reduce to the purely definitional are routed through an
analysis of the (more) mundane facts of human existence and experience; also,
frequently, they get their meaning from a critique of paganism's *analysantia* of
those facts.[7] Making God's acts the paradigms *sans phrases* puts the cart before
the horse.

Historical acts I contrasted with philosophical acts. God is not a historical
player in the biblical story, certainly not at the start. To bear out the denial, I
begin with a part of the Bible regarded by many as a foundation of the distinctively biblical view. "In the beginning ..." God's role here is a philosophical one.
Subject to the preceding qualification, God's act of creation is indeed the Bible's
philosophical event *par excellence*. "Philosophical event *par excellence*" applies
multiply. *In a positive sense*, the act of creation qualifies because its significance
is one hundred percent philosophical. And it qualifies *from an interpretive*

perspective because its analysis/interpretation serves as a guide for other more down-to-earth cases in which a temptation exists to read historically.

Creation, Major

Genesis 1's creation account is not a rival to whichever account the authorities in such matters, the scientists, advance. Accordingly, Genesis 1 cannot be criticized from the scientific quarter.[8]

I have done no more than state that Genesis 1 is not cosmogonic. So widely is the contradictory accepted that it helps, as conversion therapy, to observe the severity of the stand-off that results from reading Genesis 1 in the widely accepted way. Critics of the Bible point to the account, so read, as proof that it's not to be taken seriously. If the thinkers behind the Bible aren't con artists, they are fools or wild speculators. The Bible's defenders are under the circumstances driven to maintain that we'll find Answers in Genesis to our cosmogonic questions.

All but the most intractable critics and all but the most mystified adherents must view this breakdown as a sure sign that the thinkers responsible for the Bible are being misunderstood.[9] Why offer such an account absent any basis? Why offer it when the pagan accounts are more plausible?

The thinkers are aware that their information is insufficient.[10] They advance Genesis 1 on the strength of what they regard as a compelling being-theoretic critique of the dominant contemporary position, a critique of its categorization of things. "Whatever is right, *that* is wrong." The critique is the driver, not the belief that the world of space and time had a beginning, let alone the belief that the deity of the Bible lit the touch paper.[11]

The Bible makes the point that paganism is ontologically deficient by saying, in Genesis 1, that *God* creates the natural world. As the Bibleists will have known, this way of putting it is both *overdetermined* and *oblique*.[12]

The Bible represents God as pre-existing the natural world.[13] That the genesis of the cosmos isn't the issue is indicated by God's also being, distinctively among deities, a particular. What's this got to do with the creative role? A committee could do the job too, could it not? It's also through the representation of God as creating the physical world that the Bible conveys that God isn't part of a (pagan) pantheon. Immortal though the pagan gods are, they are (in some sense) born. The point that God isn't part of the pantheon isn't only about his non-membership in a cloud-shrouded club. It's an *irreducibility* point. As such, it's not a *causal* point regarding the relation between God and the natural world.

God's irreducibility to anything natural is advanced, *in the overdetermined way*, by saying that God pre-exists the nature into which we are born and in which we die. The writers/thinkers amplify the pre-existence by saying that the natural world is God's doing. Why make the point so *obliquely*? Since nothing is present about God besides reports of what he said and of what he did and of what he saw, the reader must gather from the background opposition with paganism both the significance of "There is only one god" and of "God is one."[14]

The Bible's use of temporal terms is misleading. A babble of the (mis)use can be heard in the springs of mainstream philosophy. On Aquinas's analysis of the modalities, "X is possible" = "X is actual at some time or other." Although Terry Molloy might find solace in the thought that if he could have been a contender, he (timelessly) is one, logicians are sent racing for the exits.

Time, as this illustrates, can easily get into an analysis where it has no place. Just so, rather than say "P is a non-natural principle," the Bible says "P precedes nature."

The representation of God is a way of *getting beyond paganism*. It does that by *giving us a particular*. Separateness (= getting beyond) is conveyed in temporal terms (= preceding), and these terms are eked out with the notion of creation, itself a temporal notion.[15]

The theoretically active ingredient of Genesis 1 is present in God's not being of the created world. Something that paganism doesn't supply is needed to account for the natural realm. God represents this something *conceptually*, through his separateness, and *ontologically*, through his particularity. It is only *dramatically* that God represents the something through his world-creativity. The creation point, since it does not involve the particularity point, cannot be basic. The creation point does involve the separateness point, though, which helps explain why those behind the Bible use it in Genesis 1.

The Bible is after the particularity point, which is made in Genesis 2. Although it is formulated in temporal terms, the particularity point is not a historical one. The *aperçu* of the biblical thinkers is that there is one-ness in the world (each person is a one) that has no ratio in extra-human nature.

God is used to make the point of principle that the natural world, the world of which pagan thought can take the measure, is lacking men and women. Why a particular? Why the lack? The Genesis 2 account of the creation provides the answers, and the story of Abraham works it out.

Creations, Minor

I will now discuss three other major events/acts in the Bible: the creation of the man in Genesis 2; the beginning of Abraham's mission in Genesis 12; Moses at Sinai. Like God's creation of the natural world, these too are philosophical acts – philosophical acts that serve to clarify and to secure the idea of the particular.

THE FIRST MAN. The creation of the first man, in Genesis 2, the simplest case of the three, shares some of the misleading quality of the primordial creation. It's sort of a middle term between the latter and Abraham's act in Genesis 12. For this reason it is theoretically less illuminating than the other two. Not even presumptively is it straight history.[16] The point of the major creation is to secure God's non-identity with nature. This it does obliquely. God's one-ness, crucial to the non-identity, is only carried by the (implicit) rejection of paganism, not by any of the many events that are described in Genesis 1. The story is granting that if God were not one, the pagan story would, from the standpoint of the Bible's thinkers, not be contested.

The story of the creation of the first man is clear in the respect in which the story of the original creation is not: God's one-ness is up front. In the act dramatized in verse 7 of Genesis 2, God imparts particularity to a part of the natural world. Yet, as I said, the story is misleading in the same way as is the story in Genesis 1. The temporal terms disguise the philosophy.

God's act too is, then, a philosophical act. The dramatic description is a way of presenting the ontological uniqueness of each of us.

The story of the transgression in Eden is now seen for what it is: a presentation of separateness and particularity. What better portrayal than one that mimics the departure of each of us from the parental orbit? "Therefore a man leaves his father and his mother …" (Genesis 2:24).

ABRAHAM. Abraham too leaves his native land and his father's house. Although most readers/interpreters see the trek from the lower reaches of the Euphrates to the region of the Jordan as a moralized travelogue, we get a similar pattern of separateness and particularity.

That God's appearance to Abraham in Genesis 12 is unmotivated in the text is as it should be. We are speaking of a philosophical departure, of strong irreducibility. It's a case of what Jerry Cohen discusses when, critiquing Marx, he distinguishes the two meanings of "no longer suited." The same goes for Genesis 1. Although the link between paganism and the biblical view is oppositional, and although the opposition was played out on the real-world stage, dialectical it is not.

When Abraham calls on the name of the Lord,[17] he is making the point that not everything is explicable in terms of the general (and instantiation). Something additional to what is currently on offer (the pagan gods and their appearances in the world) is required. Abraham is speaking as an ontologist. His position, couched in my philosophical terms, is that Greek metaphysics doesn't measure up. The name of the Lord is *the name*; it is the ultimate nonpredicable. Abraham might equally have used his God-given name, "Abraham." The addition of "h" to his pre-covenantal denomination is a baptismal equivalent of God's breath of life.

If his interlocutors were able to show that Abram could do everything that Abraham does, or that what Abraham wants over and above what he already has is sound not substance, he would have to remove his patriarchal mantle. As it is, the text represents the few members of Abraham's audience as cool to the message. This, although it seems like a historical point, can be understood as *philosophical* gossip. "They all laughed at Christopher Columbus." In two ways, it can also be seen as a parallel for Genesis 2. Both God and Abraham cause the static world to unfreeze. God, turning away from the pagan gods, creates a new man. Abraham, turning away from the unreceptive pagans, gives the members of his family a new self-image. Both do what they do vocally, God by breathing his breath of life, Abraham by calling the name of the Lord.

Why, a reader might ask, does it take from Genesis 12 to Genesis 21 for the patriarch to act on a revelation that changes how he understands everything? Wouldn't he have immediately got cracking on so life-changing an insight?

In fact, many of Abraham's acts between the incoming call from God (chapter 12) and the outgoing call to the world (chapter 21) match the Bible's philosophical thrust. Abraham enacts in the human sphere what characterizes Genesis 1 in the extra-human one: separation. Abraham departs, *separates from*, Mesopotamia. Having travelled with his extended family as far as Haran, he *takes leave of* the bulk of its members. Reaching Canaan, Abraham *shifts from* settled parts of the land to the desert. Lot he *extracts from* the warlords. He *goes yon* when his nephew goes hither. From the locals Abraham *distinguishes himself* contractually – to Abimelech of Gerar seven ewe lambs for rights to a well (21:30), to Ephron the Hittite four hundred shekels of silver for the burial cave of Machpelah (23:15) – so as to formally "set apart" (21:28) mine from thine.

Abraham's doings after he receives God's call and before he addresses the world don't therefore lie in a region of indifference to the call's meaning, as the first man's transgression doesn't lie in a region of indifference to his having been breathed into life by God. This should alert any who read the text as history that the history is of an unusual sort. God appears to Abraham in Genesis 12. "Why does it take until Genesis 21 for Abraham to act on his newfound understanding?" That the question is never asked is a further indication that Genesis 12 is misunderstood.

Packaged in the Bible as God's appearance to Abraham, the first appearance of this deity to (historical) men and women, is a development in thought about things. Men and women are separate from the natural creatures. The development in thought about things is couched theologically, in the form of Abraham's recognition of God as sovereign over the world. God is not just the authoritative source and seal of approval; more, God is the principle.

God's discovering himself to Abraham (or, preferably, Abraham's discovering God in himself) is a philosophical matter. God is a philosophical principle as are Wittgenstein's family resemblance and Kant's experience as trigger though not source of all knowledge, both of which their originators present as smashing idols in the reflectoria.

MOSES. The story of Moses addresses the practical implications of the new philosophy. But the start of Moses's career, and several of his most striking acts, are *mutatis mutandis* just like the acts of the first man and the doings of the first covenanter. In the theophany on Sinai, Moses is informed of the non-naturalness of the divine principle. In the drama of bondage and liberation, Moses enacts, in a more fraught way, both the first man's particularity and also Abraham's departure from the pagan culture. Disappointed time and again by the obduracy of the men and women whom he shepherds, Moses touches a deep place in all of us in questioning his mission. "Keep my people," he must have been sorely tempted to say to Pharaoh. The story as a whole confirms the wrong-headedness of seeing God as terminally critical of the original transgression.

The first man is an ontological representative of God in space and time. Abraham, in his life, enacts separation (in his case, from paganism). Moses's "Let my people go" is equivalent to God's extracting the man from the primordial muck – which again accentuates how problematic is the Christian reading of Eden. Men and women are ontologically transgressive.

Recently, I came across this report, on Yahoo. A pastor, perusing the offerings in the book section of the local Costco, happens upon copies of the Bible with labels reading "fiction." Voices are raised in protest. Business being business, the labels are peeled off.

In this age of ours, offence is taken at much less. But how would the aggrieved feelings be backed up? If fictions are designed to entertain *rather than* to enlighten, the Bible, although in parts entertaining, doesn't qualify.[18] The fictional status of a work is however compatible with its imparting truths. Many a pastor looks for a fictional work from which to harvest nourishment for the flock.

General bookstores often contain a smattering of philosophy, sorted with volumes on spirituality, East, West, extraterrestrial. If the section in which the books are shelved is labelled "Philosophy," should that section be adjacent to the novels, to the historical works, to the science texts, or what? Though I therefore agree with the pastor, at least in regard to the Hebrew Scriptures, this is subject to the proviso that the facts in question are of a peculiar variety.[19]

Philosophical Gossip

At the start, Abraham and Moses were set over and against Thales and Plato to give flesh-and-blood to the contrast between the philosophical gospel out of Jerusalem and the philosophical entailment of the Greeks. What I say about philosophical acts can be said also on the Greek side – in reverse. These acts *fall outside the core of the philosophy*. The principle here is compacted into the motto of a foundational text of modern philosophical thought, the *Novum Organum*. "De nobis ipsis silemus …"[20] It's not that the biblical thinkers and writers have a (collective) dramatic flair and a novelistic eye. It's that their basic principle, particularity, is most perspicuously captured through the narrative and dramatic forms. It's interesting to see that when the Greeks speak about it in the mode of gossip, they speak the Bible's language.

About the life of Thales, the father of philosophy, a few vignettes have trickled down. Socrates relates (*Theaetetus* 174a) how Thales fell down a well as, walking along, he studied the heavens. A Thracian slave girl mocked him for being so concerned with what was in the sky that he didn't see what was at his feet.

Isn't it odd that Plato should portray Thales as an absent-minded professor? But that's not it at all. Doesn't Plato himself (as portrayed in Raphael's *School of Athens*) appeal in his philosophizing to something even beyond the stars?

Aristotle (*Politics* 1259a10–15) relates an anecdote that explicitly carries the positive point about philosophy. Thales was, Aristotle tells us, derided for his poverty, the wage of his devotion to Athena. To prove that he was voluntarily impecunious, Thales, by studying the heavens, determined the time of the olive harvest. Renting all the olive presses for that time, he leased them to the harvesters at a profit.

Thales's heaven-gazing can be eked out by the story of his prediction of an eclipse. Thales (so the story goes) foretold that the moon would block out the sun in his part of the sky on (in our reckoning) 28 May 585 BCE. To have been able to divine that the lunar body would obscure the solar one on that day in that location, Thales had had to painstakingly plot heavenly movements that were recognized on a gross level to have regularity to them, and then to extrapolate.

The prediction had a practical application. Herodotus records (*Histories* Book One, 74) that the day of the eclipse witnessed a battle between the Medes and the Lydians. Having got wind from Thales of the eclipse – Thales's home base was Miletus, on the Aegean coast of Asia Minor – the Lydians were able to hold their own against the foe. Along a winding road, the Lydians held off the Medes, which led to the defeat of the Persians by the Hellenes, a defeat that resulted in the glory that was Greece.

As for falling down the well: some credit Thales with the invention of trigonometry, which enabled a problem to be solved that arose each year in the Nile Delta due to the boundary-erasing annual flood. And Herodotus (ibid., 75) tells of Thales's aiding Croesus in an armed conflict by channelling the impassable Halys River into two, each of which the forces were able to ford.

There is a pattern to the vignettes. The particular gets sunk in the general. Thales studies what's above and uses that knowledge to guide his actions down below.

Thales approached nature in a rational/scientific spirit. Plato's Forms are a yet further refinement, backed by some high-flown metaphysics modelled on mathematics. The tendency is to see both the Thalean naturalizing movement and the Platonic super-naturalizing one as exorcising superstition. But the gods reappear: as natural forces in Thales, as essences in Plato. We get a rational treatment of the natural world consistent with the pagan theology. Burnt offerings give way to smudge pots.

As to the difference from the biblical view, relevant are those lines from Proverbs 30 about the three things and the fourth. Could the Thalean constellation accommodate the last thing, "the way of a man with a girl"? Here's my contribution to the doxography: "The Thracian girl laughed at Thales. Clambering out of the well, he dusted himself off and proceeded to study personal attraction. He discovered pheromones. Distilling a vial, he anointed himself and got the girl."

Make room on the shelf, Drakkar Noir, for Eau de Thalès. But did he get her love?

The Greek side has social science in respect of Proverbs 30's four. The Jerusalem side has Talmudic case-based reasoning.

We observe here the tendency to place the human in the wider context. This is par for the pagan course: horoscopy, haruspicy, divination, the like. Good fortune, like the rainfall, is treated in the same way. Science, in its rational way, is the same. As for the Bible: the jewel-encrusted breastplate, the Urim and Thumim, that the high priest used to commune with God is more like a telephone.

Abraham's Insight: Monotheism versus Monism

L. Shamshurenkov, a self-taught Russian inventor of peasant origin, constructed in 1752 the first self-propelling or self-running carriage. The automobile, then, was a Russian invention. In 1754, M. Lomonosov demonstrated a small tandem rotor to the Russian Academy of Sciences. It was powered by a spring and suggested as a method to lift meteorological instruments. (In 1922, George de Bothezat, a Russian-American engineer, built a prototype helicopter for the US Army Air Service.) The first steam locomotive was designed by I. Polzunov in 1763, some forty years before Richard Trevithick. In 1876, P. Yablochkov, well before Edison, invented the Yablochkov candle, a type of electric carbon arc lamp.[21]

The Bible does not simply present the basic ontological novelty, it also tells a story about its discovery. Was there a person called "Abraham"? What the Bible presents had to have been presented by someone. For at one time it wasn't there. Did one person do it? Local or civic or ethnic or national pride apart, does it matter?

Was there a person called "Abraham"? "Moses"? The case of Moses is especially useful for answering, since no solid historical evidence exists either of the lengthy sojourn in Egypt or of the exodus and crossing to the Jordan that take up so much of the Torah.

A widely accepted view is that some dissident group from the region of the Nile (the basis for the Moses strain) joined a group that reached Canaan independently from the eastern part of the Fertile Crescent (the Abraham strain) and that the social and religious forms amalgamated elements of each.[22]

Of the sport in the context of biblical scholarship of scouring contemporary cultures to show that Bogdan Bogdanovitch Bogdanov wrote the Bible, I have something to say because of the thesis that the Bible is philosophy. When the scholars tell us of harbingers and glimmerings, and point to the promotion of one of the pagan deities to supremacy, they are talking about the wrong thing. That the Bible's theological view isn't the denial of polytheism is so easily shown that one scratches one's head. Plato has a communitarian view of human society. Individual men and women are parts of the wider social whole. That is the same unification as is understood by the move beyond polytheism. The idea of a social organism is however antithetical to the particularity of each and every one of us. We are parts of a wider whole only by (usually, implicit) acquiescence. Just ask how the morality of the Ten Commandments could get a (non-instrumental) foothold outside this context. The *ethical principles* here, if one wants to use the phrase to cover norms of personal conduct, are ecological, not moral.

How has this blunder come to be so entrenched? Monism and monotheism are confused. The consequences are easy to appreciate. *E pluribus, unum.* Think blobs of mercury. *Ex non-unum, unum non fit.* God's one-ness is, as Kant would have said, original. I said in past pages that God could not be a member of the pagan pantheon. That is a version of the point that monism and monotheism are mutually irreducible.

The following farrago illustrates the error:

Many deities could be given epithets that seem to indicate that they were greater than any other god, suggesting some kind of unity beyond the multitude of natural forces. In particular, this is true of a few gods who, at various times in history, rose to supreme importance in Egyptian religion. These included the royal patron Horus, the sun god Ra, and the mother goddess Isis. During the New Kingdom (c. 1550–1070 BC), Amun held this position. The theology of the period described in particular detail Amun's presence in and rule over all things, so that he, more than any other deity, embodied the all-encompassing power of the divine. Because of theological statements like this, many past Egyptologists, such as Siegfried Morenz, believed that beneath the polytheistic traditions of Egyptian religion there was an increasing belief in a unity of the divine, moving toward monotheism. Instances in Egyptian literature where "god" is mentioned without reference to any specific deity would seem to give this view added weight. However, in 1971 Erik Hornung pointed out that the traits of an apparently supreme being could be attributed to many different gods, even in periods when other gods were preeminent, and further argued that references to an unspecified "god" are meant to refer flexibly to any deity. He therefore argued that, while some individuals may have henotheistically chosen one god to worship, Egyptian religion as a whole had no notion of a divine being beyond the immediate multitude of deities. Yet the debate did not end there; Jan Assmann and James P. Allen have since asserted that the

Egyptians did to some degree recognize a single divine force. In Allen's view, the notion of an underlying unity of the divine coexisted inclusively with the polytheistic tradition. It is possible that only the Egyptian theologians fully recognized this underlying unity, but it is also possible that ordinary Egyptians identified the single divine force with a single god in particular situations.[23]

Think what they may, the scholars are not debating monotheistic trends in pagan theology. "Single divine force" does not mean "force that is, in the sense of the Shema, one." The ontological "one" is being sunk in the logico-metaphysical "unique."

The mistake of trying to understand the Bible from a theological angle ("How many gods are worshipped?") is patent in the quoted lines, the more patent as the scholars represent the departure from polytheism as a forward movement of civilization. The merging of the deities is an advance, the scholars think, because it leads to morality. Not so. It leads to a view of the sort to which science aspires. It leads to Plato. That too may be an advance. But, as Hegel said, in the night all cows are the same colour. The problem is even deeper. Why is morality a civilizational advance? Could it not be provincial? The Bible does advance a moral way because it is progressive.

Here is one last quote, whose writing is as beautiful as its thinking is wrong:

The whole history of Greek legal and moral conceptions attaching to the guilt of homicide can be studied in relation to the cult-appellatives of Zeus. The Greek consciousness of the sin of murder, only dimly awakened in the Homeric period, and only sensitive at first when a kinsman or a suppliant was slain, gradually expands till the sanctity of all human life becomes recognized by the higher morality of the people: and the names of Zeus Μειλίχιος, the dread deity of the ghost-world whom the sinner must make "placable," of Zeus Ικέσιος and Προστροπαῖος, to whom the conscience-stricken outcast may turn for mercy and pardon, play a guiding-part in this momentous evolution. Even this summary reveals the deep indebtedness of early Greek civilization to this cult, which engendered ideas of importance for the higher religious thought of the race, and which might have developed into a monotheistic religion, had a prophet-philosopher arisen powerful enough to combat the polytheistic proclivities of Hellas. Yet the figure of Zeus had almost faded from the religious world of Hellas some time before the end of paganism; and Lucian makes him complain that even the Egyptian Anubis is more popular than he, and that men think they have done the outworn God sufficient honour if they sacrifice to him once in five years at Olympia. The history of religions supplies us with many examples of the High God losing his hold on the people's consciousness and love. In the case of this cult the cause may well have been a certain coldness, a lack of enthusiasm and mystic ardour, in the service. These stimulants were offered rather by Demeter and Dionysus, later by Cybele, Isis and Mithras.[24]

The writer/writers might well ask where the sense of sin at murder comes from. Homer's warriors have no problem with killing. The obvious message is that nothing within the culture supplies a sense of the individual capable of making the idea of deliberate termination of an existence seem much different than the "killing" of day by night. Under such conditions the appeal of hot, enthusiastic cults is no surprise.

God spoke to Moses out of the bush. The final message, from this Moses ("משה" is my Hebrew name), is the same message, filtered through the Elder Bush.

It's the ontology, stupid.

Finale:
"The rest is the commentary thereof"

"VERY GOOD" indicates that "good" expresses a categorial, hence contrastless, feature of WG1. **IF** bad is absent in principle from WG1, harm-causing conflict between its occupants cannot arise. The occupants must, if so, be bound up with one another in their root identity. Since we are talking, *inter alia*, of inanimate nature, it may be inferred that WG1 is an organic-type whole. When we think of the purely physical world, and factor our own interests out, that's what we find: a system of exchanges between mutually and reciprocally dependent things. **HUMANKIND**, the species, is part of WG1. If it should be extinguished through the natural processes that brought it into being, that would be no more bad than was the extinction of the dinosaurs due to the earth's collision with an asteroid. Those inclined to shed a tear for T. rex should also light a memorial candle for the heavenly body.

> A person seeking instruction on the Bible knocks at my door. Like the applicant to Shammai and to Hillel, this person wants a short course. "Very good," I say.

SINCE it's the case that where the moral term "good" applies, the moral term "bad" has application too, it follows that our world is featured by a principle of being absent from WG1. This principle, functionally, is a principle of strong separateness. Each of the occupants that fall under it must be a thing in its own right. The principle is the principle of particularity, the principle whose first appearance in the world is through God's breathing life into the first man. **GOD**, then, isn't relevant either to WG1's nature or to its coming into being. The differentiation of WG1 into non-particular things must result from processes peculiar to it. There is therefore no issue of creation *ex nihilo* for theologians to come into conflict over – not, anyway, if the debate is about the Bible. **ALTHOUGH** it's not logically necessary for there to be bad in WG2, the absence of it would require exceptional good luck – if, for instance, the particulars of WG2 never come into contact with one another. This is too unlikely a scenario to be taken seriously in a biblical text. Moreover, the non-social style of existence would be brutish, not utopian. Conflict being a live WG2 possibility, rules are needed to adjust the interrelations among the particulars, assuming that blood in the streets isn't what one wants. These rules are the moral ordinances of the Bible. The ordinances, we see, apply to things that have an independence of one another that the occupants of WG1 do not have. It's no wonder that the Ten Commandments open with the assertion that God is your (singular pronoun) deity, and that the proscription of the other gods is part of the assertion. God is the principle of your (and of my, and of his, and of her) kind of being. The other gods? The have sovereignty over WG1. **BAD** can break out in WG2 otherwise than through inter-particular friction. It can result from interaction with W1. The interaction is unavoidable. Since God is not part of WG1, God is off the hook for this kind of (non-moral) bad. **COULD** God not be faulted for the bad in WG2? Might not (particular) men and women have been made less prone to doing it? The possibility of bad is built into the structure of things through the existence of different particulars whose interests, desires, or whatever, can't all be satisfied. Politics is not predicated on sin. Nor is morality. Both are based on difference. Native sinfulness is a Christian addition to the biblical story. However compelling

psychologically, the addition does not change the ontology. **THE** constitutions of WG1 and of WG2 differ. From this it follows that the things to whom "bad" applies, men and women, are not to be identified with WG1's humankind. **SINCE** there is no bad in WG1, and since dominion is a feature of WG1, it follows that that dominion is not a heaven-sent gift. It's a natural characteristic of one species. Also, it doesn't betoken, or justify, an attitude of domination and exploitation. **GIVEN** that WG1 has no bad in it, the sabbath must be linked to WG2. There never is (as Jesus says) rest in WG1. The winds continue to blow. But it's not God who's working. The operative point is that only a particular can rest. And in WG1 there aren't any. Given that sabbath observance, the quintessential halakhic practice, is linked to WG2, a critical examination is called for of rabbinic elaboration of the Bible's practical guidelines. For that elaboration (as the rabbinic misunderstanding of the sabbath proves) has a substantial basis in what is written in Genesis 1. **ON** a more abstract plane, the contrast with Greek philosophy is taught by my two words. There is Greek-based first philosophy for WG1: metaphysics. There is Bible-based first philosophy for WG2: ontology. The former is exhausted by the principles of generality (Plato's Forms, for instance) and individuality (space and time, Plato's Receptacle). The second introduces particularity as a separate, irreducible, principle. It introduces God.

Notes

Preamble

1 In quoting from the Bible, I default to the New Revised Standard Version (NRSV) translation. Throughout, quoted material is brought into line with "house" punctuation and spelling.

2 The Shema is enunciated at Deuteronomy 6:4. Here is how I was taught to express it in English. "Hear, O Israel! The Lord is our God, the Lord is one."

3 For the kind of broadening that Williams (2000) feels (academic) philosophy to need, he could, I believe, have looked to the Bible. Glouberman 2003 contains some earlier reflections on this.

4 See the quote at the start of the Epilogue.

5 In the class on Kant I attended that term, Strawson, it emerged, had been reading from the galleys! As soon as the book became available at Blackwell's, Strawson invited us to bring our questions to his rooms during what had been the lecture hour.

6 Adorno, *Minima Moralia*; Ortega, *The Revolt of the Masses*.

7 Among the notables whose encomiums grace the back cover of my copy is the bearer of the non-existent title "Lord Chief Rabbi of the British Commonwealth."

Chapter 1

1 In the beginning of his commentary, Rashi points out that the verse has a prepositional phrase without an object: "in the beginning of." "When" is a reasonable translation. In declaiming the opening verse of the Bible from memory, most English speakers, echoing the Authorized Version [KJ], part of the culture's literary elevator music, omit the adverb: "In the beginning God created the heavens and the earth."

2 In both verses, a cognate accusative form is used. The grasses grass; the swarming waters swarm fish. The form conveys better than the NRSV does the idea that some process internal to the region's contents generates the region's occupants.

3 "Firmament" is from the KJ. The Hebrew word is based on the verb connected to
   the idea of ductility. The NRSV's "dome" is, therefore, doubly felicitous: the sky
   appears convex as it stretches from horizon to horizon; the word looks and sounds
   like "dam."

4 "I procured some bread from our picnic basket, and threw pellets of it into the
   Vivonne which seemed to bring about a process of super-saturation, for the water
   at once solidified around them to oval clusters of emaciated tadpoles, which until
   then it had no doubt been holding in solution invisible and on the verge of entering
   the stage of crystallization" (Proust, *Remembrance of Things Past*, 184).

5 Fortuitously, the Big Bang theory supplies real-world material for extending
   the process–emergence pattern. In the beginning was an energy burst. With its
   space-creating "outwards" radiation, the temperature fell: $V_1 T_1 = V_2 T_2$. When the
   temperature crossed a threshold, the energy began, like Proust's $V_i V_{on}$, to congeal.
   Should the process reverse, matter will revert to radiation.

6 Magically, a Hebrew speaker understands "Abracadabra" thus: "As I say, so it comes
   to be."

7 "Let there be light" means "let there be light that lights the way." The initial
   condition is like the sodden condition of the (therefore inutile) sponge. Given that
   "no one can look on the light when it is bright in the skies" (Job 37:21), a different
   Bible might have had "Let there be dark."

8 Compare theoretical physicist Jim Al-Khalili ("Everything and Nothing," youtube
   .com/watch?v=rKPv8zApeeo, between 49 and 51 minutes). "Here [our universe]
   is, just a few hundred thousand years old. At this point ... the universe suddenly
   becomes transparent to visible light as atoms form. It is as though a fog has lifted
   and light is able to travel freely."

9 *Theogony*, ll. 116–18, 126–8. Tablet 1, ll. 1–9, the corresponding part of the *Enuma
   Elish*, which the Bible is quoting, is appreciably the same.

> When in the height heaven was not named,
> And the earth beneath did not yet bear a name,
> And the primeval Apsu, who begat them,
> And chaos, Tiamut, the mother of them both
> Their waters were mingled together,
> And no field was formed, no marsh was to be seen;
> When of the gods none had been called into being,
> And none bore a name, and no destinies were ordained;
> Then were created the gods in the midst of heaven

10 By what standard of comparison could the natural creation have been bad? To
   introduce an asymmetry by privileging the equilibrium state conducive (say) to
   life doesn't solve the problem. The removal of the last vestige of purpose from
   Genesis 1 distances the chapter even farther from the real scene of the biblical
   action. I explore this matter in chapter 8 of "*I AM*."

11 Chaos, Hesiod says, was born. From what? The condition expressive of the first-born's nature is *no stable form*. *Formlessness*, the absence of form, is pre-Chaotic. *It* is the Hesiodic equivalent of (godless) nothingness. Nothingness is not total absence; it's no-thing-ness, the absence of things.

12 The story about Beer-sheba has Abraham contesting with the local herders over water rights. The skirmish dramatizes the deeper issue. Does Abraham have a new source of life? Is the water of Genesis 2 different from that of Genesis 1?

13 It's illuminating to think of *Abraham* declaiming the opening of the Book of Genesis, rather than as receiving it through the ether. Abraham is the first who would have known the God-based story.

14 The Bible-based calendar designates two New Years; one in Tishrei (September/October), the other, which marks the natural world's awakening, in Nissan (March/April). Jewish tradition has it that the first man (the man of Genesis 2) was created in Tishrei.

15 The planting, which requires an actor, contrasts with the grassing of Genesis 1. This is a further reason for removing God as an actor from Genesis 1. Compare: Abraham plants a tree in Beer-sheba.

16 "Be fruitful and multiply" is said (verse 28) to the males *and* the females of Genesis 1.

17 Despite avoiding the pronoun, Alter falls into nonsense anyway. "Let us make a human in our image, to our likeness, to hold sway over &c." *A human* doesn't hold sway, *humans* do. In 1:27 a move is made from "the man" – definite article + common noun – to "them." But the singular form "the man" is a type term. Alter snookers himself by insisting that "adam" should be translated as "human." Without the definite article, "human" doesn't operate as a type term; "ben-adam," the Hebrew that comes close, has to be forced. For a finer analysis of 1:27, see pages 139–40. A future translator should scrupulously avoid using "their" as their genderless singular pronoun!

18 Genesis 1 contains a hint that the application of "made in God's image and likeness" to humankind doesn't situate the species outside nature. Like humankind, the fish receive a blessing. Compare verses 22 and 28. I discuss this in chapter 7, "'Let them have dominion.'"

19 "The genesis of the biblical way is bound up with the beginnings of the monotheistic concept; both converge in the age, and presumably also the person, of Abraham" (Speiser, xlix).

20 The range of translations can be seen at biblegateway.com. To a dragoman, the translators ignore these two facts about the original. (1) "The Lord" is a proper name. So the definite article is questionable. (2) "God" could be a proper name. Compare "our Jack is coming home soon." More likely it's a general term, like "deity." Observe the shift from upper case (singular) to lower case (plural) in most translations of the first two verses of the Ten Commandments. If the Hebrew word is pluralized, doesn't this imply "g"?

21 Akhenaten ruled for seventeen years and died c. 1335 BCE. Rabbinic Judaism gives Moses's dates as 1391–1271 BCE. Roughly at the time of Hammurabi, hence appropriately to the story of Abraham, the Mesopotamian god Marduk gets elevated over the other deities. But Marduk's elevated position is like Zeus's dominance on (so-called polytheistic) Olympus.

22 That there are many men and women shows that one-ness does not require only-ness. So if one uses "monotheism," a qualifying belief system can have many deities.

23 Augustine, *The City of God*, Book XII, chapter 20: "Ut initium esset, homo creatus est." "God created a man in order that the world should contain beginnings."

24 The custom in Judaism is for a dying person to recite the Shema. If a falling tree could vocalize, its would be a Kriat Krishna, not the Kriat Shema. "It is not born / it does not die" (*The Bhagavad-Gita*, The Second Teaching, 19).

25 The NRSV has "evil." I have substituted "bad." The Bible is speaking of a feature it regards as unavoidable in the human world.

26 Perhaps remaining in the garden is required for immortality because the fruit of the tree enlivens for only twenty-four hours.

27 Defenders of the Bible have to explain how the non-natural nature of the man and the woman, particulars, is compatible with the natural status of humankind.

28 This quotation and next: answersingenesis.org/about.

29 Aspects of Darwinism can be represented as according with commonsensical views. A niche will be occupied by creatures best suited for it. To this small degree, the Bible's naturalism is compatible with Darwinism.

30 Maimonides's evasiveness (if that is what it is) regarding the eternity of the universe might have an apologetical motivation. Close association with the ephemeral implies God's inferiority. It's a fact, though, that God gives life to particular persons; and that, *pace* Christianity, isn't eternal life.

Chapter 2

1 Roth was at the Hebrew University in Jerusalem (founded in 1925) from 1928 to 1951. The question that starts this paragraph, the title of an essay in which Roth argues for "No," serves also as the name of the collection in which it appears.

2 Compare Alexander Altmann, "Jewish Philosophy": "The term 'Jewish philosophy' denotes the attempts made by Jews, at various periods in their history, to harmonize the tenets of their religious faith with prevailing trends in the philosophy of their environment. Attempts of this kind arose, in the first place, from apologetical motives."

3 The final full stop in the sentence on 114 is reached with these words: "with the ability to survive in a sea of injustice."

4 Even if one agrees, the fact remains that the Bible conveys *all* its putative truths narratively, and some of the most important ones are quite general. Something in the quoted claim that Hazony misses is relevant to the Bible.

5 Kierkegaard is denying the competence of Hegelian idealism to make sense of the reality of men and women. Nietzsche has a genealogical view of truth. Wittgenstein is exemplifying his opposition to essentialism.

6 *The Bhagavad-Gita*, The First Teaching, 36–7.

7 "Honour your father and your mother, so that your days may be long in the land that the Lord is giving you" (Exodus 20:12). This is a version of Krishna's counsel. The men and the women who respect the culture that they inherit, respect it *inter alia* because it was robust enough for their parents to transmit, are more likely to pass it on. To change Arjuna's mind, Krishna also advances the metaphysical claim that the self is imperishable – "It is not born / It does not die." The metaphysics is relevant to the Bible's position on mortality. See note 16.

8 See note 13 of chapter 1, "Bibleism and Judaism," and note 4 of chapter 5, "On one leg."

9 Although the earliest phases supply a rather disunified system, the direction is towards unity. The omega of this movement is modern natural science.

10 The Hebrew has "male and female," not "man and woman." Biologically, male and female are inseparable, like, geophysically, heavens and earth.

11 The transgression in Eden supplies a template for much in the Bible: Terah's departure; Abraham's departure; the exodus; and so on. As I see it, the creation of the first man, an exodus from nature, is the template of templates.

12 See the story of the carpenter of Plato's ideal *polis*, quoted in note 19 of chapter 3, "'Jew' as a Category Label."

13 They, however, were taking the large step not for *mankind* but for *the man*!

14 I quoted Hazony to say that "the teaching offered by the Hebrew Scripture ... has recourse to concepts of a general nature." The generality of pronouns – each of us is an "I" – isn't conceptual generality. See the section "American gods" in chapter 6, "'Where were you?'"

15 The word rendered "humankind" is "the man." This chapter belongs to the field of Genesis 2, not of Genesis 1. See note 10.

16 Elements of systems are recycled. The assertion in the Talmud (Sanhedrin 37a) that whoever saves one life saves a world entire goes beyond saying that life is highly valued. The assertion is synchronized with the Bible's ontology. Krishna's claim to Arjuna could well be true in a world without particulars.

17 Real estate does not reproduce. Farmers who give ground are sacrificing themselves. That's why Cain is said to offer "the fruit of the ground."

18 The first woman is called by the common noun "isha," a cognate of "Enosh."

19 In *The Raven*, 71–3, I argue that the homophobic inflection of the Sodom episode heightens, rather than defines, the disruption of the family unit. In the cave, we get a bestial kind of familiality. In splitting the difference between Sodom and the cave, the Bible is drawing attention to a problem that city life poses for men and women.

20 Novak gives the verse as 1:26. It's 1:27.

21 God, Novak says (79), issues the prohibition regarding the tree of knowledge to humankind. He transliterates the Hebrew that he renders as "[to] humankind":

"al ha'adam." But this means "to the man." When humankind is created in
Genesis 1, the term first used is "adam." Novak's "ha-adam" in the extended quote is
the second occurrence of the noun. Compare: "Let's have fun. The fun was had."

Chapter 3

1 "Jewish thinker" connotes "intellectual who from a position within the Jewish
   world considers Jewish matters."

2 Philosophical significance can attach to mythic events. But events of myth aren't
   historical. If theology had a genuine subject-matter, real-world happenings could
   be theologically significant.

3 Isn't the biblical injunction regarding the Amalekites a licence to kill the members
   of a national group merely for belonging? "Killing" in the Bible's early phases always
   refers to *a way of life*: the departure from Eden, the innocent and/or the gathering way;
   Cain's killing of Abel, the shepherding way; the incineration of Sodom and Gomorrah,
   the urban way, temporarily. As he flees Sodom, Lot pleads for permission to settle in
   at least a small centre, so that "my life will be saved" (Genesis 19:20). His way of life
   is what's threatened. To assess the Amalekite injunction, we must look to see what's
   objected to in the Amalekite way and generalize accordingly.

4 Thus Wittgenstein's claim that Jews have talent but not genius. Jews are
   chameleons. Felix Mendelssohn, in effect, is a Beethoven mimic.

5 In *Anti-Judaism and the Western Tradition*, David Nirenberg, a scapegoatist, argues
   that Jews have little to do with anti-Judaism. That *individual Jews* don't doesn't
   however mean that *Jewishness* doesn't. If Charles de Gaulle had in mind Genesis 26
   when he made the remark that I quoted in the Preamble, he got it doubly wrong.
   Nevertheless, there is something in the words on the philosophical level.

6 By "the concept of a Jew" I mean "the concept, at the heart of the Jewish tradition,
   of what it is to be a person." Using "Jew" in speaking of the men and women of the
   Bible is anachronistic. My starting point is however the present.

7 The same goes for Martin Buber, also widely spoken of as a Jewish philosopher.
   Buber's ideas are powered by his experience in pre–Second World War Germany. *I
   and Thou* was first published (in German) in 1923.

8 I change "knew" to "know." Levinas is saying something that is supposed to be of
   current importance.

9 In the contest on the Carmel, Elijah uses the sacrament of sacrifice to deal with
   Baal's prophets. He speaks the pagans' language. But he has quite a bit to say on the
   positive side. A yet more serious problem for Levinas is that God gives a straight
   response to Moses's request for his name.

10 Is the world of non-traditional Jews missing the Bible's distinctive principle? True,
    Talmudic elements are absent. But (I am saying) these are different.

11 The title of Soloveitchik's *The Lonely Man of Faith* derives from Kierkegaard.
    Soloveitchik's exploitation of standard philosophical resources is more revealing
    than Levinas's. Levinas earned his living at the lectern.

12 Soloveitchik's thinking has been characterized as "halakhocentric." See Singer and Sokol, and Hartman.

13 Wittgenstein (1981, 174-5) characterized his thinking as "one hundred percent Hebraic." So averse is he to generalization that he even hedges his meaning = use principle.

14 See chapter 10, "Eat, Pray, Smoke," note 8.

15 Soloveitchik's Talmudism "refuses to relate [the mitzvoth] symbolically to a cosmic drama mirroring the inner life of divinity" (Hartman, 25). This is supposed to separate the Talmud (*qua* dealing with human life) from the Bible (*qua* dealing with God's life). *Pace* Hartman, the deity and his inner life *are* relevant to the Bible's normative view of human conduct. The relevance is however a matter of (philosophical) anthropology – of what men and women *are*. A similar criticism applies to the "cosmic drama" view of *mitzvoth* on the Hasidic side.

16 To cite Abraham's debates with God to justify such a view is an error. The animadversions should be read as the founder's debates within the foundry.

17 Sophocles is, if so, at least as much in tune with the Bible, which makes Augustine's confection (*The City of God*, VIII.11) about a stint at the feet of Jeremiah more appropriate to the confectioner himself than it is to Plato.

18 I quote from, and give line numbers in, *The Three Theban Plays*. The lines following are 995-1004.

19 Observe how a typical citizen of Plato's ideal city, a carpenter, thinks of himself. The passage is from the *Republic*, 406d-407a.

> When a carpenter is ill, he asks his doctor to give him an emetic or a purge to expel the trouble, or to rid him of it by cautery or the knife. But if he is advised to take a long course of treatment, to keep his head wrapped up, and all that sort of thing, he soon replies that he has not time to be ill and it is not worth his while to live in that way, thinking of nothing but his illness and neglecting his proper work. And so he bids goodbye to that kind of doctor and goes back to his ordinary way of life. Then he either regains his health and lives to go about his proper business, or, if his body is not equal to the strain, gets rid of all his troubles by dying.

The carpenter thinks of himself functionally. He is on that basis describing himself as a misfit. It's a short step to regarding old people as misfits. It's consistent with Plato's "to know the good is to do the good" that the misfits toss themselves onto the Kallipolitan midden.

20 How, in a drama, does one represent concepts? *Antigone* is a primer. The protagonist's conflict with Creon pits generality against particularity. Elijah's encounter on the Carmel is also an encounter between personified ideas.

21 This affirmation is present in Primo Levi's *Survival in Auschwitz*. In the camp, the incarcerated were also condemned for a transgression (being Jews). Levi's axiom is the sanctity of the particular.

22 The transgression corresponds roughly to Antigone's. Antigone is threatened with death if she violates the edict. The man and the woman are threatened with death if they eat of the forbidden tree.

23 Soloveitchik asserts that Adam I is mandated "to exercise mastery and to ... subdue the garden" (35). *Genesis 1 is not however a garden, and dominion has little to do with mastery.*

Chapter 4

1 See note 23 of chapter 7, "'Let them have dominion.'"
2 See note 5.
3 God's appearance to Abraham in Genesis 12 is (=) Abraham's coming to appreciate that he is a particular. Why not Zeus? See the set-off paragraph on page 29.
4 Hebrew does not have two cases for letters. The upper case "H" is for clarity's sake. The written language also has no vowels.
5 The Hebrew "adam" is the common noun "man." God creates H-adam, which means "the man." "Eve" is a proper name. The bearer, however, also (a little less consistently) gets the "H." Especially starting in Genesis 3, she is H-isha, the woman.
6 In one of the accounts of his departure from his birthplace, Abraham is taken by Terah. So, still known as "Abram," he leaves his native land but not his father's house.
7 The source critics are off and running. The difference is interpretively significant. So the source critics should hold their horses.
8 Javan (= Ionia) is one of Japheth's offspring. The names of the descendants of Javan mentioned at 10:4 are all associated with places in and around Greece.
9 *The Odyssey.* Locations are specified by book and line in the translated version. In Book 3 of the *Iliad*, Helen describes Odysseus as "the great tactician" (241).
10 The story of Odysseus and the Cyclops has an uncanny counterpart in Jacob's life. See *The Raven*, 153ff.
11 "Mightn't Thetis have succeeded by double dipping?" The myth's message is that even the gods can't give immortality to humans.
12 Could one not say that it is by partaking daily, as one takes a one-a-day vitamin, that the eaters stave off mortality? But the quoted words clearly imply that they have yet to eat. Besides, the two do not languish once they are distanced from the tree of life.
13 What lasts is less prone to corrosion. Plato's extra-temporal Forms are the end result of this idea. Plato's valediction in the *Republic* – "the thousand-year journey" (621d) – chillingly calls up the Thousand-Year Reich.
14 Herodotus, 2:120: "I cannot believe that Priam ... was mad enough to risk his own and his children's lives and the safety of the city, simply to let Paris continue to live with Helen." The disbeliever misunderstands the *Iliad*. Homer is plotting life as war, a struggle in which we all ultimately fall. Since the *casus belli* is the *casus vitae*, the disproportion between Helen's abduction and the mayhem at Troy falls into place.

15 To change Achilles's mind, the aged Phoenix tells a thinly disguised parallel of his story, up to the inclusion of a certain Cleopatra, whose name is an inversion of "Patroclus." The episode beautifully captures how aged ways of thinking are recycled to rationalize the present. Achilles, trying to break free, has no proper language to say what he wants.

16 Hector's isn't worrying about the personal fates of Andromache and Astyanax. The concern is the family's survival. This is a variation on the warrior ethos, with continuation through one's offspring subbing for memorialization. For the same reason that Achilles is the hero of the *Iliad*, not Hector, Abraham continues the journey and Terah is left behind. The Scrabble player of cultures might detect the makings of "Hector" in "Tera[c]h."

17 I'm referring to the tracking of the shift from pre-social "natural man" to Jean-Jacques. In Descartes's *Meditations*, the fission also occurs, though in reverse. The meditator, trying to deny his own existence, establishes that he exists when he finds it to be required by the denial itself.

18 Thetis held Achilles by the heel to gain for him what she has. Jacob held Esau by the heel to gain for himself what Esau had. The result of Thetis's attempt is a reversal too. Achilles gains what makes him better than Zeus. This corresponds to the blessing that Jacob gets over Esau!

19 The word "both" confirms the earlier point that Athena's intervention is Protean. The reference is to Hera, who, Athena explains, has sent her. Hera's contribution is to the Greek warriors' effort. Athena is acting here in part as she does in Hesiod's story, as the instrument of radical change. Her association with the head in both cases is not surprising. Zeus had a new idea, and so does Achilles.

20 As Rebekah does with Jacob. The biblical issue is, also, the replacing of the father.

21 In the absence of revelation, all this means is that biblical culture has a firmer grip on autonomous entity-hood. God is the principle – the Platonic exemplar, if you will – of autonomous entity-hood. The "firmer grip" could be an illusion.

22 Thus the claim in verse 29 that the other parts are available to the members of humankind for sustenance. The formulators would have delighted at the finding that the plants ingest CO_2 and give off O_2. "To the plants, I give the animals for sustenance."

23 For a discussion of the Bible's mockery of heroism, see *The Raven*, 207–8. Observe a deep parallel between God and Achilles. Clothing the man and the woman in battle-like gear, God sends the God-like pair into the world, where they will die. The semi-immortal Achilles does the same to the Achilles-like Patroclus. In both cases, unheeded warnings are issued.

Chapter 5

1 Babylonian Talmud, Tractate Shabbat, Folio 31a.

2 Tractate Avoth 2:5. The saying is attributed to Hillel. Might not an adjacent part of the saying, "a shy [person] cannot learn," be praise for the prospective proselyte?

3 The formulation here is symmetrical. But monotheism arises as a critique of
   polytheism. So the point is best understood as one about what polytheists do
   not see.

4 Readers of the Bible are supposed to see the earliest chapters as *Abraham's* account.
   Abraham is the first to know God. That is why the reader must wait. Did a
   historical Abraham exist? If some one person came up with the ideas at roughly
   the right time in roughly the right place, or put together ambient ideas in a form
   that compelled the right group of people, we can call that person "Abraham." If that
   person is not the same as the person who "called [in Beer-sheba] on the name of
   the Lord," we can construct a composite.

5 Whether the more mediated attitude of reverence is appropriate is a different
   matter.

6 The absence of *any* differentiation in the opening cosmogonic phase might even be
   taken to imply non-physicality. Physicality requires *some* order. On the confusion
   of aspects and elements, observe that in the first phase of differentiation, as
   Hesiod tracks it, we have the apparent absurdity of earth (Gaia) without heavens
   (Ouranos). Not that the Greeks of the time were illogical. Rather, interest begins at
   home. It is some time before the gaze is cast upwards and men and women begin to
   see the whole as having an astral part. Theogenesis recapitulates psychogenesis.

7 A Cartesian parallel will be noticed. Descartes argues for dualism on the ground
   that matter is divisible; people, infissible.

8 The formation of animals is referred to in Genesis 2, at verse 19. A creative
   translation would say that God *produced* the animals for the man to name.

9 See note 16 of chapter 7, "'Let them have dominion.'"

10 To mark the point verbally, one can say that nature has individuals but not
   particulars. In mentioning *King Lear*, I said that God does not breathe life into
   (non-human) animals. Such things are individuals, not particulars.

11 Although it commands that we should do unto others, the Bible, in the part that
   I am highlighting, only isolates a principle that morality presupposes. This itself
   is no mean feat. It is one thing to argue for moral conduct when the principle
   is absent; another, when it's in hand. Often, pagans advocate tribal *ethoi*. The
   Bible's anthropology is antithetical. Apologists for monotheism frequently state
   that their ism trumps polytheism in the dimension of morals: the one deity, God,
   speaks with one voice. Even if God speaks with one voice, why must that voice
   speak morally?

12 Plato's view of justice is a good example of pagan ethical thinking. For Plato, justice
   requires that each contribute to the proper functioning of the whole. Plato sees the
   ethical community as a system.

13 Whatever we think of Spinoza's excommunication for denying this, he
   unquestionably is afoul of the Bible. To hold what Spinoza does, and to hold it of
   the Bible, one would have to argue that Scripture is utterly metaphorical.

Chapter 6

1 The answer is put into God's mouth by the thinkers behind the text. One would have to doubt, if one reads the answer in this way, that the thinkers could be in any position to say more.

2 These lines refer back to Genesis 1:6–8. The Book of Job's imagery comes largely from Genesis 1.

3 Considered as part of a wider portion of the galaxy, an asteroid that smashes into the earth isn't disequilibrating. If the time frame is long, collisions of planetary bodies and asteroids might occur regularly in this wider portion. A companion star to our sun, Nemesis, was at one time postulated to explain a perceived cycle of mass extinctions in Earth's history.

4 Ecclesiastes observes the distinction between WG1 and WG2. Men and women come and go; the system abides. The words of the American naturalist John Muir are bang on: "neither old nor young, neither sick nor well, but immortal." Consistently with Ecclesiastes's reaction to the contrast, WG1, *qua* beginning-and-ending-less, can be regarded as lesser in value. Compare Alan Lightman: "With infinite life comes an infinite list of relatives. Grandparents never die, nor do great-grandparents, great-aunts ... and so on, back through the generations, all alive and offering advice. Sons never escape from the shadows of their fathers. Nor do daughters of their mothers. No one ever comes into his own ... Such is the cost of immortality. No person is whole. No person is free."

5 A simple way of taking this is as a reference to humankind's position atop the food chain. Its atop-ness does make humankind like God, above/outside nature as a whole.

6 The appearance that what God says in chapter 38 repeats what Elihu says one chapter before – "no one can look on the light, when it is bright in the skies" – had better not be the reality.

7 The single non-plural form in Genesis 1 proves the rule. "Him" in verse 27 is in apposition to, effectively, "humankind," which, being grammatically singular, leaves no choice.

8 God "breathe[s] into [the first man's] nostrils the breath of life." With Moses God converses "mouth to mouth" (Numbers 12:8). In the one case, God gives his non-pagan knowledge to mankind; in the other, his non-pagan sort of life.

9 God's presence in them, the Bible's explicit basis for assigning it, does not by itself establish that men and women have value. But at least their self-valuing is not completely arbitrary. Xenophanes's claim that (in effect) cows would value cows and horses would value horses is mistaken. Cows and horses are parts of the system.

10 The reverse is true too. There may be no bad in WG1. But men and women of WG2 can fish the leviathans into extinction. This, however, is not Job's angle.

11 See Quine 1960.

12 Historians of logic, puzzled by the restriction of Aristotle's logic to general forms, might look here for explanatory material.

13 For Christian thinkers of the Scholastic tradition, God exists in full. But being fully actual isn't the same as being necessarily existent as the possible world analysis has it, on which the difference between necessary existence and contingent existence reduces to that between all and some. Actual existence cannot adequately be captured by manipulating general notions. Where the Christian thinkers see *God* as special, I locate the specialness in particular men and particular women. Given how the Bible presents the latter, namely as God-ly, these are two sides of a coin.

14 The widespread interpretation of "I am that I am" as asserting that God is the principle of pure being, being *qua* being, confuses Aristotle with the Bible.

Chapter 7

1 The quote is slightly edited.

2 "Environmentalism" I understand to label the view that duty-generating non-instrumental value attaches to the natural world. Nature, that is to say, has prerogatives.

3 Steven S. Schwarzschild, 351.

4 Christenson 2005 is a word-by-word discussion of the original. The treatment of 1:16 (on 17) leaves "let them have" unexplained, which shows how profoundly the understanding of experts has absorbed the English version.

5 A non-neutral sense is present in this structurally identical sentence. "Muhammad Ali dominated Liston."

6 Meat-eating is deferred until after Noah. That's why the availability of animal flesh to men and women isn't mentioned.

7 That the Bible offers this parallel is evidence that the writers/thinkers worry that 1:26 will be misunderstood due to the harsh connotations of "וירדו." What of substance would be lost if the blessing of the fish were filleted out?

8 Aren't bottom feeders out of their depth on top? The Bible isn't contributing to ichthyology. Thus "looks to have."

9 This is discussed in chapter 8, "'Because ... God rested.'"

10 What the NRSV's commentators say here of the emergence of the animals as described in verse 24 should also have been said of the fish (there *is* a backwards reference to verse 20: a sense of logic dictates a forward reference at 20 to 24). "[They] are immediately bound to [the water] and only indirectly ... to God." The point is that the inhabitants result from reorganization of the material that makes up the regions. This might however be taken as a dry run in the wet for an *Origin of Species*.

11 If this is regarded as simply too heterodox, a middle path is available. With, for example, Southgate, read Genesis 1 deistically.

12 "God," most non-scholars will agree, "creates the heavens and the earth, and as part of his cosmogonic activity forms Adam." Although scholarly readers weaned on the

Documentary Hypothesis never tire of telling us that Genesis 1, which contains "In the beginning," and Genesis 2, in which is found "God formed [the] man," come from different sources, that does not prevent even them from running the two chapters together.

13 The claim is part of the Genesis 2 story's sequel. Nonetheless, it mixes in elements of Genesis 1. Verse 1 of chapter 9 deliberately echoes 1:28. The world is starting up again after the flood. It is as it should be that elements of Genesis 1 and of Genesis 2 are intermixed.

14 The description of the fish is false. In chapter 8, "'Because ... God rested,'" I explain that its untruth is known to the describers and doesn't harm their case.

15 The NRSV, unaccountably, has "in mortals" for "באדם."

16 Non-human animals, Aquinas states, use nature; it's only fitting that men and women should do the same. *Pace* Aquinas, it's as true to the mechanism of the Genesis 1 story to say that flowers use bees to get pollinated as to say that bees use flowers to get nectar. Aquinas anthropocentrizes the creation of Genesis 1.

17 Since in the world of Genesis 1 there is only recycling, Schwarzschild's gibe at the environmentalists that "nature is a fickle mother ... she kills many of her own children" (356) is conceptually flat-footed. How does Ecclesiastes put it? "The earth remains forever" (1:4).

18 "Tu B'Shvat" means "the 15th day of the month of Shvat." Although this holiday, Arbor Day in effect, is Talmudic, Leviticus 19:23–5 seems to plant the seed. "Lag Ba'Omer" means "the 33rd day in the counting of the days between Passover and Shavuot." Shavuot, the Feast of Weeks, celebrates the giving of the Torah. See Leviticus 23:15–16.

19 A position can't be anthropocentric if there is nothing besides the *anthropos* to be the centre. And since the world contains non-*anthropoi*, the centre cannot be people as we ordinarily think of them. For Kant, the centre is the transcendental subject, spinning the unity of the objective realm out of the unity of self-consciousness.

20 In Glouberman 2010, I argue that the Bible can be used to correct Kant.

21 For the former, see *The Raven*, chapter 4; I discuss the tower in "Hero, Israel." Two parts of the Tanakh focus on the natural world: Genesis 1 and the Book of Job.

22 Schwarzschild, had he understood the text, would have understood that the pot is as *schwarz* as the kettle. The doctrine of Israelite exceptionalism backslides towards (pagan) Genesis 1 from Genesis 2.

23 Anything with clear identification and reidentification conditions counts as an individual. Abstract things like redness and honesty qualify, as do concrete ones like trees and automobiles. In *Individuals*, Strawson analyses concrete things (non-general individuals) into (1) abstract properties and characteristics, and (2) spatio-temporal positioning. Particulars are non-general things that resist this analysis. The Bible's God is the epitome of a particular. That explains why the man

of Genesis 2 is said to come into being when inspired with God's breath of life. Strawson's metaphysics, a philosophical version of paganism, conflicts with his deeper, more biblical, thoughts.

Chapter 8

1 "EL[o]H[i]YM" transliterates the appellation in Genesis 1. "Y[a]HW[e]H EL[o]H[i] YM" transliterates the appellation that figures in all but verses 2 and 3 of Genesis 2. The first appellation the NRSV renders as "God"; the second, as "the Lord God."

2 One might rest on the first day in preparation for what's next. A musical composition can begin with a rest.

3 The difference in Hebrew between "man" and "mankind" isn't as marked as it can be in English. Hebrew does not have an indefinite article. I say "can be" because the simple noun form is available as a type term in English too. "Man is born free, and everywhere he is in chains."

4 The Bible couldn't have in mind here various species of fish. The ubiquity of people is *not* a function of species differences.

5 The NRSV does not have the definite article before "man," even though in verse 8 it translates as "the man" the same Hebrew. This illustrates the failure to appreciate that Genesis 1 and Genesis 2 have different subject-matters.

6 The Bible navigates between the horns of the dilemma of Plato's *Euthyphro*. Neither is something holy because God deems it so, nor does God deem something holy because it is. Holiness is internally connected to Godliness.

7 This has to be understood, though, as the human version of God's Genesis 2 creation of the first man, not the creation of a member of the species *Homo sapiens*.

8 Thus the legends of the Sambatyon. According to Pliny the Elder's informants, the river flows less swiftly on the sabbath; Josephus's sources report, contrariwise, that it flows exclusively on that day.

Chapter 10

1 Amikam was interviewed in Haifa, Israel, in 1995.

2 For the documentation, I am indebted to Morton Rappaport, the Goldsteins' chronicler/genealogist extraordinaire. I'll add that the tight labour market in the 1930s seems to have had little effect on the admission of Americans and of British subjects.

3 https://pewforum.org/2013/10/01/jewish-american-beliefs-attitudes-culture-survey

4 Frankel (1801–1875) founded the historical school of Judaism. Schechter (1847–1915) was an early advocate of Zionism, a position that met with opposition in Jewish circles on the grounds, *inter alia*, of its lack of spirituality; and, in a less theoretical way, because only the adventurous felt a call to roam.

5 He does not take the view that relative to *their* understanding of *halakhah*, the leaders were wrong to issue the Responsum.

6 In her fifties, my mother, crossing Décarie Boulevard, made the move from the family's long-time Orthodox synagogue to a Reconstructionist congregation, which she attended much more religiously.

7 I quote from the extensive set of letters appended to Gordis's essay.

8 Levinas (1990, 136) writes: "To be a Jew is to believe in the intelligence of the Pharisees ... It is through the Talmud's intelligence that we accede to the Bible's faith." And the Pharisees' politics? "Pharisee," incidentally, means "Separatist."

9 In *The Beginnings of Jewishness*, Shaye J.D. Cohen locates the origins of the halakhic criterion in the second century BCE. In the Bible itself, it's patrilineal lineage that counts.

10 See Barcsak. The NRSV, compounding the confusion, translates both "oto" and "otam" as "them."

Chapter 12

1 As Cohen notes, his surnamesake Leonard was of this body.

2 "To meaningfully recite the Shema" means "to recite the Shema understanding its meaning and meaning it." Any act the meaningful performance of which has the same truth-content would do, mindful sabbath observance for instance.

3 The Enlightenment gave us the idea of the rights of man. Whence the idea of the bearer of the rights? Its origin in the thinking that plays into the Bible is occulted by the Enlightenment critique of naive religiosity.

4 Re "final homage": the dying person, as Cohen indicates, is, if possible, to recite the Shema. Below, I'll explain the internal connection.

5 From the Jewish perspective, suffering also comes from unavoidable interactions with (sinless) nature. Early on in *The Assistant*, the storekeeper, Morris Bober, voices the non-Jewish view: "The world suffers."

6 Christian Wiman, 25. And earlier (20): "I'm not sure you can have communion with other people without these moments in which sorrow has opened in you, and for you." You'll have to ask Wiman whether he is inviting suffering into the lives of others. Certainly, he isn't discouraging others from opening their own doors.

7 The authorities in the formative Jewish frame, recognizing the allure of self-denying conduct, took steps to manage it.

8 "Adherent to Christianity," "Christian," and "person who is Christian" *are* interchangeable.

9 Gerald Tulchinsky quotes an RCMP operative tasked during the 1930s with observing the Jewish communities in western Canada for signs of Communist sympathies. "[The Jews of Saskatoon] all considered themselves capitalists and at least potentially wealthy" (124).

10 In the primary grades, Cohen attended the socialist/Communist Morris Winchevsky School, which confirms the assertion. A Communist, Fred Rose, was elected to Canada's Parliament in 1943 and again in 1945. The motivation of the

largest part of the supportive Jewish voters of the Montreal riding of Cartier was the view of the Soviet Union as the main hope for the Jews of Europe, not Rose's redness.

11 The gradations of (non-Communist) leftism in Canadian Jewish life are described in Tulchinsky, 132–5.

12 Whether ties should be obligatory on the premises was a greater bone of contestation between Talmud Torah's administration and the PTA than whether we boys should wear *kippot* outside the classes of religious study.

13 Cohen will have found the kibbutz movement appealing. Plainly, though, the collectivist mentality is unfriendly to some of the values that I listed. Many early Zionists had leanings at odds with the Bible's anti-paganism. The Zionist element to which I refer stresses self-determination in a hostile world. This, in personal rather than national terms, goes back to the sequel of the story of Genesis 2.

14 Abraham's annals contain seeds of the various elements. He insists on his property rights (a well in Beer-sheba, a burial cave near Hebron). A family man, he is quick to assist kin when they're in need (the redemption of Lot). His basic act is an act of self-determination: the departure from his father's house and (pagan) culture. These things are all done under the sign of a new deity, God.

15 The Eichmann trial took place in 1961.

16 While Zionism, the modern political movement, I endorse, I am critical of any link with the idea of Israelite exceptionalism.

17 Aren't rejecters of God rejecting a certain view of their own nature? If that view is important for flourishing, it's not to be wondered that their problems are handed down to subsequent generations.

18 Hegel's criticism of Judaism's conception of the deity is really a criticism of Platonism, which links necessity to timelessness. But few belief-systems are as anti-Platonic on this matter as the Bible-based one. Many scholars of Judaism misunderstand God's transcendence. Suffice it for here to observe that its denial that suffering is structural to human existence sets the biblical conception of God's presence apart from the Christian idea of divine incarnation.

19 Since God's existence is not relevant to this, the thankfulness has to be understood not as gratitude *to* someone but as gratitude *about* something. To adapt the words of Psalm 118:24: "we are glad in our (mode of) being."

20 Doesn't an asteroid that smashes into the earth upset the equilibrium? See note 3 of chapter 6, "'Where were you?'"

21 Above, I quote Samuel Beckett's *Murphy* version of Ecclesiastes. Modern absurdism extends Ecclesiastes's point to men and women.

22 The idea of a deathless particular is not self-contradictory. The point here is that "and to dust you shall return" (Genesis 2:19) does not apply to non-particulars. They never leave it. Ruth's assertion that she will die as well as live with God now becomes clearer.

23 Marxism denies an independent moral position. It sees only a system whose changes follow an inexorable dynamic. As to the idea that some might, on moral grounds, deliberately swim upstream, the Marxist assessment is that opposing the current puts one in an internally inconsistent position.

24 The story of the Tower of Babel expresses biblical opposition to collective ("totalitarian") arrangements. Observe that the pronouns that the earthly creatures of the episode use are all plural: "they," "us," and "we." God's breath is absent "upon [the] plain in the land of Shinar" (Genesis 11:2).

25 The being who asks Cain "why has your countenance fallen?" is a being whose countenance has fallen. *God* is unhappy about the development. The proposition that if Cain does well he will be accepted applies to the proposer too.

26 Being a Jew might be described as an ethnically inflected form of being a human being.

27 Similar remarks apply to the claim, at Deuteronomy 7:7, about God loving the Israelites. The assembled at Sinai were at the time the only men and women who accepted God.

28 The Greek-derived "monotheism" misleads in implying that what counts is the cardinality of deities, rather than whether the deity is strongly separate or a part of a system. Providing that each deity is a particular, Commandment One can be in the plural. Proponents of the cardinality view should reflect on the fact that at the start of Hesiod's *Theogony*, there is but one god, Chaos.

29 We see here why sabbath observance is a correlate of **the** Shema. The sabbath is taken out of the natural temporal flow as the man of Genesis 1 is taken out of the natural world. Mindful sabbath observance is a way of acting the relevant difference.

30 Levinas refers to this as "the dissymmetry of the interpersonal relationship" (1998, 91).

Chapter 13

1 This is the refrain of Samuel Butler's "A Psalm of Montreal." Provoked by the sight of a Discobolus gathering dust in a Montreal lumber room, Butler is protesting the way that flesh is treated when God is prominent in the public space.

2 If the Oratory of the Paris of North America is likened to Sacré Coeur, the Orange Julep qualifies as its Eiffel Tower.

3 Three such could I am sure be found in any large North American city. But consider. Montreal's official name is "Montréal." Isn't it on Moriah that the Bible's word reposed?

4 What prevented pagan societies from endorsing the Bible's moral code? What does Commandment One have to do with the prohibitions on murder and on thievery? Entry to the philosophical side can be gained through these questions.

5 In this regard, the imagery of the story of Frankenstein's creation is pleasingly pagan. The chief pagan deity, Zeus, generates its animating agency, electricity.

6 Epicureanism is according to Taylor an exclusively humanist position. He's mistaken. Epicureanism is not humanistic, exclusive or otherwise.

7 "Accept only God" isn't identical with "Do not accept other gods before God." The worship of other gods is not the same, also, as bowing down to idols. The Bible objects to nature worship because it sees it as stupid.

8 Recall Schwarzschild's claim that the doctrine of incarnation is a reversion to paganism. The corresponding thing said of Plato's insertion of Forms into space and time would not elicit *my* criticism. Plato is some kind of rationalist pagan.

9 Taylor frequently mentions Émile Durkheim, whose sociological analysis of religion is classic. If Taylor's anti-ontological slant were due to the Durkheimian influence, he could be charged with sleeping at the philosophical wheel. As is indicated by my talk of confusing an effect for a cause, I think that Taylor's position has its basis in a philosophically more interesting error.

10 This is rather like the claim that Jackie Robinson, when he joined the Triple A Montreal Royals, corrected an error that MLB had committed.

11 Taylor attended Balliol, which was in its way as "Jewish" as was McGill. In Dorothy Sayers's *Five Red Herrings*, the Balliol man Lord Peter Wimsey, asked about a contemporary from Trinity, responds: "I never knew any Trinity men. The Jews have no dealings with the Samaritans."

12 Rabbi Akiva (50–135 CE), a giant of rabbinic Judaism, doesn't disapprove of the Samaritan. But the critique of Jewish exceptionalism that underlies the story he would reject. In the next section, Taylor's idea of fullness is examined. As we'll see, Taylor's line of fullness aligns him with Buddha rather than with Judah.

13 Taylor underestimates Platonism's influence on Christianity. "Christianity throughout history has identified more with its Hellenic roots than with its Semitic ones" (Meyers, 91). More important here is Taylor's failure to appreciate that the absence of the category of the particular, which the Bible supplies, makes "living the full span" senseless in the Socratic case.

14 The shift described above is an *imitatio Dei*, and hence is revealing about God's nature.

15 Tocqueville gives a more abstract argument of this kind about American religiosity. Transplanted Europeans retained in their consciousnesses a hankering for social hierarchicality.

16 Muhammad too has an equine ascension. The name of the horse, Boraq, means "lightning," "blitzen" in German.

17 The text reports that Elijah "repaired" the altar of the Lord (30). "Repaired" can be rendered as "doctored." A word with the same root, translated in the NRSV as "physicians," appears at Genesis 50:2. The physicians in this case are Pharaonic embalmers – deceptively enlivening the dead.

18 Taylor's handling of the noun "god" commits the same mistake that I signalized in discussing Hitchens.

19 In 2 Kings 2, Elijah also parts the waters.

20 Chapter 3, "'Jew' as Category Label," explains why representing naturalism as idiotic is objectionable.

21 Compare Jacob's corresponding hard lesson at Bethel. See page 44.

22 Elusiveness is even part of Elijah's political story. Ahab seeks him everywhere, but he is nowhere to be found. "He is not here" is what is always said of Elijah. See 1 Kings 18:10.

23 The rabbinic explanation is that the cup will be drained when the messiah comes. Why not allow the Baalites to say that Baal will respond in time?

24 Like Zeus, Baal is (*inter alia*) a rain deity. So this is a part of the challenge to the Baalites.

25 The 1 Kings 17 episode of Elijah's bringing the boy to life by warming him up is a variant of what God does in Genesis 2.

26 See Glouberman 2011.

27 "God," one might say in the Bibleists' name, "is love. Zeus is sex." As a midwife would, Arina focuses on biology. Fruitful multipliers are, as Saul Bellow puts it in *Augie March*, "in the clasp of nature, and in on the mission of a species."

28 The case is sketched in chapter 7, "'Let them have dominion,'" in the proposition that (2) is true though (1) is false. See page 100.

Chapter 14

1 The words, of Steven Pinker, are quoted in Brean.

2 As Nagel (2012, 5) observes, rejection of materialism and of Darwin, like the denial of climate change, is politically incorrect.

3 Here's a line from the publisher's description of Nagel's *The View from Nowhere*. "Excessive objectification has been a malady of recent analytic philosophy, claims Nagel, it has led to implausible forms of reductionism in the philosophy of mind and elsewhere."

4 Nagel's teleology is separate from the matter of intelligent design. He confesses (2012, 12) to lacking "the *sensus divinitatis* that enables – indeed compels – so many people to see in the world the expression of divine purpose." Compare Paul Dirac (Kragh, 257): "It might be that it is so difficult to start life that it has happened only once among all the planets … Let us consider, just as a conjecture, that the chance of life starting when we have got suitable physical conditions is 10^{-100} … Under those conditions … it is almost certain that life would not have started. And I feel that under those conditions it will be necessary to assume the existence of a god to start off life."

5 McGinn's view is that we lack the cognitive wherewithal to grasp the material (neural) property that brings consciousness into the world. McGinn's point is epistemological. There is however no great distance between saying that we do not have the wherewithal to understanding the link between matter and consciousness and saying that they are not linked in the general way that we believe them to be. In his 1999, McGinn salutes Nagel.

6 *Critique of Practical Reason*, 99. Kant has *his* Pinker, and a real stinker he is. Kant's killjoy, A.O. Lovejoy (1906) begrudges Kant the "once great."

7 Nagel (2012, 49) is candid, but one-sidedly. "It is not enough to say 'Something had to happen, so why not this?' I find this confidence among the scientific establishment ... hard to understand." Nagel levels against Darwinians the criticism that the evolutionary story lacks world enough and time to play out. "[There is] much more system and less chance in the sources of genetic variation" (48n9). Consider the notion of valence. Doesn't Pauli's exclusion principle place restrictions that explain the jumpy periodicity of the elements? Nagel adds (ibid.): "But such facts would also have to be explained ultimately." Why can't such principles be ultimate? In any event, there is no more pressure to explain the evolutionary restrictions than the valence ones.

8 Why doesn't the meditator, in criticizing his beliefs at the outset, include the quite mundane "I am in pain" and "I seem to see the sun"? Doesn't the premise of Descartes's emblematic question express something that is among the meditator's everyday beliefs? Shouldn't that halt the doubt immediately?

9 What could "essential precondition" mean? Nagel doesn't believe that as a philosopher he can bring to the issue nothing besides the distinctive capacity to work at a level of great abstraction. I will later give a reading of Nagel's words on which it makes sense to say that the descriptive results are essential. But the results that I have in mind are not Strawson's. They concern the B-question.

10 This invites the charge of verificationism against Strawson's position. Ontology is read out of epistemological constraints.

11 Within Strawson's tradition, Locke is the philosopher who pursues the issue on its own terms. Locke updates Aristotle's categorization.

12 A modern writer might begin the Bible with God's appearance to Abraham in Genesis 21. At the end, Abraham would be represented as saying "Now, friends, lend an ear to how the world really came into existence. 'In the beginning ...'"

13 In evaluations of the Bible from the secular perspective the increase in technological rationality isn't acknowledged. Advance prejudice aside, the reason is, I think, the presence of purpose. What I say below, and what I said in "Bibleism and Judaism," support the view that the storytellers don't take final causality to be the final word on the creation.

14 In the pre-scientific era Lucretius tells such a story, as, at the infancy of science, does Descartes. Compare Herbert Spencer's "complete definition" of "the true idea of evolution" (*First Principles* §57): "Evolution is a change from an indefinite, incoherent homogeneity, to a definite, coherent heterogeneity; through continuous differentiations and integrations."

15 Here is verse 4 of chapter 2: "In the day that the Lord God made the earth and the heavens." In effect, the world as in Genesis 1, which contains humankind, is up and running.

16 In Hitchcock's *Vertigo* and in Almodóvar's *The Skin I Live In*, the confusion is explored in the opposite direction. The substitute, *known* to be one, is treated like the particular. In both cases, obsession is at work.

17 The mix-up of newborns in the maternity ward is not treated like the exchange of cars from the lot, even if we alter the example so that the car whose keys you're handed has more attractive features. The newborns are bone of their parent's bones, and flesh of their flesh.

18 Aristotle is a pagan. His answer is that a person is a specific kind of animal. Aristotle does not have the category of the particular.

Chapter 15

1 Ayer's attack on (the phenomenologist) Heidegger's "nothing noths" as "mere verbiage" (16) is legendary in the discipline.

2 Intention and intension are, some will say, as different as "t" and "s." But then we have H.P. Grice's reductive analysis in "Meaning." Sentence and word meaning can, Grice argues, be analysed in terms of what speakers mean, and speakers' meaning, in turn, in terms of speakers' intentions.

3 Kant, taking the view expected from a critic of pure reason, maintains that "everything ultimately gravitates towards the practical" (1974, 94).

4 In bygone days of post-secondary pedagogy, I've seen not a few cigarettes disintegrate as teachers applied them to a blackboard, and observed the flame of more than one match charring a stick of chalk,

5 "Descartes," an interpreter might react, "*is* arguing that a mode of belief-formation is flawed if beliefs of the same kind as it generates can be formed along other routes. The mode of formation of beliefs about one's mental conditions he finds to be free of this flaw." Unfortunately, the deliverances of the latter mode have nothing to do with information of the kind that the senses supply. On this reading, the certainties that Descartes finds are disconnected from the uncertainties he is seeking to correct.

6 "Rationalism" is a typological term used by historians of philosophy. Descartes does not self-apply the ism. He says that the senses should not be relied upon.

7 The Descartes volume listed in the bibliography contains *The Search After Truth*.

8 The madness argument retells the story of the emperor's new clothes. Aristotelianism has convinced most folk of a false story about themselves and their world. Descartes is awakening the world from this collective dream.

9 The "all" lacks a well-defined meaning. Still, indirect evidence never runs out.

10 "Why are they used if they are superfluous?" They *model* what Descartes believes our ordinary situation as world-experiencers to be.

11 It would not be an acoustic illusion to hear echoes of Kant here; of Leibniz, too.

12 Numbers, which are non-general, have well-defined identity conditions. They, though, are abstract. Descartes would grant that selves ("thinking things") are

particulars. Distinctive to Merleau-Ponty's phenomenology is the claim that the body has transcendental status. His position, non-Cartesian in this regard, looks a bit like Strawson's. *Individuals* was at the centre of English philosophical discussion in the early 1960s. This, then, is my conjecture about the inclusion of Merleau-Ponty's book in the *Library*.

13 For Quine's position, see 1960; for Strawson's, 1971.

14 The main text is Strawson, "Freedom and Resentment."

15 The disobedience in Eden is an expression of autonomy from the system. It is no accident that God, answering Moses's request, gives his name in terms of the first-person personal pronoun: "I AM."

Epilogue

1 youtube.com/watch?v=AHxKvxqs9qs, at minutes 42–43.

2 "Historical activity" is circuitous. No activity occurs essentially in the past.

3 Natural *for us* to view it so. It's a substantial assumption that the original recipients viewed the text as we tend to, or had our difficulties understanding it. See note 12.

4 Our understanding is that what we have of Aristotle is, largely, lecture notes. This strengthens the view that a perspicuous philosophical exposition doesn't require Plato's dramatics. Despite the occasional splash of colour, the dialogues, anyway, are pretty undramatic.

5 There are many analytic truths (hence, according to Kant, conceptual truths) about space and time, for example the truths about time that successive instants can't be simultaneous and that "later than" is transitive. The mathematical truths stated earlier are, according to Kant, synthetic.

6 "Lowest level." Let us say that instances of concepts, for *falling under* the concepts, are *lower* in level. From the fact that "Instances of C_1 are instances of C_2" refers to something lower in level than C_1 and C_2, it doesn't follow that it refers to non-concepts. For there are concepts of concepts. So Kant's claim that the arithmetical necessity is more than a function of the concepts *septet* and *quintet* does not by itself mean that the necessity is *non-conceptual* in nature. God's being non-conceptual in nature makes it plain that on the biblical side of the parallel the lowest level reached is not conceptual.

7 If men and women were entirely natural, claims about God that the Bible makes would be forceless. God is not an object of worship merely because he exists. The same goes, *mutatis mutandis*, for the pagan deities. They inspire attitudes like awe and fear because their power harms and benefits.

8 It is unfortunate in this regard that in its broad outlines the early account of the cosmos in Genesis resembles the Big Bang account.

9 Although not by itself a decisive reason to read/interpret in some other way, this is *a* reason. Hazony says that the thinkers behind the Bible have no good grounds for believing true what they advance about the creation. Doesn't he represent the Bible

as a work of reason? A construal that does not impute lapses is superior to one that makes the construer out as superior.

10 It might even be said that they hedge their bet as to whether the natural world came into being at all. Genesis 1 can be read so as to grant that a chaotic state pre-existed God's creative activity.

11 Not that (1) paganism is ontologically incomplete, and (2) the natural world in which we find ourselves has a starting point, are unconnected. But the connection is too weak. If the natural world in which we find ourselves had a beginning, and if what began was not absolutely everything, it can be inferred that the natural world in which we live doesn't exhaust the whole of (concrete) reality. Our world could still however be one in a succession of natural worlds, each of which has a beginning.

12 "Oblique" might be excessive. Wouldn't the target audience have been hyper-conscious of the dialectical context?

13 The term "pre-exists" is temporal. While philosophers of religion struggle with God's relation to space and time, I do not think it's a worry for the Bible's thinkers. *Qua* principle of particularity, God and temporality are related.

14 This confirms that God's basic role is not the Genesis 1 role. It is possible for A to create B when the two are of the same type. Indeed, some metaphysicians argue that causes and effects must be type-identical. Why could not a B-irreducible A emerge in B; emerge, then, after B is up and running?

15 "God created the spatio-temporal world" seems to require that God be extra-temporal.

16 By contrast, the Genesis 1 account of the emergence of humankind, though not scientifically credible, is on a par with biological treatments of the origin of species.

17 A similar claim is made in Genesis 13:4. This is however the first occasion on which the patriarch is called "Abraham." The earlier occasion is pre-covenantal.

18 Can one not imagine a book like the *Morte D'Arthur* being taken as history? The compilation "respond[s] to the issues, aspirations, and anxieties of readerships in every different time and place that they touch" (Bryan, x).

19 In Glouberman 2007, readings are offered of Jesus's miracles as tropes with a conceptual thrust.

20 "Of myself I say nothing: but in behalf of the business which is in hand I entreat men to believe that it is not an opinion to be held, but a work to be done; and to be well assured that I am labouring to lay the foundation, not of any sect or doctrine, but of human utility and power."

21 See https://en.wikipedia.org/wiki/List_of_Russian_inventors.

22 The labels heard here are "Hapiru" (or "Habiru") and "Hyksos." The first is said by some to be cognate with "Hebrew." Its meaning, they say, is "[from] over [the river]," a reference to the group's geographical origin in Asia. The Hyksos, also from Asia, settled the eastern Nile Delta. They were expelled at about the (conjectured) time of the exodus. The Egyptian historian Manetho identified the coming of the Hyksos with the sojourn in Egypt of Joseph and his brothers.

The latter are referred to as "Hebrews" at Genesis 39:14 and 41:12. Some scholars speculate that "Moses" is (as Freud speculates that Moses is) of Egyptian origin.

23 "Unifying Tendencies." crystalinks.com/egyptreligion.html.

24 Entry for "Zeus." Encyclopedia Britannica. 1911.studylight.org/encyclopedias/bri/z /zeus.html.

Bibliography

Akenson, Donald. *Surpassing Wonder: The Invention of the Bible and the Talmuds.* Montreal and Kingston: McGill-Queen's University Press, 1998.

Allen, James P. "The Natural Philosophy of Akhenaten." In *Religion and Philosophy in Ancient Egypt,* Edited by Allen et al. *Yale Egyptological Studies* 3 (1989): 3–89.

Alter, Robert. *Genesis: Translation and Commentary.* New York: W.W. Norton, 1996.

Altmann, Alexander. "Jewish Philosophy." *Encyclopædia Britannica,* 1962.

Aristotle. *Metaphysics* [1924]. Translated by W.D. Ross. Oxford: Kessinger, 2010.

Augustine. *City of God.* Translated by Henry Bettenson. London: Penguin, 1984.

Ayer, A.J. *Logical Positivism.* New York: The Free Press, 1959.

Barcsak, Janos. V. "Love as the Divinity of the Human." *International Journal of Philosophy and Theology* 76 (2015): 249–66.

The Bhagavad-Gita. Translated by Barbara Stoler Miller. New York: Bantam, 1986.

Bible. *The New Oxford Annotated Bible.* Edited by Bruce M. Metzger and Roland E. Murphy. New York: Oxford University Press, 1991.

Brean, Joseph. "What has gotten into Thomas Nagel? Leading atheist branded a 'heretic' for daring to question Darwinism." *National Post,* 23 March 2013, A1.

Bryan, Elizabeth J. "Sir Thomas Malory." *Le Morte D'Arthur.* New York: Modern Library, 1994.

Christenson, Duane L. *Reading Genesis 1–2 in Hebrew.* BIBAL, 2005.

Cohen, Gerald A. *If You're an Egalitarian, How Come You're So Rich?* Cambridge, MA: Harvard University Press, 2000.

– *Karl Marx's Theory of History: A Defence.* Oxford: Oxford University Press, 1978.

Cohen, Shaye J.D. *The Beginnings of Jewishness.* Berkeley: University of California Press, 2001.

Descartes, René. *The Philosophical Writings,* vol. 2. Translated by John Cottingham, Robert Stoothoff, and Dugald Murdoch. Cambridge: Cambridge University Press, 1985.

Dostoyevsky, Fyodor. *Notes from Underground.* Translated by Jesse Coulson. London: Penguin Books, 1972.

– *The Possessed*. Translated by Constance Garnett. New York: Barnes and Noble Classics, 2004.

Enuma Elish. *The Seven Tablets of Creation*. Edited by Leonard William King. Luzac, 1902.

Glouberman, Mark. *"I AM": Monotheism and the Philosophy of the Bible*. Toronto: University of Toronto Press, 2019.

– "'I am the Lord your God': Religion, Morality, and the Ten Commandments." *The Heythrop Journal* 52 (2011): 541–58.

– "Israelite Idol: The Proto-Humanist versus the Proto-Philosophers." *Philosophy and Theology* 19 (2007): 57–78.

– "Noman's Land: Bernard Williams Performs CPR on Philosophy." *Iyyun: The Jerusalem Philosophical Quarterly* 52 (2003): 3–40.

– *The Raven, the Dove, and the Owl of Minerva: The Creation of Humankind in Athens and Jerusalem*. Toronto: University of Toronto Press, 2012.

– "Transcendental Idealism: What Jerusalem Has to Say to Königsberg." *Dialogue: Canadian Philosophical Review* 49 (2010): 25–51.

Gordis, Daniel. "Conservative Judaism: A Requiem." *Jewish Review of Books* (Winter 2014).

Grice, H.P. "Meaning." *Philosophical Review* 66 (1957): 377–88.

Guttmann, Julius. *Philosophies of Judaism: The History of Jewish Philosophy from Biblical Times to Franz Rosenzweig*. Translated by David Silverman. London: Routledge and Kegan Paul, 1964.

Hartman, David. "The Halakhic Hero: Rabbi Joseph Soloveitchik, Halakhic Man." *Modern Judaism* 9 (1989): 249–73.

Hazony, Yoram. *The Philosophy of Hebrew Scripture*. Canbridge: Cambridge University Press, 2012.

Herodotus. *The Histories*. Translated by Aubrey de Sélincourt. London: Penguin, 1954.

Hesiod. *Theogony, Works and Days, Shield*, 2nd ed. Translated by Apostolos N. Athanassakis. Baltimore: Johns Hopkins University Press, 2004.

Hitchens, Christopher. *god Is Not Great*. New York: Hachette, 2007.

Homer. *The Iliad*. Translated by Robert Fagles. New York: Penguin, 1990.

– *The Odyssey*. Translated by Robert Fagles. New York: Penguin, 1996.

Kant, Immanuel. *Critique of Practical Reason*. Translated by Lewis White Beck. Indianapolis: Bobbs-Merrill, 1956.

– *Logic*. Translated by Robert Hartman and Wolfgang Schwarz. Indianapolis: Bobbs-Merrill, 1974.

Kragh, Helge. *Dirac: A Scientific Biography*. Cambridge: Cambridge University Press, 1990.

Kreisel, Howard. *Judaism as Philosophy: Studies in Maimonides and the Medieval Jewish Philosophers of Provence*. Boston: Academic Studies Press, 2015.

Kwall, Roberta. "Saving Conservative Judaism: The Case for Ballasting the Tent Rather Than Widening It until It Collapses." *Commentary* 143 (2017): 31–5.

Levinas, Emmanuel. *Beyond the Verse: Talmudic Readings and Lectures*. Translated by Gary D. Mole. London: Athlone Press, 1984.

- *Of God Who Comes to Mind*. Translated by Bettina Bergo. Stanford: Stanford University Press, 1998.
- "Simone Weil against the Bible." In *Difficult Freedom: Essays on Judaism*. Translated by Sean Hand. Baltimore: Johns Hopkins University Press, 1990.

Lightman, Alan. "A Brief Version of Time." *New York Times*, 8 February 1993, A17.

Lovejoy, A.O. "Kant's Antithesis of Dogmatism and Criticism." *Mind* 15 (1906): 198–214.

Malamud, Bernard. *The Assistant*. New York: Farrar, Straus and Giroux, 1957.

Markfield, Wallace. *To an Early Grave*. New York: Simon and Schuster, 1964.

McGinn, Colin. "Can We Solve the Mind–Body Problem?" *Mind* 98 (1999): 349–66.

Meyers, Eric. "The Challenge of Hellenism." *Biblical Archaeologist* 55 (1992): 84–91.

Nagel, Thomas. *Mind and Cosmos*. Oxford: Oxford University Press, 2012.

- *The View from Nowhere*. Oxford: Oxford University Press, 1989.

Nirenberg, David. *Anti-Judaism and the Western Tradition*. New York: W.W. Norton, 2013.

Novak, David. *Athens and Jerusalem: Gods, Humans, and Nature*. Toronto: University of Toronto Press, 2019.

Plato. *The Republic*. Translated by G.M.A. Grube, rev. C.D.C. Reeve. Indianapolis: Hackett, 1992.

Proust, Marcel. *Remembrance of Things Past*, vol 1. Translated by C. K. Scott Moncrieff and Terence Kilmartin. London: Penguin, 1985.

Quine, W.V.O. "Two Dogmas of Empiricism." *Philosophical Review* 60 (1951): 20–43.

- *Word and Object*. Cambridge, MA: MIT Press, 1960.

Rosen, Ilana. "Ukrainian-Jewish Relations as Depicted in Narrative Accounts of Former Carpatho-Rusyn Jews in Israel." In *The Ukrainian-Jewish Encounter: Cultural Dimensions*. Edited by Wolf Moskovich and Alti Rodal. Jerusalem: PhiloBiblon Project, 2016.

Roth, Leon. *Is There a Jewish Philosophy?* Liverpool: Littman Library, 1999.

Sacks, Robert. 'The Lion and the Ass: A Commentary on the Book of Genesis.' Installment I, chapters 1–10. *Interpretation* 8 (1980): 29–101.

Sandel, Michael. *Liberalism and the Limits of Justice*. 2nd ed. Cambridge: Cambridge University Press, 1998.

Schwarzschild, Steven S. "The Unnatural Jew." *Environmental Ethics* 6 (1984): 347–62.

Singer, David, and Moshe Sokol. "Joseph Soloveitchik: Lonely Man of Faith." *Modern Judaism* 2 (1982): 227–72.

Smart, J.J.C., and Bernard Williams. *Utilitarianism: For and Against*. Cambridge: Cambridge University Press, 1973.

Soloveitchik, J.B. *Halakhic Man*. Translated by L. Kaplan. Philadelphia: Jewish Publication Society of America, 1983.

- *The Lonely Man of Faith*. New York: Doubleday, 2006.

Sophocles. *Antigone*. In *The Three Theban Plays*. Translated by Robert Fagles. New York: Penguin, 1984.

Southgate, Christopher. "Re-reading Genesis, John, and Job: A Christian Response to Darwinism." *Zygon* 46 (2011): 370–95.

Spadoni, Carl. "Great God in Boots – the Ontological Argument Is Sound." *Russell: The Journal of Bertrand Russell Studies* 23–34 (1976): 37–41.

Speiser, E.A. Introduction to the Anchor Bible Genesis installment. New York: Doubleday, 1964.

Spencer, Herbert. *First Principles*. London: Williams and Norgate, 1867.

Strawson, P.F. "Freedom and Resentment." In *Freedom and Resentment and Other Essays*. London: Methuen, 1974. First appeared in *Proceedings of the British Academy* 48 (1962): 1–25.

– *Individuals*. London: Routledge, 1959.

– "Singular Terms and Predication." In *Logico-Linguistic Papers*. London: Methuen, 1971. First appeared in *The Journal of Philosophy* 58 (1961): 393–412.

Strawson, P.F., and H.P. Grice. "In Defense of a Dogma." *Philosophical Review* 65 (1956): 141–58.

Taylor, Charles. *The Ethics of Authenticity*. Cambridge, MA: Harvard University Press, 1991.

– *A Secular Age*. Cambridge, MA: Harvard University Press, 2007.

Tulchinsky, Gerald. *Branching Out: The Transformation of the Canadian Jewish Community*. Toronto: Stoddart, 1998.

van Wolde, Ellen. "Why the Verb ברא Does Not Mean 'to Create' in Genesis 1.1–2.4." *Journal for the Study of the Old Testament* 34 (2009): 3–23.

Wardlaw, Terence Randall, Jr. "The Meaning of 'ברא' in Genesis 1:1–2:3." *Vetus Testamentum* 64 (2004): 502–13.

White, Lynn, Jr. "The Historical Roots of Our Ecologic Crisis." *Science* 155 (1967): 1203–7.

Whitehead, Alfred North. *The Function of Reason*. Princeton: Princeton University Press, 1929.

Weinberg, Steven. *The First Three Minutes*. Updated edition. New York: Basic Books, 1988.

Williams, Bernard. *Descartes: The Project of Pure Enquiry*. New York: Penguin, 1978.

– "Philosophy as a Humanistic Discipline." *Philosophy* 75 (2000): 477–96.

Wiman, Christian. *My Bright Abyss: Meditations of a Modern Believer*. New York: Farrar, Straus and Giroux, 2013.

Wisse, Ruth. *If I Am Not for Myself ...* New York: The Free Press, 1992.

– *The Modern Jewish Canon*. New York: The Free Press, 2001.

Wittgenstein, Ludwig. "Conversations with Drury." In *Ludwig Wittgenstein: Personal Recollections*. Edited by Rush Rhees. London: Blackwell, 1981.

Wolfe, Tom. *Bonfire of the Vanities*. London: Picador, 1987.

Index

Material in endnotes is indexed by chapter and note number. "5n4" refers to chapter 5, note 4.